Religion, Liberation Theology and Modern Godmen

Religion, Liberation Theology and Modern Godmen

Editors

UDAY MEHTA

RAM PUNIYANI

KALPAZ

ISBN: 978-93-8639-740-9

First Published, 2018

Published by

Kalpaz Publications
C-30, Satyawati Nagar,
Delhi - 110052
E-mail: kalpaz@hotmail.com
Ph.: 9212142040

Printed at: G. Print Process, Delhi

Cataloging in Publication Data—DK
Courtesy: D.K. Agencies (P) Ltd. <docinfo@dkagencies.com>

Religion, liberation theology and modern godmen / editors, Uday Mehta, Ram Puniyani.
pages cm
Includes bibliographical references.
ISBN 9789386397409 (HB)

1. Religion and sociology—India. 2. Hinduism and state—India. 3. Liberation theology—India. 4. Gurus—India. I. Mehta, Uday, editor. II. Puniyani, Ram, editor.

LCC BL2015.S6R45 2018 | DDC 306.60954 23

Contents

Section - B

RELIGION IN INDIA

Section - C

RELIGION AND POLITICS IN CONTEMPORARY INDIA

Section - D

RELIGION AND LIBERATION THEOLOGY

Foreword

Religion has come to the fore in last few decades not only in India but World over. Be it the terrorist violence; outcome of the politics of control over oil wealth of West Asia; or be it the very discourse of politics in South Asia religion is the cover for political discourse. In India the very phenomenon of Hindu Nationalism, Hidnutva is to the fore. With this also have come a large number of Godmen, the breed which is sharp and efficient in drawing the popular attention, gathering lakhs of devotees and millions of rupees. Unlike the Saints of medieval times they are affluent to the heights, associated with those in power and wielding mass following. Many of their escapades have come to light. How come this phenomenon became so prevalent from the decades of the 1980s is the question dogging us. How some of them who have been exposed are mortals with the entire human weaknesses and who have exploited the weaknesses of average people of the society to expand their material empire or how have they are masquerading their carnal desires in the practices which they have designed or how they exploit their followers, needs a much deeper investigation.

At the same time the broad phenomenon of Religion has come to the fore in a new and modified form, encompassing newer horizons. Historically religion has been a big umbrella, under which so many social phenomena have been incorporated. The philosophy, social reality, the social norms, the social rituals, the mythology all has their place under this umbrella. Among religions again Hinduism has the specialty as there is no single prophet or a book or a deity. Liberation theology has been part of most of the religions; happily many scholars have delved deep on the theme.

Historically Hinduism has progressed and changed its expression over times, its diverse components; sub sects have played different roles over period of time. In Hinduism again the appeal of Ram story has been magical. Gita, though has been looked at from different perspectives, has emerged a major scripture in current times. These are all the facets/questions which we had in mind while putting together some of the essays and articles for this compilation. We look up to the syncretic traditions, as the path for the future and, and could lay our hands on brilliant essays outlining the syncretism in Indian traditions.

We hope that the essays in this volume will raise the level of debate on the issues, theological and political, related to religion and will help us grapple with the social reality in a better way. The contemporary phenomenon does require a better grasp, which is possible only if we can understand the multifaceted aspect of religion. Surely current times do require the spirit of Bhakti, Sufi, and liberation theology to bring better harmony among people of society with diverse identities. The impact of linking up religion with the global project of control over oil resources needs to be unraveled to rid humanity of the cycles of intense violence. The society also needs understand about the Godmen in their true reality.

Uday Mehta

Ram Puniyani

Acknowledgements

The present times have witnessed a massive increase in religiosity in the society. There is a mushrooming of Godmen in society. These Godmen are of different hues, all with special characteristics. On one side there is a rise in the politics in the name of religion, orthodoxy in the society and on the other are these Godmen. Not many studies have come to understand the nature of these Godmen. We wanted to begin this effort by taking a look at historical and contemporary aspects of the phenomenon. Since the enterprises of Godmen derive their following from some aspects of religion, it was important that we study these facets of religion. We are very thankful to the contributors to this volume. We also thank the publishers, who published some of these. We owe a debt of gratitude to Frontline (Ungodly Men-Unholy Activities), Mumbai University (The Historical Development of Bhagwat Gita), Monthly Review (Religion and the Left) from where we have taken these essays.

Introduction

The political and social history of late twentieth century and the beginning of Twenty-first Century is laced in the language of religion. While religion, a complex ensemble of social phenomenon, the mirror of society, has been a crucial facet of human history from times immemorial, during last three decades the politics has been adorning the garb of religion, so to say. As such from last three decades, multiple political, social and economic changes like the decline of the might of Soviet Union, the collapse of socialist economy, the adverse impact of globalisation, the coming into being of Uni-polar World, Religion has become much more prominent in social space. One recalls different other processes taking place in the name of religion. The occupation of Afghanistan by Soviet Union and the promotion of Madrassas in Pakistan indoctrinating youth for terrorism was another major landmark. The political acts were done in the name of jihad, to kill kafirs and what have you.

In parallel, the politics in the name of Hindu religion, Hindutva asserted itself and Babri demolition; post-Babri violence shook the very foundations of democratic polity in India. The attack on World Trade Centre, 9/11, 2001, resulted in the killing of 3000 innocent people, and Osama bin Laden announced at the same time that this is what jihad means. Not to be left behind George W. Bush pronounced the word Crusade for attacking Afghanistan where Osama was living.

The blatant phenomenon of invasions of Afghanistan at global level and the violence in the name of religion at various places, more so in India, kept the religion in the forefront. At the same time one witnessed the rise of Christian Right in US and some other western countries, political Islam, Wahabi and Salafi Islam in the Gulf region. Sections of population coming in the grip of conservative, orthodox values went up by leaps and bounds. The religiosity at social level became more pronounced. We also witnessed the societal culture getting modulated by the expressions of religion. Globally, intimidated by the regular attacks on Muslim countries a large section of Muslims felt threatened and intimidated, many of them receding into their ghettoes.

In India, the religiosity was visible in the rise in pilgrimages to Vaisno Devi, Tirupati Balaji Temple, and Shirdi Sai temple amongst others. More and more people started joining these pilgrimages. The donations to temples started going up during this period of time. For major sections of society religiosity became the central norm. The television channels on one hand took up unending serials which show the conservative values in the glossy way, the family decisions are incomplete without the family priest and the astrologer, while the struggling people were gradually eased out from the issues to be presented in this media. The plethora of channels with proliferation of religious programmes to begin the day got supplemented by special channels dedicated to the devotion to the supreme powers. Sections of people, who were glued to the television sets when the mega serials like Ramayana and Mahabharata were relayed, got their further dose of spirituality through the channels like Astha, Sanskar, Sadhna etc. Not to be left behind the newspapers began the spirituality columns, the speaking trees and coverage of discourses of Sadhus became the part of newspapers in the more refined papers while the mofussil press, the language press, the regional one's started devoting more space to the importance of a particular ritual or the discourse of one or the other Acharya, Dharm Guru.

At the time of independence, Nehru put his foot down and disallowed any official or prominent trips of leaders to the temples. Now temples and Dargaahs became the places of regular visits by the politicians, on every conceivable occasion. The social functions become more heavily tinged by colour religious. While political discourse changed its language to the one of religion, those basing their politics in the language of religion started becoming more assertive and prominent in social scenario.

The issues taken up by these political outfits had more to do with the issues of political identity, the real issues related to peoples' survival and livelihood took a back seat. The interesting observation was that the politics based on religious identity raises the mass hysteria and can throw up issues resulting in violence at the drop of the hat.

II

During this time the Godmen, Acharyas, Bapus and Gurus proliferated dime a dozen. While no authentic census of these Holymen is available, one can safely say that while on one hand there are big players drawing national attention on the other there is plethora of local one's spreading their net far and wide. There are many a characteristics of these holy men, one being their well adorned sartorial pattern. They also pull the crowd in big numbers are good orators, have excellent grasp on psyche of individuals and social groups. Those from the political arena seek to be close to them; industrialists seek their blessings and also seek their divine mediation for their business disputes. They proliferated in all parts of the country, and many of them also made headlines for frauds and sex scandals, what of children dying in their ashrams under mysterious circumstances. What is common amongst them is their closeness to the affluent in the society, their amassing huge wealth and acres of land.

While some of them specialised in improving people's health, others gave spiritual peace by taking them for long sea cruises for discussing matters divine. There are hues and hues of them probably coming in all diverse specialties, astrology and other varieties of faith based discipline. Some of them do assert aggressively that what they are practicing is science, in real fact they do promote blind faith of sorts. What is common is their reach and affluence, their confidence in what they tell people, irrespective of its basis being true or not. While some of them may be having some inkling of holy texts many of them resort to religious language without much grounding in the philosophy of that particular religion. What is common amongst them is their extreme proximity to the political streams working in the name of religion. Many of them talk the values of Manu Smriti in modern language, some others while providing emotional succor are counselors par excellence. Each of them has a unique quality.

III

Religion as such is probably the broadest phenomenon in the society. Its expanse and spectrum is vast and encompasses most or many aspects of human life. Many a thinkers have tried to understand it as a part of their philosophical system, so we have religion explained as the mirror of society, religion as the opium of the masses and also the expression of sigh of the deprived sections in this heartless world. Its linkages with spirituality are very much their. Most religions talk of supernatural power, only few of the religions deny the existence of the overarching ruling authority over the world. The mode of worship in most religions is different; it again depends on sects and sub-sects and is also affected by geographical regions. The religions propounding the concept of supernatural powers also have *the* book, which is the divine revelation. In the phenomenon of religion clergy is the central pillar, the interpreter of the Word of God, the holy book. Historically clergy had been close to the powers of society and harps on status quo, on following the established norms, rituals etc. This is in contrast to the founders of the religions who were rebels of the time.

Prophets were disturbed by the prevalence of violence, oppression, injustices and thereby called for new values which can give respite to people from the wrong practices of the time. Once the religions got accepted by the powers of the society, they mostly became conservative and the rebels were threatened with hell, a strong deterrent against rebellion. Charvak who challenged the divine nature of Vedas was threatened and people were told that the followers of Charvak, the Lokayat tradition will become jackals in the next birth. During the early part of renaissance many a scientists were condemned to hell and a couple of them were burnt alive for defying the dictates of the clergy in the matters related to knowledge.

While the concept of God itself underwent a big transformation over a period of time, the nature worship of Adivasis, the polytheism with one God or Goddess supervising one of the aspects of nature or social life or personal virtues, to the concept of God with Body and Superhuman quality to the one of formless God transcending physical existence values to the concepts attributed like Truth, Non-violence, Knowledge, the spectrum is too vast to analyse.

Religions' other aspects like, rituals, places of worship and pilgrimage have their own importance in the society. Clergy are the one's who shape this aspect of religion.

From times immemorial, in contrast to the clergy the saints have emphasised more on moral values, have undermined rituals and socially associated with the poor in the society. There has been a big cult of renouncers and many other social groups orienting their lives around religion. As such Sadhus in India are a special category by themselves.

Today we see a plethora of the Godmen, totally in contrast to the saints of medieval times. While people use the word saint loosely, they may mean different things by the same word. For some the teachings of prophets, is the religion, for others the holy books are the religion while for another group the institution of religion and authority of the clergy defines the religion. One can very well point out that the moral values emerging from religions are supplementary while the differences are there in identity-related issues.

The contemporary scene is more for using identity as the marker of the religion. While in India the issues related to temple and mosque has dominated the scene, the moral values taught by religions have been relegated to the background. In India, Hindutva, in some Muslim countries the likes of Maulana Maududi and Taliban have resorted to the identity issues again.

At global level the biggest policy in the name of religion came, when religious identity was presented as the core foundation of civilisation and the global politics was presented as the clash of civilisations. Samuel Huntington, in a way explained the US policy of invasion of oil rich countries, as the battle against backward Islamic civilisation which according to Huntington is opposing the developed Western Civilisation. This Clash of Civilisation theory was built up from the 'End of History' thesis by Francis Fukoyama who pronounced that with the decline of Soviet states the threat to freedom and democracy from communism has ended, so history has ended. This thesis was taken further when Huntington pronounced that the clash between socialist world and Free world has been substituted by the clash between the Islamic civilisation and Western civilisation.

So this Communism, which was propagated by the imperialist West as the major threat to freedom, was substituted by Islam, as the major threat to the World. All this further intensified the presence of religion in political space. So far communism, political system was the other of Western model, now with Islam being the 'other', religion was very much at the political centre. Along with this the race between different fundamentalisms intensified. Christian Fundamentalism in US and some European countries, Hindu fundamentalism in India and Islamic one in the some Muslim majority countries asserted themselves. While these political streams boost each other they are also upholders of status quo in a very aggressive way. They do resort to the birth-based hierarchy of caste and gender, pushing the lower sections of society and women in particular to the margins of society. In the whole game of lust for oil wells, domination of the World politics, Islam, Muslim were the worst sufferers and large sections of Muslims felt insecure due to the political events which took place.

IV

How do Kingdoms-States treat the religion, has been a question which many a kings earlier faced and later nation states had to deal with. The Kings did use the identity of religion to expand their empires, Jihad, Crusade, *Dharmyudh.* Also Kings had to deal with diverse religious communities. In India, while Kings like Akbar followed the policy of Sulah-e-Kul, amity of religions, the Kings like Aurangzeb were intolerant towards other religions at some levels. Despite this Kings in India had alliances cutting across religious boundaries. People did celebrate religious differences by throwing up syncretic traditions, picking up bits and pieces from each others' religious traditions. Sufi and Bhakti are the highest example of the same in Indian context.

During colonial period the British rulers played the game of 'divide and rule' and used a communal version of history to sow the seed of divisiveness amongst religious communities. It is this policy which led to the partition tragedy and further worsened the leftover of communal problems in Independent India.

With different types of transformations to nation states, diverse attitudes were displayed by the rulers towards religion, to be more precise towards the institution of religion. In countries where democratisation process was complete, the religious institutions were relegated to the backdrop and walls were put between the state and religious institution. In a way religion became the private matter of the individual.

In nation states where the democratisation process was not complete, the grip of religiosity dictated a prominent place of religion in political and social sphere. While in countries like Pakistan religion came to become the ally of dictators, in India, it was a waxing and waning relationship. State did want to confine religion in the private sphere, treating all religions on par. Unfortunately, the political formations with religious identity wanted to bring in an alliance of clergy of different varieties with political power, in the process various clergy and Godmen become much more dominant.

Socialist states had a different attitude to religion they took up the first part of the sentence; Religion is the opium... and classically in Russia banned the churches. This could not stop the religiosity, and with the collapse of Soviet system, churches bounced back with vengeance. Can such social phenomenon be curbed by dictat? Lot of confusions has come up in current times about role of religion in the modern nation states.

In India, there are two major confusions prevailing. One is around the Kings, labeling them as secular or communal. This is a futile exercise as the very notion of secularism is related to the nation state. In Kingdoms at the best we can use the word liberal or intolerant king. The second is an imagined notion of conflict between two notions of secularism, Sarva Dharm Sambhav, equal respect for all religions on one hand and iron wall between religion and state. As a matter of fact, secularism essentially means that religious clergy will not dictate the social-political policies. State can very well look after the secular aspects related to religious congregations, Kumbh Melas, Haj pilgrimage etc. People are free to follow whatever religion they like in their lives, and the practices which do not violate the laws of the land. And that's where the matters should end.

V

The essays in this compilation are the one's which cover different facets of the phenomenon of religion. One major aspect of religion is clergy, godmen, saints and various other prefixes which describe a diverse set of people with different roles in society. Uday Mehta in his perceptive essay, Modern God Men and Gurus: Sociological Appraisal, points out that influence of religion is visible on all aspects of life. One of the aspects of society has been renunciation of material life and many of the renouncers set out to set up alternate society, alternate life style. In ancient India, Parivrajaks were wanderers, who moved in groups and were opposed to the authority of Brahmans and Vaishnav Dharma. They came up with decline of tribal society and adopted Tantric rituals, in opposition to Brahminic rituals. In mediaeval period Bhakti saints were having attributes which are in striking contrast to the Godmen or Gurus emerging in Post-independence India. Bhakti in South India came up in the middle of sixth century with the new wave of Aryan influence. Shaivism and Vaishanivism coincided with the rise of feudal monarchy. The saints did not have the support from the rulers, Kings and landlords. Bhakti in North was a response to Mughal oppression, was an attempt to reform Hinduism. Kabir symbolises it very well, in the philosophy of such saints there is absence of abstract philosophical ideas. One can say that the opposition to Brahmanism takes puritanical forms and right from beginning Buddhist, Jaina, Ajivika monks are opposed to Brahminic orthodoxy. For Bhakti saints true devotion, seeking of God is inside, God is within, in daily routine life, they do reject the organised religion.

In his second essay, Gurus in India, Uday Mehta focuses on the phenomenon of Godmen. After independence the phenomenon of Gurus has become prominent, more so from last three decades. The word Guru is absent in Vedic religion. It comes up during Upanishadic period. The emphasis is that Guru is needed for all occasions, from sacrifice rituals to *gnana* (knowledge). Ashram system comes up during this time. Guru also gives a mantra called as Bija. Gurudom is extremely authoritarian, he is also regarded as one above God, and he is a teacher giving direction. For continuation of the lineage, Gurus were married and had children. Guru system is very peculiar to India and is mainly due to the nature of Upanishdic religions, authoritarian structure of family and society and absence of printed books. Guru played the role of an intellectual and spiritual guide. Mehta points out that according to the Taittroiya Upanishads; the teacher is the first letter the student is the last letter and knowledge is the meeting place. Instruction is the link. The nature of Gurus is related to the religious traditions to which they belong. As in India there have been two major traditions, Atmavadi (Idealist) and Dehvadi (materialist). Atmawadi tradition is broadly represented by Upanishadic, Smriti literature and Dehwadi trend as evident in Tantric, Lokayat and similar traditions. Tantricism and the Natha Siddha tradition and Nathism originated among persons belonging to the lower ranks of Indian Society. This tradition was influenced interestingly by Jainism and Ajivikism and on the other by Tantrism. All over North India, in the Maharashtra region of Western India, also in parts of South India the followers of Nathism had their centres. Bhakti saints came generally from low caste and stood against the caste hierarchy prevalent in the society. During last three-four decades the changes in economic scenario has resulted in the rise of Hindutva politics and these Godmen are closer to the affluent sections of society, corporate sector, and ruling strata of society.

The present activities of Godmen are far from Holy or Godly. K.N. Panikkar in his essay 'Unholy Men: Ungodly activities' points out that there is lot of deception and sexual abuse associated with many Godmen. At times their religiosity has communal connotations. Playing music before the mosques is out and out used for communal purpose. Religious processions, at times, are also sites of communal violence. Godmen primarily exploit irrationalism and superstition and there is a nexus between Godmen and politician. Nehru's scientific temper has been kept in the cold storage and Godmen are increasing their clout though blind faith.

Ram Puniyani in his Religion, Politics and Godmen, sharply contrasts the role of Bhakti saints, saints in general as the one's speaking for weaker sections of society, while the Godmen-clergy allying with affluent and powerful currently. All the saints emphasised the values of love as the core of religion, while the clergy is stickler to the rituals and traditions. He takes up the incidents associated with Baba Ramdeo, Asaram Bapu and Shakracharya of Kanchi Kamkoti Peetham to show how these people are not only away from the poor and oppressed of the society, but also as to how they are close to the politics of status quo, are close to the centres of power in their own way. He relates the dominance of religion in social space to the global economic changes, its adverse impact on the society as well. Interestingly most of these Godmen keep quiet about the social ills prevalent in the name of religious traditions.

Krishna Mohan Shrimali, 'Religion, Ideology and Society', in his broad survey of the phenomenon, its role in society and the nature of Hinduism makes various significant points. His emphasis is more on multi-dimensional character of the phenomenon of religion. To begin with he says that there are various levels on which religion should be analysed. There is a strong presence of supernatural in most religions, then there are various universal categories of religious behaviour, which include elementary practices of rituals: prayer, songs, physiological exercise, exhortation, recitation of texts, simulation, mana (touching things), taboo, feast, sacrifices, congregation, inspiration and symbolism, Religion is a phenomenon of human world-a segment of a larger human reality. Author points out that Religion emerged at a certain stage of human development on earth and will continue to survive till the functions for which it was created, have not disappeared. Religion is a historic category. It is manmade, not something which has emerged from the forces outside of nature and human society. It is distinct type of natural phenomenon. Human beings have invented supernatural and created gods and not the other way around as is believed. The author does a broad survey of different scholars of religion and analyses their viewpoints. He also delves deep into analysing different religious traditions. The expression of religion does change with age and time, and with changing times, religion needs to be understood in the context of its changing social functions.

With the rise of politics in the name of Hinduism, Hindu religion has been a matter of discussion at different levels in society. Laxman Shastri Joshi in his exhaustive essays takes up most of the facets of Hinduism. There are several ways of looking at this religion. One is that it is a set of norms for preservation of the order and stability of society. Second is that it is a path to attain God in this and the other world. Then there are those who regard Hinduism as the religion of spirit. The focus of different scriptures is different. The Vedas talk of worship of different Gods, related to different material virtues, while Vedanta is spiritualistic in content. As per Joshi the religions emphasising materialism are primitive while the one's focusing on spiritualism are more advanced. It is not easy to define Hinduism as it is a curious mixture of numerous religious forms and conflicting and contradictory tendencies. It has peculiar social customs or laws of social life are its main aspects or features; and various consistent or even conflicting spiritual sects are its other aspects. The four-fold Varnas, the caste system, the marital rituals, the norms of family or caste life, the laws of succession or the joint family system, they all represent the social side of this religion. Hinduism in this way stands for the rules of a particular social structure. Varna is the core of this structure. During the last two thousand years and more, Hinduism has always meant the religion founded on caste system. All religious texts, for example, have used the concept of the birth along with the doctrine of Karma in order to defend the laws of the social structure. The domination of Brahmin and subjection of Shudra has been there right from Vedic period. Joshi also points out that movement based upon human reason and rational thinking were developing in India when Buddhism arose. It was an age of social transition. He de-links the varnas from the concept of race. As society is in flux, the contemporary changes are bringing new institutions which may be more equipped for engaging with the contemporary reality.

Kosambi in his in-depth analysis of Bhagwat Gita, song of the blessed one, points out that it is a book in which diverse interpretations are possible and each can find something for one self. Currently Gita has also been presented as the major Holy book of Hindus. It does stand for Varna system. Philosophically it is a powerful exposition as it does equip a reluctant warrior to take up arms against his own kith and kin. There is a class bias in the fascination for Gita. While the saints like Kabir were very much aloof from this Holy Scripture, the likes of Aurobindo, who withdrew from the peoples struggle found a deeper attraction in this. The class bias is very clear in this book. Kosambi points out that Gita is sung for the upper classes by the Brahmins and only through them for others. Lord Krishna says "For those who take refuge in me, be they even of the sinful breeds such as women, vaishyas, and shudras....". That is, all women, and all men of the working and producing classes are defiled by their very birth, though they may in after-life be freed by their faith in the god who degrades them so casually in this manner. Gita is the strongest defense of caste and gender hierarchy, which continued strongly till independence and is prevalent even now in some form. Kosambi is scathing in his analysis and breaks many a myths about this Holy Scripture. The treachery and deceit advised during the war is far from the moral and ethical values which religions should be upholding.

Nagindas Singhavi, in his exploration of Ramayana shows that the collection of tales of Lord Rama are prevalent in different part of the sub-continent, from Afghanistan to Sri Lanka to Thailand, so there is nothing Hindu about it. There are infinite versions of Ramayana. These versions can be classified into three major groups. One, those books written in the languages like Sanskrit, Pali and Ardha-Magadhi which are not used now, Two, Ramayana written in modern Indian vernaculars in various regions of India, and three, the literature in non-Indian languages. The mention of Rama comes much later. While in Vedic literature Krishna is there Rama is missing. Sources from which Valmiki put together this epic is unknown. The diverse accounts of Rama, Hanuman and Sita are astounding. Hanuman as Brahmchari is a later concept, in Valmiki Ramayana his house is teeming with beautiful women. Sita is presented as daughter of Mandodari. Jains have their own version. The eastern spread of Ramayana has mainly been due to the spread of Buddhism in that region by the propagators sent by Ashoka. In Buddhist version, Dashrath is Sita's father also. A panel depicting this version of Ramayana was seriously objected to by the communalists, who attacked an exhibition showing this version of Ramayana. Singhvi remarks that such versions of Ramayana have a shocking effect on the orthodox that have been using the particular version of Ramayana and also putting it to political use.

Irfan Engineer in Undermining National Institutions to Create Regimented Minds takes up the issue of the policies of BJP government as far as the Institutions of importance are concerned. These moves of government may also reflect on the overall pattern of appointments in top positions of scientific, cultural and educational institutions.

Taking the case of Film and Television Institute of India, he shows that the major criterion for appointments as the intitutions' heads; those having loyatly to RSS-Hindutva ideology are being selected. The professional achievements of the individuals have been given a go by and only those with affiliation to RSS controlled organisations and subservience to Hindutva ideology is given the primacy.

In 'Hindutva Politics and Democratic Norms' Ram Puniyani takes up three points related to contemporary Hindutva politics. First is the journey of Brahmanism over a period of time, its becoming the dominat part of the religion Hinduism, which is constructed by putting together different religious traditions of sub-continent to begin with. Later; in late nineteenth century; with the rise of dalit-Bahujan, the word Hindutva (a politics with Brahmanical core) comes up. The second issue is the forcible conversions of Adivasis and Muslims into Hinduism in the name of Ghar Wapasi (Home coming) and Love Jihad. The third point is the attack on scientific temper by killing of reationalists like Narendra Dabholkar, Govind Dabholkar and M. M. Kalburgi. The Hindu right wing is perturbed by voices of reason, and in its desperation is not only threatening and abusing the progressive thinkers, it has also undertaken to kill three major voices of secular, democratic voices articulating reason.

Uday Mehta in his 'Role of Hinduism in Modern India' lays a broad backdrop of role of religion in modern times. This varies from the role of Buddhist monks in Thailand, Sri Lanka, role of Church in Polish solidarity movement, revival of church in ex-communist Russia and its role in Iranian overthrow of Raza Shah Pehlavi. He points out that the need for religion would be felt in all human societies, irrespective of their cultural or technological levels, or socio-economic systems. Religion did fulfill some basic urges, emotional needs and also provides a sense of security to individuals and groups. He states that the interpretation that Marx's view of religion as the opiate of masses does not give the correct picture as Marx also sees that religion can provide an expression of rebellion also; expression of social discontent has also been articulated through religion. As India has seen a whole lot of politics in the name of religion, it has been founded on a new wave of religious revivalism. What is being projected as Hinduism in recent years is a novel concept based on crude amalgam of various contradictory set of beliefs, rituals and practices. Mehta aptly brings out the relation between the changing social economic situation and the practice and application of religion. Material conditions created as a result of the introduction of modernisation process by the British in the nineteenth century were the ones which laid the ground for the emergence of religion-reform movement which in a sense also articulated the aspirations of the rising bourgeois. The crisis of economic- social system during last three decades has resulted in a crisis and has created conditions giving rise to new aggressive, religious fundamentalism particularly since last decade.

In an introductory essay on the theme of Left and religion, the author raises three pertinent questions. First, how are we to understand the character and content of religious beliefs and practices? Secondly, how are we to account for the recent religious upsurges in Latin America, the Middle East, Asia, Africa, Eastern Europe and United States? And third, in which ways can these upsurges enrich and enhance-or delimit and deter – the international struggle for human freedom and democracy? In a way these facets present the kernel of the dilemmas of left vis-à-vis Religion. Marx's oft debated formulation Religion as the opiate of masses is taken up here again. For Marx and Engel's religion constituted alienated forms of human cultural practice under circumstances not of people's own choosing and so it is a phenomenon related to alienation not primarily because it often overlooks the socio-economic conditions which shape and mould its expression and thereby delimits human powers and efforts to transform these conditions. For Marx it is not an apriori philosophical rejection of religion; rather it is social analysis of and historical judgment upon religious practices.

Ironically major figures of Western Marxism took the cultural aspect very seriously but none of them took up religion for deeper appraisal. Interestingly part of the phenomenon of current revivalism of religion is also in opposition to the rebellion against West. Religious revival, along with nationalistic and ethnic ones, fundamentally result from the inability of capitalist civilisation to provide contexts and communities wherein meaning and values can be found to sustain people through the traumas of life. Rather than shunning away any mention of religion, the need is to find the liberatory expressions of some of these movements. Author is forthright in is criticism of the left in pointing out that it is, in part, the inability to believe in the capacities of oppressed people to create cultural alternate culture in which stands between contemporary Marxism and oppressed people. And it is due to this arrogance and snobbery due to which Marxists are unable to take religion seriously, to look at it as a crucial element of the culture of the oppressed.

Asghar Ali Engineer's essay on liberation theology, 'Religion, Ideology and Liberation Theology: An Islamic Point of View' explores the topic in historical and contemporary perspective. Engineer notes that people in Asia and Africa are trying to transform their societies. Such societies should raise certain questions for themselves. First, important question is transformation for whom? Second, question is transformation for what and thirdly, how to bring about this transformation? His focus is on role of religion in social transformation, in contrast to the role which perpetuates, status quo. He points out that most religions are very radical instrument of change in the beginning, like Buddhism, Christianity and Islam. Later these come under the grip of vested interests and play the role contrary to the original one. As per Engineer the Marxists of Third World countries have not shown much sensitivities to the cultural aspects of social life and so have been unable to make a serious impact on social and political life of society.

He opines that religion should be taken pretty seriously as an ally of revolution, progress and change. In that direction it must be divested of those theological aspects – which at best are later accretions – and were made part of it to serve not the oppressed but the oppressors. So 'liberation of theology' is needed to develop 'theology of liberation.' Theology today by and large is monopolised by those who swear by status quo. Reemphasising on the core humane teachings of Islam for social change he states that Islam was both a religion in technical sense and also a social revolution which posed powerful challenge to the oppressive structures of its time in and outside Arabia. Its basic thrust was towards universal brotherhood, equality and social justice. And that's what needs to be restored.

In his second essay on Sufism, he takes off from these premises of Islam to show that Sufi tradition has been closer to the poor people. There are many versions of origin of Sufism. Some consider them as the first Sufis who were deeply concerned about spiritual aspects of life and were known in Islamic history. Some Sufis were also concerned with just governance and setting up just social order in keeping with the Quranic teachings and hence participated in political struggles for this purpose but not in struggle for political power. However, most of the Sufi saints maintained their distance from political Islam and concentrated on spiritual side. As Sufis had maintained distance from political Islam, there were also differences with orthodox Ulama who concentrated on Shari'ah Islam i.e. legal Islam. The most significant part of the phenomenon of Sufism has been the closeness of Sufis to the poor people. They preferred to be close to poor and weaker sections of society instead of courtiers and upper class nobles. Also they did not observe religious boundaries and could acquire much popularity. They were highly respected by the masses, both Muslim as well as Hindu. It is due to them that many low caste Hindus converted to Islam as they found more dignity and acceptability at their hands.

What happen to the nature of religious traditions when two of them live close by, are there conflicts or is there interaction? This is what Uday Mehta sets out to answer in his contribution, Syncretism: Indian Context: while there are elements of diversity, the religious interaction results with a newer synthesis which takes up from both the religions. Syncretism word stands for this amalgam of religions. As religions keep drawing from the prevalent norms, all religions can be said to be syncretic in one sense. As such syncretism can be classified in various categories, (a) Defensive Syncretism, (b) Aggressive Syncretism, (c) Recessive Syncretism, (d) Adaptive Syncretism and (e) Pragmatic Syncretism. Some scholars point out that this term ignores the multiplicity of meaning which human agency seeks to comprehend in the cosmos around, and restricts itself to a binary opposition of 'Syncretism' and 'anti-syncretism'. Hence, they prefer to use the term liminality – a term that takes into account a third space that seeks to transcend the binary mode of thought and understanding. In a sense, it also does away with the sacred – profane categorisation through a peculiar combination of reverence and irreverence to the gods.

Another concept which comes closer to this intermixing is that of 'hybridity', this expresses the intercultural encounter. Hybridity implies how two entities combine to produce a third, with specific reference to cross-cultural kinship / marriage. The intermixing is expressed in different aspects of social life. One major expression of this is shrines, which have become decisive meeting points of religious communities in the Indian landscape. These shrines determine the importance of sacred places vis-à-vis religious syncretism and continue to be centre of power, interaction and legitimacy in the realm of the lived religious experience of people. With the half way process of secularisation come into the Indian society, the debate has also gone on to encompass the notions of secularism and religion in Indian society.

VI

In grasping the present social reality one has to grapple not only with the obvious phenomenon of Godmen, but also look at the social political realities which have created the atmosphere for the rise of such phenomenon. The process of globalisation has taken a very anti-poor form in the last three decades, and this has on one hand created a sector of affluent class, wanting the social status quo of social relations of caste and gender, and on the other created a destitute sections living the life of total deprivation. The politics in the name of religion creates an atmosphere where by the affluent sections benefit from this politics and the destitute sections are utilised as foot soldiers of the politics in the name of religion. So one section benefits from it and another section is fed with the emotional opium to make them keep quiet even in their deprivations. One can say that Godmen have a unique functionality for keeping the status quo in the society.

Only few in-depth studies are available to grapple with this phenomenon of Godmen. One is also surprised that the liberation theology which was heard of few decades ago is totally missing from the social scene. The syncretic traditions which can provide and inclusive social system are also being attacked by the divisive orthodox people currently. One has to look for the way out from the present impasse created by vested interests. The deeper understanding of role of Godmen and the use of religion in political space needs to be analysed to find the way out.

SECTION - A
GODMEN IN INDIA

1

Gurus in India: Historical Perspective

Uday Mehta

Religion since almost pre-Vedic period has exercised tremendous influence on Indian society. Religious influence is evident in practically all aspects ranging from art, dance, music, theatre, sculpture, painting, to all important events of Hindus life, such as birth, marriage, death and other social, political as well as economic sphere of Indian society. If it was true of traditional Indian Society, even in modern Indian society impact of religion in some form or the other hardly needs much elaboration.

Cult of Renouncers in Indian Society

In this essay we focus on the relevance role of the Gurus, Sants or, as Romila Thapar so aptly suggests, the cult of renouncers, in Indian society since Vedic times. In her paper on "Renunciation: The making of a counter culture", she argues that the organised groups of renouncers of the post-Vedic period were neither negating the society to which they belonged nor trying to radically alter it, but rather they were seeking to establish a parallel society. Inherent in this attempt was the notion of dissent, but its articulation was often ambiguous. In early India, this role is enmeshed with the complexities of caste and with the nature of dissent.

The renouncer does not necessarily represent a religious sect but often an order constituting an alternative lifestyle, in many ways contradictory to that of his original social group. For instance, he cannot observe caste norms, must be celibate, cannot own property, and may be requested to break various food taboos.

The focus, as she suggests, is on the social manifestations of these groups and their role in historical change. Initially, it seems asceticism arose from groups which questioned the ritual of sacrifice as the means of acquiring magical power. Proponents of asceticism believed that tapas and dhyana were more effective. Gradually the idea was extended to more than magical power to absolute freedom. This was seen primarily as the freedom of the soul or consciousness to achieve a state of ecstasy, to receive knowledge from experience and meditation rather than from the claim or revelation.

The Mid-first Millennium B.C. and Proliferation of Sects

The mid-first millennium B.C. saw a proliferation of sects in the Ganges valley. Many of these were pariwajakas wandering in groups under the direction of a teacher or loosely affiliated to sects, but preferring to wander by themselves, alone. The wanderers were often dissidents. The question of the orthodox tradition had started prior to this period, but what was new was the emergence of various sects such as Nirganthas, the Ajivikas and later the Buddhists, as well as various Carvaka sects. The dissidence of these groups was however qualitatively different since they were not individual dissenters but had organised their dissent into sects whose identity was based on an opposition to the orthodox doctrines as expressed in the notions of the sanctity of the vedas, the authority of the brahmans, Varnasrama dharma and the worship of the Gods.

The proliferation of sects has been explained as due to the breakup of tribal society and its consequences. The cushioning effect of kinship was declining with the impersonal relations of post-tribal society coming to the fore. The increasingly hierarchical ordering of society had been hostile to the wanderers. This was further reiterated by the growth of towns and cities during this period with the anonymity and alienation encouraged by urban institutions. Inevitably there was a breach of methods of adjustment. The introduction of iron technology also brought profound change in prevailing socio-economic structure. Its description as the age of transcendence was not accidental. Economic prosperity made possible by the new situation permitted the maintenance of such large groups of renouncers. The Buddha spent more years at Rajagriha and Sravasti than anywhere else and the early and important monasteries were located at both these towns and at Kausambi. The earlier Jaina tirthankara Parasvanatha is also associated with towns. It was the towns which provided the renouncers with an audience and later with patronage.

The main body of monks came from the lower social orders such as artisans, fishermen, hunters, and basket-weavers. Similarly, the Mathura inscriptions of the pre-Gupta period indicate support for the Jaina also coming from trading groups, artisans and castes low on the social scale.

The Tantric-Yogic Combination

The Tantric-Yogic combination was predominant in the relatively less Hinduised border regions around Assam, being a channel by which foreign elements were assimilated into Hinduism, giving rise to the substratum culture of obscure families and castes and therein assimilation into the political and economic vortex of the Great Tradition via, the system of land grants. The Siddhacaryas of this cult were mostly of low castes. The association of Trantricism with yoga was in all probability an undercurrent of one strand in the ethos of renouncers since early time. This would be true also of Nathpanthis. The substratum culture was opposed to the orthodox tradition, an opposition which came to be symbolically expressed in Tantric rituals much of which is a reversal of Brahman values.

Thus, as Romila Thapar so aptly brings out, the appearance of renouncers as an organised section of society occurs historically at periods of change when there emerge within society not only religious but social and economic sanctions to maintain such groups, for example, the growth of urban centres and the expansion of the agrarian economy. The religious impetus may come from the need to institutionalise a way of life that is new (The Ajivikas, Jaina and Buddhist Sanghas), as a strategy for proselytising (the Dasanami Sanyasis and the Bairagis) or as a means of crystallising a popular religious ethos and providing it with status (the Tantric sects and Yoga). Not all such sects were opposed to orthodoxy, but the technique of using social heresy was employed to organise a religious identity, and the sects therefore registered various degrees and stages of non-conformity. The Buddhist, Jaina and Ajivika monks were opposed to bramanical orthodoxy but the expression of their dissidence took on a puritanical form, in which certain social mores were ultimately strengthened but the manifestations of Brahmanical religion were discarded. The groups influenced by Trantricism accepted some of the religious symbols but discarded many of the social mores. The Dasanami Sanyasis supported Brahmanical orthodoxy, but did not conform to the Brahmanical view of Sanyasa in the setting up of monastic centres.

The renouncers, as she argues, were above and beyond the conventional laws, for they conformed to their own laws and these were often in contradiction to the accepted social laws. This gave them added prestige as it also gave them freedom to protest against the laws of normal society. The form which their protest took was the flouting of social convention. The accommodation of this protest and the investing of it with charisma and moral authority have been in a sense characteristic of Indian society.

(Renunciation. The making of a counter culture: Essays from Ancient Indian Social History, Romila Thapar pp. 63-104. Orient Longman Ltd. 1978. New Delhi).

Romila Thapar's appraisal provides vivid and critical understanding of the cult of renouncers in the context of socio-economic and political transformation experienced by Indian society right from vedic to post-vedic and Mauryan period.

Bhakti Movement

Bhakti movement which largely prevailed during the medieval period also deserves close appraisal as it sharply differs from the earlier cults of renouncers. It also needs special attention as its major proponents pose striking contrast to the cults of Godmen, gurus and other varieties that emerged during the post-independence period. Although the initiation of the Bhakti movement could be traced to sixth and seventh centuries with Alwars and Nayanars movement in South India, in medieval India its spread was far more extensive and exercised deeper impact in many parts of the country.

Indian scholars, Marxists as well as others have exhaustively and critically examined significance of the Bhakti movement. Within Marxist circles also there are sharp divisions, and evaluations differ widely. We don't see any relevance of referring to such controversy in this appraisal. Our attempt here is only confined to brief appraisal of the major thrust of the teachings of the leading Bhakti saints in Southern, Western and Northern India and their impact on the medieval Indian society.

The Bhakti Movement in South India

The Bhakti movement in South India, especially in Tamil region, began sometime in the middle of the sixth Century A.D. and continued till almost upto the tenth century A.D. As brought out by G.S. Harayan and V. Kesavan, this movement represents a new wave of Aryan or Hindu influence. The two main currents of the Bhakti movement are Shaivism and Vaishnavism, and their saints are known as the Nayanar and Alwars respectively. The movement created cultural links by cutting across political boundaries and promoted a new Tamil consciousness. It coincided in time with the rise of a new Feudal monarchy in the South. Initially, it had to confront the already established orders of Jainism and Buddhism. But the growth of Shaivism was so rapid that the kings became its patrons and even went to the extent of persecuting the followers of the heretical sects. Thus, Brahmanism returned with a vengeance, along with its institutional base in temples. The support for temples came from the grant of agrarian settlements in the adjoining areas. In a sense, as suggested, rivalry between the Bhakti movement and heretical sects also reflected the conflict for socio-political dominance between the land-owning and the trading classes. It also should be noted that the Bhakti movement eventually took over Jainism and Buddhism not only because of royal patronage, but also due to its use of several media that evoked popular enthusiasm, such as song and dance and its egalitarian and democratic ethos so vividly expressed in poems and other workings of Nayanar and Alwar saints at the initial stage. This was strikingly different from the rigidity of the classical Brahminical approach. As the authors contend, the Bhakti movement in the South did deviate a great deal from the orthodox philosophy of Brahminical Hinduism and provided impetus to intellectual activity at both secular and spiritual levels. There was a rejection of abstract metaphysical as well as caste regulations. This could be seen in the fact that untouchables and outcastes have also been recognised as saints. Vedic ritualism was thus considerably changed and diluted by the addition of several other folk, local and regional elements. It made the individual and groups aware of some basic equal rights that they could claim at the cultural and religious levels. Similar freedom was also extended to women who had been denied such rights before.

Warkari Movement in Maharashtra

In Maharashtra, several devotional sects came up of which the Warkari sect proved to be the most influential. Dyaneshwar, Namdeo, Ekanath and/Tukaram were the major exponents of the Warkari sect. The Warkari sect was mainly concerned with the Shudras and the untouchables. It was thought necessary to chalk out a practical path as the Jains and other sects like Mahanubhavas emphasised ascetism which had hardly any attraction for common people. Such path had to be found which would not disturb their day-to-day duties and household responsibilities and yet enable them to attain spiritual progress. The path of devotion did not mean either retirement or renunciation and not even spending one's time in performing bhajans all the time. These saints never accepted any conflict between day-to-day life of house holders and their spiritual pursuits. The Maharashtrian saints exhorted their followers to immerse themselves in the pursuit of their occupational and family life without in anyway losing sight of spiritual life.

The devotional cult of Vithal was not monopolised by any one sect. It had incorporated various sects like the Nath, Datta, Chaitanya, Anand and Sufi. Vithal was worshipped as a deity and Poetry (pads) of Dyaneshwar, Eknath Bhagvat, of Namdeo and Tukaram were accepted as authoritative literature and that is how centres associated with Vithal and Dyaneshwar, Eknath and Tukaram are acclaimed as holy centres of pilgrimage which have contributed to the solidarity between persons belonging to different castes and regions and sub-regions within Maharashtra.

From Dyaneshwar to Tukaram, no saints from the Warkari sect felt the need of kingly or princely support, nor were they interested in any kind of gift of land. They did not depend on the generosity of the wealthy. Through their own living example, the performance of Kirtans and the exposition of philosophy and religion, they carried on the work with a missionary zeal. But once a religious movement becomes well organised, it gives rise to vested interests that alienates the leaders from the followers. That is why the Maharashtrian saints did not start Maths. Tukaram had exhorted Kirtankars not to accept food where they performed Kirtan and renounce all kind of pride and hypocrisy.

Soon after Tukaram's death, the devotional movement was on the wane, probably due to the revivalist trends which were reflected in the thinking of Hemadri, Vidyaran and Narasingh Saraswati that became dominant since the period of Ramdas.

Nevertheless, the saints contributed to the sophistication of the Marathi language and that is why Marathi literature can boast of a long tradition. The Sanskrit Gita was translated into Marathi by Gyaneshwar for easy access to people.

Bhakti Movement in North India

While referring to the Bhakti movement in North India, Savitri Chandra aptly remarks, scholars have paid little attention so far to take social context of the Bhakti movement which developed in North India from the fifteenth century. If some critics regard the Bhakti movement as a reaction to Mughal oppression, others see it as Hindu reform movement that arose in order to counter the challenge of Islam. Yet others see the radical wing of the

Bhakti movement as representing the protest of the influential growing number of artisan groups which came into existence as a consequence of city life developing under the Turks.

Kabir is the most outstanding exponent of the Bhakti movement in Northern India. He laid stress on the fundamental equality of man as reflected in the earlier writings of the Sidhas and the Nath Panthis and this tradition continued in the later sixteenth and seventeenth century writings of Guru Nanak, Dadu Dayal and other saints as those of Bihar. Such social ideas, especially those of Kabir, invited sharp reaction from both Hindu and Muslim orthodoxy as they were very radical for that period. Bhakti literature indicates the absence of abstract philosophical ideas; ideas instead are placed in a simple language which made a deep and direct appeal to the common man. Kabir often expressed these ideas by making fun of the Brahmanas or other established strata in Indian society.

While Kabir, Raidas or Rohan Dadu and others believed in basic equality of all especially in terms of access to religious scriptures, Surdas and Tulsidas upheld the position of the Brahman in the caste hierarchy. In other words in Bhakti movement there are two contradictory currents; i.e. at the religious level there is no discrimination based on caste in terms of one's devotion to God, but in secular society social distinctions were not disapproved.

Of course, all of them maintain that the intrinsic qualities of the varnas rather than birth status should be stressed. These ideas did make an impact on society because the exclusive rights of the Brahman were diluted and after the sixteenth century the low caste saints were respected by all sections of society. Kabir disapproved of beggary and emphasised the virtues of working for oneself. For most of northern medieval saints, it was evident that the trader-cum-money lender was exploiting the poor, and other officials including the divans and the kings; perpetuated injustice and sufferings of the masses. Bhakti saints also do not approve of asceticism of those orthodox sects which advocate renunciation of the world. For the Bhakti saints true devotion implies seeking god within oneself, in the routine daily life and their approach based on mysticism is fundamentally humanistic and individualistic. Hence, logically the rejection of a formal and organised religion based on authoritarianism was natural. However, such sacred books as the vedas and the Quran were not entirely rejected, but knowledge based on personal experience was given preference. They stated quite clearly that various rituals and practices were evolved by the privileged in order to control the common man. This approach also perpetuates the animosity between the Hindus and the Muslims. The various saints differ in their attitude towards the scriptures and the role of the priests. Unlike Kabir, Tulsidas and Surdas do not disapprove of the vedas. Dadu, as the dissenter, did not consider himself, to be either a Hindu or Muslim and invited hostility from both sides. On the other hand, Kabir, Raidas, and Nanak, during the fourteenth, fifteenth and sixteenth centuries considered scriptural knowledge secondary to personal knowledge and devotion to God.

Basically, the saints expressed disapproval of social distinctions by seeking to identify themselves with the sufferings of the common man, although they chose to express themselves in religious terms. The movement was thus ideologically against the prevailing socio-economic ideas and institutions which had sharpened the distinctions between the haves and have-nots.

(Reference Indian Movements : Some Aspects of Dissent, Protest and Reform Ed by S.C. Malik Articles by M.G.S. Narayanan, V. Kesaran, G. B. Sardar and Savitri Chandra – Indian Institute of Advanced Study, Simla, 1978).

Sufi Saints also played a similar role during the medieval period. They opposed the tyranny of the powerful. They preached against social inequality and struggled against the prevalent orthodoxy and blind faith. Their following also predominantly came from the lower strata, irrespective of religion. Miyan Mir, Baba Farid, Shaikh Salim Chishti and Nizamuddin Auliya are some of the prominent Sufis who are respected by all for their humanistic preaching.

Godmen, Gurus in Post-independent India

In post-independent India, as we mentioned earlier, there is prolific growth of Godmen, gurus, Sants and Bapus. Apart from Godmen and Gurus, there are other numerous categories as palmists, astrologers, Vastu Shastris, Chhaya-Shastris, Tantrics, visionaries and others who commanded large following. They have proved to be the largest audience pullers as their discourse is attended by lots of people, cutting across caste-class borders.

Post-eighties Spread

Post-eighties have witnessed extensive spread of this phenomenon. It is not accidental that post-eighties period has witnessed profound change in economic policy and political and social orientation of our major political parties. National Congress also under late Indira Gandhi's rule in eighties openly adopted strategy of Hindu appeasement on the one hand and on economic front opted for liberalisation policy, giving up its earlier thrust on self-reliance and attaining development through expanding role of public sector and protection to domestic industries. This shift in policy should also be viewed in the context of structural crisis of the world capitalist economy since the end of sixties, its repercussion on Indian economy, our energy crisis in late seventies and the pressure of the world monetary institution for greater access for the growing Indian market. It is also not surprising that since eighties the ruling parties also stopped giving up even lip-sympathy to earlier pronouncement of socialist pattern of society and pro-poor stance. Thus, the decisive shift in Congress Policy and open overture to placate Hindu sentiments have to be viewed in the context of its open advocacy of world monetary institutions i.e. pro-American policy, since eighties, culminating in its criminal silence on demolition of Babri Masjid in 1993, under Narasimha Rao Government. Thus, the changing scenario since eighties and especially after 1990 when India openly opted for the new economic policy of structural adjustment advocated by the World Bank and IMF has to be kept in view while examining the government policy of promoting Hindutva agenda.

The decisive influence of the shift to the so-called market oriented Liberalisation policy as advocated by American Imperialism also could be seen in the type of Godmen and Gurus who exhibit all the features of an effective marketing Manager of a successful CEO in the corporate world.

Keeping this perspective in view, we will try to sum up the broad features of modern Godmen or gurus that dominate the scene since eighties and nineties.

(1) The number is so large, it is impossible to keep track of them as many of them operate at local level, some district, some at state, some at interstate, while some operate at national and global level.

(2) Many of them operate through some formal committee or trust but the entire control is monopolised by them.

(3) Sizeable number of them operate through institutions, like Ashrams established by them and also engage in social welfare activities and provide various types of social services, such as educational and relief operations, charitable dispensaries, modern hospitals, educational institutions, etc..

(4) It is very difficult to have correct estimate of the wealth acquired by them, cash as well as estates, business they control, their total income and its distribution and also mode of investment. Recently newspaper stories of their investment in stock

market, being cheated by some followers were published. But it is a matter of serious investigation.

(5) Sources of accumulation are also not known. Most of them, especially in Gujarat and Mumbai, are more like Kirtankars with proficiency in story narrations, based on Tulsi Ramayan, Epics like Mahabharat and Gita. By and large source material is based on puran as Bhagwat Puran with occasional reference to Upanishads and vedas.

(6) Bhagwat Katha or religious discourse at times would be only a small part of the total narration. Most of the time they talk of current problems, family situation, decadence because of western culture, glorification of imaginary Hindu, Vedic, traditional value system, institutions, family structure, spiritual values and past glory and greatness of Indian or Hindu nation.

(7) Most of them know several languages. Apart from the mother tongue, they talk well in Hindi, with limited knowledge of English and Sanskrit. Almost all of them know, and quote from Sanskrit slokas, Gita, Purans and lucid explanation of the same. These are characteristics of all popular gurus.

(8) All of them stress the prime importance of attending Sankirtans. Sankirtans alone could pave the way for moksha, liberation, would give peace of mind, could resolve their followers' problems and Gods also would come to their rescue provided they regularly attend kirtans and internalise Guru's teachings.

(9) All of them are good orators; understand mass psychology, people's mind-sets in general, their problems, agonies and have the art of presenting solutions acceptable to the audience.

(10) Katha, pravachan, discourse intertwined with music, songs, poetic recitals, jokes to the extent that Katha's actual content proceeds very slowly

with so many types of interventions. Satsang and the time spent with Guru, search for real Guru and once found Guru is endowed all ability for liberation. Guru can find solution for all their woes. Trust in guru and worship of guru, guru regarded as God, as incarnation of God on this earth.

(11) Disciples' expectation of satsang and from Gurus are all based on this-worldly worries, anxieties, problems, ranging from health and various ailments to marriage, obtaining progeny, and especially male progeny, finding suitable job, educational career, wealth, success in occupation, business – all are predominantly this-worldly and Guru also understands such expectations, responds appropriately. There is hardly anything spiritual about this. Peace of mind is important but that is all for better health and better family or business management.

(12) All these godmen or gurus invariably suggest some herbal treatment or some simple remedies for various ailments, as also for serious health problems. They also suggest some yogic exercises.

(13) Discourse is always in a very loud language full of anecdotes, stories, humour and entertainment. It is very light. They also use various other devices. Bhajans at short intervals is popular. It could be folk; or classical, often based on Filmi tunes and expression of bhakti, especially Krishna-Gopi Raas in a highly romantic style. Most of them also expect audience participation, with clapping and dancing as if they also are in a state of trance, some of them do act or feel that they are in a state of semi-romantic, semi-devotional state of ecstasy.

Music forms very important part of discourse of practically all gurus. Guru sings but also accompanied by a band of musicians, with musical instruments and singers. This technique in psychotherapy described as technique of dissociation, which is highly effective, is very cleverly used by all successful Gurus.

Most of them invariably drop hints of their miracles, their supernatural powers and ability to cure or resolve all problems. Very often, it is also common practice in case of some eminent Gurus to present half a dozen or more disciples who would narrate how miraculously they have been cleared of fatal illness or disease or could resolve their family or business crisis.

Some of the Gurus are in such heavy demand that their discourse dates have to be booked much in advance; may be one year or more. Since booking the date to arrangement of the programme, publicity campaign, advertisement, posters, hoardings, accommodation, pandals, arrangement for Guru and his guests for stay, food arrangement – organisers have to arrange all this much in advance including travel, mode of journey of gurus and sometimes a large number who also accompany guru.

Apart from this, guru may also charge his fees for discourse which could be also quite exorbitant. Even when they go abroad, the same pattern is followed.

Most of the established Gurus maintain extremely good political, administrative and corporate connection. They are highly influential and often are in close touch with higher-ups in political and corporate circles. They often help them and also get favour in return for the assistance they are able to render due to their eminent public position.

The stage from where they address public gatherings is usually very opulent, with display of Gods and Goddesses, usually Ram, Sita, Krishna, Radha, Hanuman, Shiv-Parvati, Vishnu-Laxmi – their expensive statues, idols.

On the basis of our observation of various T.V. channels that broadcast such devotional programme all the time, we found that now we have Gurus of all age groups. Some could be as old as in their eighties, while many are middle aged and also a sizeable number of very young and quite attractive. One almost gathers the impression that they must be spending a lot of time in selecting their wardrobe: costly dresses, even some kind of rings, for every discourse. One could see they have special costumes and very often when they speak about Krishna Radha Gopi-Raslilla, from their gesture and the way young girls respond and dance; there is hardly anything spiritual, but very much romantic with the kind of gestures which are seductive.

It is also widely reported that most of them are womanisers. About their money rolling practices, also investment in stock exchange and other such speculative or profitable avenues is widely suspected. Their involvement in various scandals, even criminal, is also reported.

In concluding remarks, we wish to point out the sharp difference between the ancient cult of renouncers and medieval Bhakti Saints and modern Gurus. Renouncers in ancient Indian society, right from Upanishad to Mauriyan and Gupta period, played a significant role in articulating the socio-economic and political transformation that was taking place in Indian society at various historical junctures. Not only did they articulate this transformation but registered their dissent or protest by evolving on alternate style of living, evolving some parallel philosophy or school of thought, entering into debate with what they considered outdated established religious schools. The protest started with challenging vedic formulation, animal and human sacrifice associated with Yagna, to a philosophy that Buddhist called middle path which facilitated trade and commerce and also provided some semblance of solace by starting Sangham based on equality, simplicity and high ethical values vis-à-vis the destruction of the tribal communities that took place with the emergence of the state as established political institution in early Indian society. Similarly other schools or sects as Lokayat, Siddha and Nath cults and some other Tantric sects also articulated sentiments of the lower strata of Hindu society and in a sense also could channel the discontent and register protest of lower strata against the dominance of upper castes and their established schools of religious philosophy.

Medieval bhakti movement also, beginning with Alwars and Nayanars movement in South India and subsequently culminating in medieval period in practically all parts of the country also articulated the dissent, protest and the desire for reform of lower strata against the oppression and domination of upper and particularly Brahmin castes in Indian society. Medieval saints, most of whom, came from lower poor strata, popularised Bhakti by the use of vernacular media also by simplifying devotional practices, by encouraging women to participate in religious worship. Bhakti saints set up a unique precedent by their lifestyle. Practically all of them had simple life, most of them earned their own living, preached simplicity and never accepted any gift, even food, from their followers. They even despised kings, nobles and such other dignitaries and by and large taught that they are the root cause of people's misery. They set up a strikingly different model of religious pursuits, which included austerity, honesty, transparency, simplicity of language, life style and exclusive stress on lower strata and women for worship.

Modern Godmen, however, pose a striking contrast to them with the fabulous wealth, support from corporates and political and administrative hierarchy, with their huge institutional setup, their corrupt practices, and hypocrisy they appear more as charlatans compared to medieval saints.

It is no wonder, in modern Indian and also global order, with its moral, intellectual and economic decadence, its thrust on neoliberal market economy with Bush, the previous American President, ideally representing this decadence, the kind of modern Godmen or Guru we have, are also perfect exhibit for such system. This contrast also enables us to understand contrast in the role of cult of renouncers and medieval saints in Indian society.

The above observations are quite disturbing and probably too sweeping. But operation of many Godmen and women deserve serious appraisal. Recent mysterious deaths of two kids in Ahmedabad Ashram of Asaram and two more in Chhindwara district of Madhya Pradesh in Asaram Bapu's Ashram Schools are extremely shocking phenomena.

In Ahmedabad and Chhincdwara both protest against the activities of the Asaram Ashram has acquired a massive form. In both places people in thousands displayed their hatred against this Bapu by violent demonstration and mass hunger strike. Protest is also directed against the state government and the police officials with whose connivance Asaram Bapu is able to conduct his legal and illegal activities.

These recent incidents in these states also indicate the imperative need for closer, perusal of modern Godmen and women's activities, basis of their appeal, their mode of operation and network through which they operate. Of course, there would be quite a few of these spiritual gurus – honest, committed and sincere in their beliefs and intention. But a proper appraisal of their impact on society becomes all the more imperative.

We shall conclude our paper with the reproduction of a critique of Godmen and women and Guru Das, a deity in Kerala.

A century back it was Swami Vivekananda who characterised Kerala as a lunatic asylum. It was the most deplorable social situation arising from the worst form of untouchability, highly irrational rituals, superstition led by caste-feudal forces that prompted Vivekananda's sharp comment. However the renaissance movement led by Sreenarayana and Ayyankali followed by initiatives on the part of democratic and left forces did succeed in transforming Kerala to a socio-political situation which was far better than that in other Indian states. Obviously, the formation of the first Kerala Government led by the communist party after state re-organisation took place in this historical context.

However, ever since the notorious liberation struggle of the late 1950's led by Congress party mobilising reactionary, casteist and religious fundamentalist forces with imperialist dollars and due to the ideological and political weaknesses of the left, the above mentioned progressive stream had been experiencing reversals which assumed a new dimension consequent on imperialist globalisation since the 1990's. One manifestation of this has been mushrooming of fake godmen and women or what is called spiritual mafia in the guise of charity, philanthropy and religions throughout the length and breadth of the state. Along with funding, neo-liberalism with its ideology of post-modernism whose affinity towards cult and identity are well known has been propping up these fake god-men and women belonging to different religious denominations. Backed by immense foreign funds and sponsored by the various ruling fronts in Kerala, almost 2000 fake god-men and women are flourishing in various parts of the state. Invariably, under the cover of religion, charity and philanthropy, they are engaging in mafia land deals, fake money transaction, sex crimes, exorcisms and so on. Unparalleled growth of speculative finance and the all-round degeneration that it has created and above all the further decay of organised religion along with growing parasitism associated with imperialist crisis are all providing fertile fields for the growth of spiritualist mafia. As agricultural land is increasingly becoming a speculative asset, there is an unholy relationship between land mafia and fake godmen. More often, the latter prefer the company of ruling class political leaders, bureaucrats, police officials, film stars and of course the wealthy.

While even official estimates put the number of fake god-men and women in the state at more than 1500 among whom 200 are having obvious criminal background, investigation has proceeded against 25 only. Out of this, charge sheet is prepared only in the case of three including Santhosh Madhavan and Himaval Bhadrananda. Though existing provisions of law empowers the police to frame cases on its own, the policy of appeasement towards different religious groups and sects by the government hampers investigating agencies to pursue the matter freely.

An interesting aspect is that while the government investigation is confined to small guys such as Santhosh Madhavan, spiritualist mafia such as Amrithanandamayi and K.P. Yohannan left scot free. For instance, Amrithanandamayi is reportedly running a financial empire worth Rs 20,000 crores. The tentacles of this spiritualist mafia have spread over everything from charity and philanthropy to rehabilitation and real estate business throughout the country. It is just like a parallel government in spite of several criminal allegations against it. Another case is that of K.P. Yohannan who, with the funds coming from America and Germany, runs two institutions, viz. Gospel for Asia and Believers' Church as cover organisations for his underworld financial and real estate deals. Even the Kerala Government's own records put the recent funds that he earned from foreign sources as 1,040 crores. A part of this money is used for purchasing about 2500 crores of land in Kottayam district from the Goenka Group which is illegally possessing about 76000 acres of estate lands in various districts of Kerala in violation of land lease agreement with government. He is also reportedly operating parallel telecommunications network at his headquarters in Tiruvalla with the connivance of those in power. No serious investigation is going on against his unlawful activities.

(Reproduced from Red Star Central organ of CPI (M) July 2008 pp. 30-31) Article by P.J. James. titled 'Proliferation of Fake Godmen and women in Kerala'.

2

Modern Godmen:
Sociological Appraisal

UDAY MEHTA

Historical Resume

Since the Vedic period Gurus have been with us. Suddenly they have been in great demand in last three or four decades. As Mangalwadi aptly remarks, millions of people, young and old, rich and poor, illiterate and sophisticated, bow before them. Agnostics are baffled, sociologists surprised and psychologists seem curious by this phenomenon. Gurus have become influential even in the decaying western culture ('World of Gurus', Mangalwadi).

As a matter of fact, the rise and popularity of Gurus have to be viewed also in the broader context of the revival and resurgence of the indigenous art, music, dance, medicine and language boosted up by the official and non-official institutions especially since independence.

Origin and Relevance of Gurus

According to some observers early Vedic literature does not refer to the word Guru. Even the idea of Guru is absent as the vedic religion essentially revolves around sacrificial rituals. The word was first used and the concept developed during the Upanishadic period, when the emphasis shifted from sacrifice to Jnana as the means to liberation. Guru was needed to impart Jnana. During the Upanishadic era, the ashram system was also established. The acharya who taught students in such Gurukuls was also called the Guru.

With the advent of Pauranika and Tantrikay religions, the founder who initiated the sect or creed also began to be called Guru. His followers who preached and propagated his doctrines were also referred to as Gurus. For the followers of Tantrika sects the giver of a mantra was Guru. The secret mantras were communicated in the ears of the disciples and were called Bija or the Guru Mantra... It was in these Pauranika and Tantrica sects that the lineage of Guruship was established. For the continuation of the lineage, it was considered essential that the Guru be married and have sons.

While tracing the origin of the institution of Guru as a peculiar product of Indian society, Mangalwadi holds following five sociological factors as of special significance for the acceptance of Guruism, namely (1) the nature and place of education in Aryan Society, (2) the esoteric nature of Upanishadic and later Indian religions, (3) the class or caste system with Brahminic dominance in religious affairs and sporadic reaction to it, (4) the authoritarian structure of Indian family life and the repressive puritanism of Indian society and (5) the absence of printed books.

Peter Brant, another noted Western scholar explains the origin of the cult of Gurudom in terms of psychological motives, authoritarianism and puritanism. Right from his earliest days the young Indian was expected to conform absolutely to his father's wishes and commands for the rest of his life. The average Indian is almost incapable of doing anything of which his father disapproves. In this situation, the Guru can appear as rescuer. For with him, the whole conditional mechanism of happy slavery can come into operation without conflict. He is the father who has been chosen. In this way, the disciple remains free in his bondage, bound in his freedom. Taught to be non-attached he can cut himself off from his family without guilt. (P. Brent, 'Godmen in India' p. 287)

Mangalwadi, on the basis of his own observation about the life style in the ashrams of the divine light mission at Haridwar and New Delhi, also draws similar inference. Young people were found to be doing manual labour almost slavishly but happily in this ashram. They cannot step out of the ashram nor answer the question of visitors without permission. Yet they testified that they had peace and contentment now, which they did not have before. The author, however, suspected that some of this peace came because of the fact that their three meals a day were guaranteed in the ashram and not necessarily so at home.

The second factor closely connected to the first is also rooted according to Brent in the repressive puritanism of Indian society. The contempt of sexuality and the strict segregation of sexes led to repression of normal emotions. These feelings were often transferred towards a Guru as to a deity, resulting in intense devotion. In the West, as Brent argues, they are free to work for the approval of those they love or respect and whom they would like to love and respect them. Not such is the case with Indians, who fit into family situation and his social stratum as inevitably as a part of a machine – for the average and particularly the middle-class Indian, there are often only two directions he can go to prove that he can love, that he can be loved. One is towards homosexuality, the other towards the Guru. These are not of course, as Brent suggests, mutually exclusive. Instances of some widely respected Gurus in India of having sexual relationships with their young disciples were cited to substantiate such contention.

The above observations of Mangalwadi and Brent though quite valuable, provide only partial explanations for the emergence and popularity of the cult of Gurudom in Indian society. For the better and more comprehensive understanding of the Guru phenomenon, we would prefer to refer to more vivid and descriptive account of the role of the Guru in vedic and post-vedic society.

In ancient times, as brought out by William Cenkker, the transmission of learning was oral. Teachers repeated to their students texts that they themselves had received orally. In the whole of vedic literature there is no reference to writing because that literature was transmitted entirely by mouth. The oral transmission of the sacred literature continued longer in Indian than any other civilisation.

Later religious literature explicitly forbids the writing down of the vedas. The Mahabharata, for example, condemns to hell anyone who would write the Vedas; the Narada Smriti claims flatly that learning the vedas from a book, unlike learning it from a teacher, is utterly worthless. There is an adage that the text must be learned from the lips of a teacher and not from a manuscript because religious education takes place through hearing and memorising sacred wisdom. Kumarila Bhatta (eighth century C.E.) describes the learning of the vedas from written sources as equal to not comprehending it. The oral transmission of the veda continued till the eleventh and twelfth centuries C.E. (A Tradition of Teachers Sankara and the Jagadgurus Today; William Carkner, pp. 3-4).

Further, the same author remarks 'the hymns of the Rigveda are now classified according to families of authors. Each unit of the Rigveda authored by a particular family possesses a significant homogeneity of authorship. While there existed no system that could be identified with a single teacher, the poets and philosophers of India's earliest religious literature did achieve a marked individuality. The religious preferences of each family of authors can be detected in the hymns by their reference to cult of deities and by creation of hereditary class of teachers. This enabled Indian society to make strides in education.

In early times, as suggested, the teachers usually were householders and did not charge any fees for their teachings. Various types of teachers existed in ancient India: Guru, acharya and Upadhyaya were common types. The gurus after performing various rites gave instructions in the vedas. Upadhaya, although often called the first teacher, along with a disciple's parents taught only some portion of the veda and expected some reward for his instruction.

The Gurus in Upanishads

The guru in Upanisads played a dual role of an intellectual and spiritual guide. A teacher as per the Upanisads is a self-realised person. The Mundaka Upanisad describes the guru as one well-versed in vedas and absorbed in Brahman. A significant portion of early Indian literature is enigmatic. The early teachers sharpened their skills in debates on the basis of the Sutra literature. The Chandogya Upanisads refer to the teacher as one who gives the direction. During the times when the Upanisads were composed, it was not unusual for teachers to be both householder and ascetics. In contemporary Jain and Buddhist education, only an ascetic could become a teacher. However, by the end of Upanisads, it appears only an ascetic could be a teacher.

According to the Taittriya Upanishads, the teacher is the first letter. The student is the last letter. Knowledge is the meeting place. Instruction is the link.

The unique contribution that the Upanisads make to educational method in religious development are the threefold operation of hearing (Sravana), reflecting (manana), and concentration (nididyasana). The focus on hearing, reflection and concentration obviously acquire significance especially in the context of oral transmission of religious knowledge in ancient Indian society.

Meditation is, however, separated from the above threefold method. The Upanisads do not offer a technical definition of meditation. The Upanisads use various words for meditation, of which it seems, the most common are Upasana and Vidya. Upasana virtually means to come near a thing or to approach the realisation of the self through concentration on an object of meditation. Meditation may be made for instance, on a syllable, such as OM or on a more material symbol.

The Guru in the Upanisadic tradition is a realised individual, one who is intellectually supposed to know the Veda and experientially dwells on the absolute Brahman. The epics, in contrast, highlight the divinity of the Guru and the consequent reverance and worship of him. Krishna in the Geeta is addressed as father, lord and most venerable Guru. In the puranas, it is stated that the Guru was regarded as the highest divinity in a particular sect, the Bhagvata Purana which regards the Guru as a deity who is worshipped because liberation comes only through him. In much of this literature the action of the Guru is equated with the action of God.

The ascendency of the Brahmana class along with the heterodox teachers of Buddhism and Jainism gave impetus to the ascetical groups within Hinduism and the indispensability of the Guru is stressed in all Smriti literature. But it is only among the Gurus of the Tantra this imperative was strong because as William suggests, esoteric and secret aspects of their salvation process could be known only through the preceptor (ob.4. pp. 8 to 27).

The ideal teacher in the Upanishads is supposed to be a figure of an intellectual astuteness while in Tantra his personality is presumed to be dominated by mysterious power.

Two Parallel Religious Traditions

In this context it would be quite pertinent to bring out two almost parallel religious traditions in Indian society since very early period. These two trends may broadly be categorised as (i) Idealist and (ii) Proto-materialist or Atmavadi and Dehwadi traditions. Atmawadi tradition is broadly represented by Upanishadic-Smriti literature and Dehwadi trend is evident in Tantric, Lokayat and similar traditions. The relevance of this basic distinction is needed for proper understanding of the Guru phenomenon in Indian society.

Tantric Tradition

The Tantra as argued by N.N. Bhattacharya, categorically asserts that without diksa or initiation all efforts are bound to be futile. This aspect has been elaborately treated in all Tantria texts. "The word diksa is derived from the root *da* (to give) and *ksi* (to destroy) and hence, as per the Tantric tradition, *diksa* confers divine knowledge and destroys sin. Most of the Tantric works provide that the knowledge conveyed by the Guru must be kept secret. In the Tantras any qualified person, irrespective of caste or sex, can act as guru and for this purpose He or She may have to wait for years. He must possess a quite mind and be well versed in scriptures. The disciple should solely rely on him and be ready to surrender everything to the guru. Buddhist Tantras also have the highest praise for the guru, but also warn against false gurus who pretend to know the truth and give false instruction motivated by a greed for money.

According to Mahanirvana Tantra, persons belonging to sects like Sakta, Saiva, Vaisnava and Ganapatya may have sectarian guru, but in order to become a *kaula,* initiation from a proper Kaula teacher is necessary. There is a difference between diksa and Upadesa. While the former includes abhiseka or complete consecration, the latter means communication of mantra in solar or lunar eclipse, at a tirtha, or a Siddakestra or in a temple. On the day of initation the novice, after a bath, is supposed to offer gold, or its substitute, to the guru for the removal of his sin. Then the guru draws a Sarvato bhadra mandala on an altar, sanctifies the five makaras or the tattvas, places an auspicious Jar and fills it with wine. The guru consecrates the novice by sprinkling holy water and uttering mantra invoking the deities and then gives a new name to him as a symbol of his new life (p. 146).

This type of initiation is quite in accordance with the entirety of the Indian tradition of initiation in which the idea of death and rebirth is the driving force. The rebirth of the initiate is often represented dramatically by a magical representation of the act of dying and being born from the womb.

Many features of the vedic-upanayana and Tantric diksa are, as suggested, sophisticated versions of the primitive tribal rites of initiation.

The importance of initiation at puberty becomes evident when we look at the primitive secret societies headed by tribal elders. These societies bear distinctive totems, traditions and rituals and in many cases they have magico-religious functions. Admission to such group is restricted to those who have undergone the appropriate rites and rituals.

The idea of primitive secret societies reminds one of the Buddhist Guhya Samaja. The name itself has the same meaning. Tantric converts to early Buddhism, although they professed a belief in the Buddha Sangha and Dharma, did not give up the traditional beliefs and rituals which they used to practice in secret. The secret conclaves which thus grew within the monastic order developed, in course of time, into organisation known as the Guhya Samajas. Their teachings and practices were not sanctioned in early Buddhism, but they were not slow to find means of obtaining the sanction. They tried to introduce their doctrines into Buddhism by composing a new Sangiti or collection or verses which came to be known as the Guhya Samaja tantra and attributing these doctrines to Buddha they were able to secure many followers within the Buddhist Sangha.

The Siddhacaryas, Buddhist Tantric Influence

Within the fold of Buddhism there developed distinct Tantric ways, the aim of which was to attain *siddhi* or supernatural power. The followers of this path were opposed to Brahmanism and the caste system. In fact, many of them came from the lowest castes. In different Tantric texts, there is reference to Siddhas and the sects like Siddhakula, etc. According to this tradition there were 84 siddhas who were endowed with supernatural power which they achieve through meditation and physical exercises. These 84 Siddhas were also well known in the literature of medieval Indian alchemy for their valuable contribution. The lower ranks of Siddhacaryas are also evident from their names like Dombi, Sabari, Tanti, Camari, Teli and Kumari. They came from the castes of carpet carriers, leather-workers, washermen, oilmen, tailors, fisherman, wood-cutter etc. The Nath siddhas are also included in the list. These Siddhacaryas did not bother for social distinctions and the caste system.

The Siddhas also believe in the divine power of the guru, who initiates the disciples according to their potential. There are five kulas or brands of the Siddka culture, Dombi, Nati, Rajaki, Candali and Brahnani. These are symbols of five female forces or Sakti. The way of the Siddhacarya is basically that of Kaya Sadhana or the way of the body. According to Sidha, there are 32 nerves in the body through which the Sakti flows from its main centre below the naval region. The aim of the aspirant, in short, is the realisation of Sahaja. Sahaja is the root of all existence, the source of eternal bliss and pleasures. When all the senses are merged in it the aspirant has the feeling of absolute non-dualism. He then sees everything as an integral part of his own self.

Liberation here is conceived as not of soul. It is of body which can be attained within the span of human life. The followers of the siddha way use the term Jivanmukti. It means the attainment or immortality which is possible by Kayasadhana or disciplining the body.

All believers in the Tantric Kayasadhna, including the siddhas believe that the body is the microcosm of the universe. Mountain, sea, moon, sun, river all that of which in the world is composed are within the human body. It is by Hathayoga that one is able to have mastery over the body and mind; Siva and Sakti reside in the body.

Tantrism and the Natha Siddha Tradition

Nathism originated among persons belonging to the lower ranks of Indian society. This tradition was influenced interestingly by Jainism and Ajivikism and on the other by Tantrism. All over North India, in the Maharashtra region of Western India, also in parts of South India the followers of Nathism had their centres. In theoritical outlook they have been influenced by the Saiva and Sakta Agamas. In practical field their aim was to attain Siddhi or miraculous power and they characterised the method of attaining it as rahasya or esoteric. Nathism probably developed in the lower regions of the Himalayas. The Natha sidhas had a general predisposition towards acute practices and acquisitions of supernatural practices and supernatural powers. Some of them also believed that by the yogic control over breath, disciplining of the body and the use of drugs made of mica and mercury it was possible to attain immortality. In many places in North India, the Nath Panthis are known as Kanphat yogi because they were a pecular earring known as Mudra, or Kundala. They use Siva symbols and observe the Sivaratri festival and their religious theories and practices contain many Sakta-Tantric elements. Their deities include Niranjana, Sunya and Adinatha. In Nathism one finds diverse influences as Saiva, Sakta, Buddhist, Jain and Ajivikas. Ingredients of

Islam and Vaisnavism are also evident in the Natha way of life. Their religious discipline was based on Hathayoga. However, over a period one also finds among some Nathpanthis a trend influenced by the Brahmanical fold.

Medieval Period – Bhakti Movement

Religious Gurus of the medieval period were influenced by Sahajiya ideals. Etymologically Sahajiya implies that which is same as human instinct itself. In popular version it was understood as God, by whatever name or attribute he may be characterised, resides in the heart of man. The realisation of God as identical with one's own self has become the basis of all forms of Sahijiya cult. This realisation is called by the Sahajayani Buddhists as Mahasukha which is possible through the union of Sunyata and Karuna or Prajna and Upaya. The Natha-panthis understand mahasukha in terms of immortality which is possible through Kayasudhana. All forms of Tantric teaching insists on the symbolic union of the male and female principle – the efficient and material causes of creation – within the body and this concept has influenced all types of medieval religious ideas. The Sahaja ideal has also influenced Sikh religion. Sikhism is anti-Brahmanical; it has no room for caste system. Like the Sahajiyas and the followers of the Tantric way the Sikhs also believe in the absolute authority of the guru (p. 302).

In the medieval age several Vaisnava, Saiva and Tantric sects launched religio-reform movements and fought for the religious rights of the sudras and women. Nevertheless, there were few exceptions in medieval Bhakti-movements such as Tulsidas who was a champion of Hinduism. He was critical of the Telis, Kumars, Candals, Kiratas, Kolis and others belonging to despised castes who became gurus by just shaving their heads, meditating, observing vows and reading the puranas and expected that the Brahmins should be subservient to them.

Such observation of Tulsidas was a reflection upon the popularity of teachers like Rabidas, Dharna and others who belonged to the so-called lower castes and professions. (p. 303). Of the North Indian leaders of the religio-reform movement, Ramananda of the fourteenth and fifteenth century belonged to the Vaisnava Sect. In the Granth-Saheb, one comes across a song attributed to him in which, he states that God (Rama) cannot be found in any external object, he is not in the vedas, one should seek him in one's heart. Among his disciples Rabidas was a chamar (cobbler) by caste and profession, who attracted numerous disciples due to his liberal religious ideas. Kabir himself held Rabidas in high esteem. The Granth Saheb contains more than 30 songs composed by him. Jhali, Queen of Chittor, was his follower and the celebrated Mirabai was also his disciple. Thesena, another disciple of Ramananda was a barber.

Apart from Rabidas, the most celebrated disciple of Ramananda, as widely accepted, was Kabir, born in 1398. He learnt from Ramananda the futility of the caste system, Idolatry, pilgrimage, vows, fasts and all external formalities of religion and earned his livelihood by weaving. He advocated that everyone must work, he must earn to help others, but he should not accumulate wealth; should be truthful and accessible to all, he should realise the truth within himself, truth is in the form of love and compassion. One's religious system is different from another's only in name, God may be called by any name and external formalities in spiritual quest are meaningless.

One of the best exponents of the way of Kabir, was Dadu (1544-1603) who was born in Rajasthan. His objective was to synthesise all forms of religion, the sect founded by him was known Parambrahma Sampradaya. He made a selection of devotional writing from all forms of religion and this compilation was unique of its kind. Dadu did not believe in any scripture. According to him, the realisation of the self should be the aim of human life. His sons Garibdas and Maskindas and daughters, Nanibai and Mutabai composed many devotional poems. Of his disciples,

Sunderdas and Rajjab deserve consideration. Rajjab founded a sect; the teachers of this sect could be either Hindu or Muslim. Of the other medieval saints who pursued the ideals laid down by Kabir and Dadu, Dharamdas, born in Chapra in 1556, Laldas, coming from the meotribe of Rajasthan, Puran Bhakat and Babalal of Punjab and Narsingh Mehta of Gujarat deserve special consideration.

Among the liberal religious teachers who flourished in North India in the first half of the Eighteenth Century. Bhan Sahab, a follower of Kabir, formed a salvation army. His important disciples were Jivandas and Rabi Sahab. Carandas, who was born at Dehar near Alwar in 1703, started a sect of his own, was against caste system and all forms of superstition. Sivanarayana born in 1710 in Belia district, sought to Synthethise Hindu and Muslim religious ideas. Jagjivan who flourished in the last quarter of the seventeenth century, founded the Satyanam or Satnami sect. The Satnamis were against idolatry, untouchability and the caste system. Similar views were held by the Alakhnamis, a sect which flourished in Bikaner under the Leadership of Lalgir.

In Maharashtra, saints like Jnanadeva, Ekanatha and Tukaram and others believed in absolute devotion and simplicity in religious life. Personally, many of these gurus were free from caste prejudices, but they did not launch any socio-religious movement as did their counterparts in North India.

Bengal, Assam and Orissa were basically the strongholds of Saivism and Tantra. Jagannatha of Puri was originally a tribal god, although he is now in Vaisanava garb but his rituals indicate tribal influence.

Nathism in Bengal, Assam and Orissa is also known as yogi-pantha due to the influence of the medieval reform movement.

From our appraisal of the guru phenomenon in Upanishad and the subsequent period, it becomes somewhat evident that the classical type of the vedic guru imparting training in vedic texts with all their complexities in terms of its oral transmission with exclusive stress on their proper pronunciations, style of recital and memorisation of these texts, with long duration of the stay of pupils in Gurukul, often located in forests areas, away from community, gradually loses significance and almost withers away, since Mauryan and post-Mauryan period, till bold attempt for its revival with some alterations by Shankaracarya in eighth and ninth centuries A.D.

Since the advent of the Mauryan period and the emergence of the centralised state power inaugurated by a series of changes in social, political and economic structure, with rise and spread of Buddhism, Jainism, Ajivikas, Lokayats and host of other religious and philosophical sects, one witnesses varieties of religious teachers challenging the old Brahminic, vedic style of gurus in Indian society. This period also witnesses the emergence and spread of different religio-mystical cults sponsored largely by the lower social orders with their primitive legacy. The influence of variety of the Tantric sects with their preoccupation with Yogic practices or Kaya Sadhana on all major religions and sects ranging from Buddhism, Jainism, and vedic sects apart from other sects like Nath, Kapalika, Siddhacarya and others, is quite evident.

Advent of the British rule and Guru phenomenon

With the advent of the British rule, the guru phenomenon based on earlier Nath, Sidha and other Tantric sects and subsequently evident in medievel Bhakti movement lost its earlier prominence. There are numerous social, political and cultural factors responsible for the Guru or sant phenomenon receding into background in Indian Society. It is not possible to examine these factors at length at this juncture. We will attempt to briefly mention some of the more significant factors which we think contributed in sidelining Guru Sant phenomena.

First major factor that vitally influenced this development was the approach of the British administration and scholars in assuming and accepting the dominant social and cultural ethos of the traditional Indian society. They favoured the version given to them by the Brahmin scholars about the religious and social traditions of Indian societies. Thus, the Brahminical and the vedic perception and interpretation based on such presumption was accepted as the appropriate perspective for understanding Indian society.

Secondly, even Indian scholars and social reformers who were exposed to Western ideals, development and value system based on liberal and democratic framework of European and particularly the British society also protected classical Vedic ideals and the social order as having all ingredients of such liberal outlook and society. Here the slogan advocated by Raja Ram Mohan Roy and his supporters was restoration of old Vedic ideals. Indian society had experienced social and cultural decay because of the impact of all alien systems of Mughals and others. They advocated social reforms in Indian society evoking imaginary ideal social order that prevailed during the Vedic period. They welcomed with zest the Western liberal value system and spread of the Western educational system and social order for the progress of Indian society and polity.

Swami Dayanand Saraswati who founded the Arya Samaj went to the other extreme of rejecting outright the Western value system and liberal order by advocating that we had much better society and cultural and social order based on vedic ideals that we have hardly anything new to learn from the western world.

The nationalist movement and large number of our national leaders from the Indian National Congress subscribed to such outlook. They also found it convenient to popularise the demand for self rule and political independence on the basis of such premises. The British advocacy of India as a backward country and justification of the British rule for the emancipation of Indian population from such primitive, barbaric legacy also found an effective rejoinder from such glorification of the Indian past heritage by Indian leaders. The nationalist leaders who also by and large coming from higher castes and better off section of Indian society also found it quite convenient to adopt and advocate such Brahminic version of Indian society. Such backdrop hardly left any space for the rival religious or cultural groups as was the case in medieval and earlier phase of Indian society to project and propagate their alternate religious and social position and practices. Guru phenomena thrived in this cultural and religious interface.

Post Independence Period

In post-independence period also during the earlier phase, over the first decade of independence, when this country could attain comparatively new threshhold of economic, political and social development, one hardly notices any significant spread of the guru phenomena. It is essentially during the last three or four decades, one witnesses an extensive spread of the guru phenomena all over the country. The widespread growth of the guru phenomena is largely linked up with the rapid spread and growing influence of the Hindutva forces in this country. Several other factors must have also contributed in the rapid and amazing spread of the guru cults in recent years. We can only enumerate some of the significant factors which we think have played more vital role in this direction.

It won't be much of an exaggeration to say that factors which explain the fast growing influence of the Hindutva forces in all probability account for the extensive spread of the guru phenomena. Of course, it is not our contention that these factors are identical. But the correspondence between the two could not be overstressed.

It is not possible in this brief appraisal to highlight all factors which are instrumental for the growth of growing influence of the Hindutva forces. Nor we are competent enough to tackle such task. Since eighties the BJP and its associate organisations as VHP, Bajrang Dal, Durga Vahini, Sant Sammelan, and several other under the banner of the RSS have witnessed rapid rise on account of several political, economic and social factors. We can briefly mention some of the prominent factors responsible for this development. Since seventies Indian economy witnessed deepening energy crises, with a paradox of Indian path of "independent, self-reliant path of development culminating in severe crisis of foreign exchange along with growing structural crisis of the global capitalism. Late Indira Gandhi coming into power in eighties shifting from her earlier thrust of Garibi Hatao, nationalisation of financial institution and Independent foreign policy opted for or had to opt for the policy of neo-liberalisation as advocated by the institution like IMF and World Bank under the pressure of American imperialism. Indian economy and polity had experienced a severe jolt since mid-sixties and this got articulated in political upsurge in West Bengal, Andhra, Bihar and other parts of the country in the form of Naxalbari revolt, peasant agitations and workers struggle culminating in recurring state and Bharat bandhs. This growing discontent got articulated in growing influence of communists and socialist along with the rightist political parties like Jan Sangh and similar formations in different parts of the country and their posing serious challenge to the Congress monopoly of power. Indian National Congress could not continue to retain its political hold over the electorates on the basis of its earlier umbrella character based on alliance of upper caste, Muslim and other minority votes and dalit castes, especially at regional levels. Emergence of new social classes with their expanding economic base and also numerical strength posed serious challenge to the Congress rule. The new social class largely recruited from the middle and backward castes also benefited from the expanding industrial base in rural and urban areas. In order to retain its political hold the Congress openly started playing communal card in 1980 general elections. This became blatantly evident in Jammu and Kashmir elections.

This sharp turn in the Congress policy also provided golden opportunity to BJP to use communal card for more effectively and also skillfully. Since 1980s, Rathyatra and Ram Mandir politics with the support of the newly emerged entrepreneurial classes and other middle castes who had not found any space in the Congress rule, enabled the BJP and allied forces to rapidly expand their influence in the country.

Electronic media, its extensive spread since eighties with the relay of Mahabharat and Ramayana serials also significantly boosted the appeal of communal forces to gain larger foothold in Indian society. Along with the use of the television, other devices as manufacturing of audio and video cassettes based on religious mythology, devotional songs based entirely on Hindus scriptures and god heads, also could be used effectively to spread the influence of the Hindu communal propaganda. Such religious propaganda with its blatant communal overtones helped not only communal forces but also contributed in a big way in providing social base for the growing flocks of gurus in many parts of the country.

The rise and extensive spread and popularity of the guru and gurumai phenomena in last over three decades all over the country could be attributed to this favourable environment. The extensive patronage they received from the corporate sector and the ruling strata has facilitated the popularity and influence of the cult of gurudom in no small manner.

Apart from this, the forces unleashed by neo-liberalism with its exclusive stress on unregulated market mechanism have facilitated the spread and popularity of the Guru phenomena. The world of gurus, gurumai, with its infinite variety of appeals cultivated by its seasoned operators has become a big attraction cutting across caste, class borders and thereby has successfully created a huge entertainment market. As reported, the sale of audio and Video-cassettes alone fetch over Rs1400 crores annually in Indian entertainment market. If one takes into account the huge money generated through T.V. and other and serials based on infinite variety of mythological figures, probably the total financial market and profit generated from such programmes would exceed the total capital generated from all other entertainment market put together.

As Prof. Panikar has aptly argued that since independence the extensive spread of religiosity and commodification of religion largely account for the rapid rise of the guru-gurumai phenomena in last over three decades in this country.

The state patronage, open admiration and presence of the prominent political leaders, at the central as well as state level, irrespective of the allegiance to any particular political party is also largely responsible for the rise and institutionalisation of the guru / gurumai cults in this country. Corporate sector has also extended large scale support by the presence and sponsorship by industrial magnates and business tycoons of Ramkathas, Bhagwat Sapthas, Shiv Parayans, Radha Krishna celebrations, Gayatri yagnas, and similar religious discourses and festivals initiated by modern gurus / gurumais all over the country. Apart from this, other major and vital factors instrumental in rapid rise and popularity of the modern guru / gurumai phenomena are increasing insecurity, alienation, despair experienced by practically all sections of Indian population cutting across caste and class lines as a result of cut-throat competition, inflated consumerism let loose by global policy of neo-liberalism based on unregulated market mechanism. Modern Godmen and women cater to their needs. Most of over modern guru / gurumais' success and increasing popularity could be attributed to their art of oratory and skill to manipulate their audience mind-sets and provide effective escape mechanism from their routine world of sorrows and anxieties.

3

Ungodly Men, Unholy Activities

PROFESSOR K. N. PANIKKAR

Indians have the reputation of being the most religious and spiritual people in the world. Whoever invented this stereotype for whatever reasons has only created an alluring myth Indians still seem to savor. Spirituality is the only capital Indians possess and invest. At the World Congress of Religious, Swami Vivekananda is believed to have accomplished spiritual conquest which is often invoked as a high watermark of Indian attainment. Contrasting the materialism of the West with the spiritualism of India continues to be a profitable past time, despite the acquisitive fervour currently gripping society. A pretended indifference to this worldliness is still an obsession.

Spirituality has been a useful commodity, both for export and for internal consumption. The exporters can be ignored, for they only create a false image abroad and in the bargain indulge in some welcome material pursuit of earning a few dollars! The internal purveyors of spirituality are too insidious and far too many today. Their spirituality is suspect and religious knowledge is superficial. Honourable exceptions though, are not wanting. But exceptions are few and pretenders are many.

The former do not vie for public attention, instead they lead a secluded life and engage in silent pursuit of mystic power through meditation. The latter strive to amass riches, enjoy social prestige and exercise political power. They are the modern incarnations of traditional *sanyasis* – godmen, who in the guise of representing Indian spirituality and religious tradition, indulge in political maneuvers, sexual abuse and trafficking in arms and a host of other anti-social activities.

In 1802, Raja Mohan Roy, popularly perceived as the 'Father of Modern India', but in practice a theist, unhappy with the then prevailing religious conditions in India, had traced religious superstitions and obscurantism to the vested interests of Hindu priests. He made a distinction between religion and the religious system and argued that all religious systems are systems of deception. The manipulation of faith attuned to serve the interest of the priestly order is central to the system. The dogmas and rituals invented for this purpose do not necessarily reflect the essentials of religion nor convey religious knowledge. Thus, magic is traded as supernatural power, lust for lucre is conceived in elaborate ritual practices and sexual abuse is interpreted as divine benediction.

The deceptive nature of the religious system is actually unraveled only when believers become alive to it. It does not happen so easily, as it requires transgressing the ideological barriers set by religious faith. Take the examples of the Vallabhachari sect in Bombay. There was hardly any conceivable exploitation, including sexual abuse of devotees, which their Maharajah or head, did not indulge in. Yet, it went on unchallenged for a long time till a court case exposed the Maharaja's demeanors. It administered such a shock to the members of the sect that they could hardly recover from it.

More despicable is what goes on among the godmen today. Recently there has been a spate of incidents of sexual abuse involving sadhus and saints. A few of them have even resorted to murder to preserve their privileges.

The official godmen, Chandraswamy, who is reportedly thick with more than one prime minister, is accused of criminal connections and even of pimping. Yet, not only has he not been arrested, but he continues to enjoy the proximity of the politicians in power and even publicly performs *yagnya*, which in popular perception is a holy act. While people felt enraged in the nineteenth century by the exploits of the Maharajah of the Vallabhachan sect, scores of much worse instances do not arouse the social consciousness of the people today.

This indifference and acquiescence is partly posited in the increasing hold of religiosity and superstition. Religion is an intensely personal experience and as a practice has been confined to homes or to places of worship. In recent times there is a visible change, marked by a tendency to demonstrate religiosity through public organisation or religious functions and ceremonies. Hardly a day passes now when the streets are not invaded by one religious procession or the other. This public display of religiosity, among others, is conducive of a social consciousness on which, godmen thrive.

The extension of religious events formerly confined to one religion or to other parts of the country is another recent phenomenon. The Ganesh procession is a case in point. Prior to Bal Gangadhar Tilak invoking Ganesh as a symbol for political mobilisation during the beginning of the century, Ganesh festival was hardly known as a public event. At best, it was a legal community celebration. Over the years worship has not only been replaced by public processions but has also been extended to other parts of India. In Tamil Nadu, for instance, Ganesh (Vinayaka) procession was almost unheard of about ten years ago. Now it has become a major event and unfortunately carries a communal connotation. This is true of other regions also. At many places, including Chennai, the processions occasioned communal tension. Even if Tilak's invocation of Ganesh had unintended communal consequences and also underscored religious consciousness, it was essentially different from what is happening today. Unlike in the past, the Ganesh festival is now an occasion to affirm religiosity and to arouse communal sentiments.

That religious processions have been the sites of communal violence in the past is worth recalling. One singular cause for many a communal conflagration has been the music before the mosque performed by religious processions. The British government banned religious processions whenever law and order was at stake. Why not the Indian secular state disallows all religious processions which are more often than not public exhibitions of vulgar and communally motivated exhibitions of religiosity? That they do violence to the sentiments of true believers should be an added reason. At any rate, religious processions are now being used to perpetuate practices contested by the reform movements in the nineteenth century.

The irrationality and superstitions which the godmen exploit and perpetuate are generally attributed to the uneducated. That they easily fall pray to the miracles of godmen is undoubtedly true. But godmen draw their main support and legitimacy from the power-hungry, guilt-ridden and ambitious elite, who are constantly looking for a solution to their personal anxieties and professional uncertainties. Among them are politicians, professionals and bureaucrats. Without them a Chandraswami or a Sai Baba is not possible. They prop up the image of these godmen, provide patronage and bolster their social acceptance. What they gain in return is profitable enough to ensure their fealty, often exhibited in ways repugnant to reason. For instance, prominent politicians of the country, including prime ministers, cabinet ministers and speakers of parliament do not hesitate to touch their feet in public or receive blessings in humiliating postures. Gone are the days when Jawaharlal Nehru used to exhort his countrymen to develop a scientific temper. In contrast, what the present day political leader projects are superstition, obscurantism and irrationality. Rather than a reflection of individual aberration and personal beliefs, this indicates the ideological bankruptcy and electoral opportunism of contemporary politics.

In recent years hundreds of well educated young men and women 'competed' for an opportunity to participate in the *Putrakameshti yagam* which would help them beget a progeny. They are unlikely to be oblivious of elementary knowledge about the human reproductive process. Yet, they chose to succumb to temptation offered by religious merchants who, if newspaper reports are to be believed, charged the aspirants a hefty fee. More recently, among those who queued up to offer milk to the obliging Ganesh were a large number of educated and enlightened elite, some of whom waited for darkness to fall to be a party to the miracle.

The Indian society appears to be in the grip of cultural backwardness and intellectual bankruptcy which largely accounts for the current scenario. The former is partly a legacy of the colonial past and the distorted social development it had engendered. It is also rooted in the limitations of our national movement which did not succeed in integrating the cultural and political struggles. As a consequence, independent Indian inherited a culturally backward social consciousness. While the nationalist leaders failed to evolve adequate strategies to overcome it, the present politicians, most of whom do not possess any idealism or vision are exploiting it in their pursuit of power. The godmen keep their company, encourage them and provide 'spiritual' sustenance. In the process, they contribute to the perpetuation of a socio-cultural situation in which their 'spirituality' could reap rich harvests. They are ungodly men indulging in unholy acts.

Discussing the practice of Hinduism in India, Max Weber had observed that 'religious behaviour is not worship of God, but rather coercion of God, and invocation is not prayer but rather the exercise of magical formulae'. If alive, Weber would have perhaps made the same statement today. What distinguishes the contemporary scene, however, is that godmen have greater clout and social acceptance.

4

Religion, Politics and Godmen

RAM PUNIYANI

Last few years has seen a rise of a variety of Godmen who have a vast following. Most of these are talking in the language of spirituality, ignoring the issues of average people. In history we see that on one hand there are clerics, Priests, Maulana, Acharya who had been associates of the landlord-Kings and gave legitimacy to the rule and oppression exploitation of landlord-Kings. The saints talked the language which related to the problems and travails of the people. These saints cut across religious lines, bhakti, sufi and liberation theology in particular. Many a religious traditions began as the syncretic traditions like Sikhism.

Today we see a plethora of Godmen who have mushroomed along with increase in religiosity all around. The rise in the impact of identity politics and mushrooming of Godmen has been running in a parallel fashion, one does not see too many saints articulating the problems of poor people today. These Godmen talk in a mystical language and propound some of the conservative values while keeping quiet about the social ills prevailing in the name of religions.

While these Godmen have increased in number Topics related to religion and Godmen cannot be easily brought under the scrutiny of reason. Today innumerable social phenomenon have thrived which derive their name from religion. The whole politics, global as well as local is wearing the clothes of religions. While in earlier times also the clergy and saints were the two faces and two sides of the phenomenon of religion, the one related to power the other to the powerless, today the contrast is more visible today but more complex than before.

Politics Today

The social-political scene in India during last two decades has witnessed one or the other political issue, which has its base in the religion. Religious conversions, Shahbano case, Ram temple movement, Babri demolition, and 'Islamic terrorism' present a picture of India, which is much different than the one seen in the earlier decades of the republic. This scene is duly backed up by the rise of religiosity in different walks of life. The religious cults, Asaram Bapu, Aniruddha Bapu, Pandurang Shastri Athwale and their ilk are drawing large followings. The temple visits and temple functions have become the major events of communities. The media is devoting more and more space on the discourses of swamis and saints, columns on religious values and religious functions are a plenty in the media.

Television serials depict the 'guiding role' of clergy and there are special channels like Astha and Sanskar to propagate particular versions of religiosity. The struggling middle class hero of the previous decades is replaced by the stinking rich patriarch constantly in touch with the priest for guidance in his regular affairs. "Current events in India reveal the continuing importance of religious nationalism...the religious aspects of Indian Nationalism have yet to receive adequate attention." (Peter van der Veer, 1998)

Globally one is witness to the phenomenon of terrorism, couched in the words like Jihad. The US attack on Afghanistan took place under the banner of crusade. The theory of Clash of Civilisations, which has been much in vogue and does represent the undercurrent of religion as the core of civilisation, also presents the political interests in the language of religion. This phase of World politics has seen the overarching presence of religion all around.

Religion: Mirror of Society

Religion being a total mirror of society has multiple facets, which are complexly interwoven but diverse. On one side we have the facts which have more to do with belief in supernatural, holy books, and rituals, places of worship and places of pilgrimage. All these are well articulated by the clergy, official or de facto of that religion.

These have more to do with identity aspects. As such understanding of religion fluctuates between religious identities and religious community on one hand to the moral values of the religions on the other. Somewhere the role of clergy, with different prefixes like Acharya, Mahant, Guru, has always been a dominant one. Their social power has also risen along with rise of religious cults and their following amongst diverse sections of society.

Moral aspect of religions, have a great deal of overlap, like love, non-violence, dignity, tolerance, truth, justice etc. The saints, the ones' who were with the average people of society do act as vehicles of this aspect of religion, in different forms like Bhakti sainits in Hinduism, Sufi saints in Islam and liberation theologian in Christianity.

Clergy and Saints

Of all the aspects of religion the role and power of the clergy has been most striking. In societies where agricultural mode of production led to the rise of feudal classes and Kingdoms the clergy played a role which was that of defender of the system of exploitation based on the feudal relations of production.

The association of clergy with the feudal lords in different settings has been the hallmark of feudal power structure. Here the expressions are different. The structure of clerical organisation also remains diverse. In Christianity, one sees the most organised Church standing in close relation to the power of Kings. In Hinduism the King had a Rajguru (Royal Priest) and the landlords had the blessings of the local priest.

"The opposition to clerical power in Europe took the form of mysticism, open heresy, or armed insurrection, all depending on the conditions of time. Sixteen century reforms heavily leaned on mysticism, this, was directed against the clergy whose wealth and political power it affected". (Mehta, p. 32) The revolts of poor peasants took the form of deriving the strength from pre-hierarchical Christian society and medieval mysticism. This was as opposed to the power of Church, which was oppressive to poor peasants. Munzer deriving values from mysticism led the poor peasants and attacked the hierarchic church structure. He repudiated the concept of Bible being the only and infallible revelation. The role of Saints vis-à-vis clergy is manifested in different forms; there is no universal pattern in this. The opposition to exploitative systems also assumed the forms in a religious language, "Revolutionary opposition to feudalism lasted throughout the middle ages. It took the form of mysticism, open heresy or armed insurrection, all depending on the conditions of the time. As for mysticism it is well known how much sixteenth century reformers depended on it. Munzer himself was largely indebted to it." (Engel's, 1982, 88)

The oppressed masses found their pain and sorrows addressed in a sympathetic way, which acted as a sort of healing balm by set of people who were saints. "The impoverished masses who in the earlier phase of civilisation were simply slaves and who in the advanced phase, became the propertyless working class were henceforth confronted with a dual uncertainty and dual misery; those coming from still uncontrolled nature and those coming from the exploitative machinery of ruling class. This made the life of masses too painful of suffering and uncertainness to be born without some palliative remedy, this was supplied by religion-the belief in God who alone could assure justice, if not right now at least sometime later, if not in this world at least in the afterworld." (Chattopadhyay, 1987) Religion on one hand had this role of offering a solace to the deprived sections. It is the saints who at a positive note offered solace to the deprived. The saints in a way challenged the power of clergy. But this challenge was always articulated in a very positive language. They were critical of the established norms of religion at the same time they evolved their own spiritual language, which while totally opposed to the one of institutional religion did create a bond of harmony amongst the poorer sections. Lokayat type traditions, which again were away from the dynamics of social power opposed the caste system, opposed the concepts of heaven and hell and the blind faith constructed by Brahminism. This blind faith was the instrument through which the dominant classes, feudal lords, were exploiting the poor. Lokayat like traditions called for resorting to reason.

Mostly Saints did not practice rituals, did not conform to religious scriptures and neither did they invoke the established traditions. Their concept of God or Super Natural power is like that of a friend, who is not much to be feared; as projected in the tradition of clerics. Thus, two parallel traditions keep running in the name of religion, the one of clergy and the other of saints. The clergy is with the oppressors and saints with the toiling masses. "To the extent that the subjugated and oppressed class is able to resist the dominance of their oppressors, their ideological hegemony and are able to pose a serious challenge to oppressive religious doctrines, the oppressed can insulate their beliefs which later continue to symbolise defiance...The philosophy of Charvak, Siddha, Nath Tantra ran parallel religious traditions to the Brahminical religion, more popular amongst the oppressed, right upto Bhakti movement." (Engineer, 1998) Interestingly in due course many of these traditions themselves are co-opted again by the elite religious traditions. Sai Baba who was a Muslim sufi, with following amongst both religions, has currently been Brahminised Sai baba of Shirdi as well. Lord Jagannath of Orissa was worshipped by Advasis but now it has become the God of dominant class and castes.

India: Bhakti and Sufi Traditions

In India the major Saint traditions have been Bhakti and Sufi. Both these coming from different religious streams had a strong impact on Indian masses. Bhakti is probably the outstanding example of the subaltern trend in Indian religious history. Bhakti movement began in Tamil Nadu and spread northwards. The Bhakti saints came from different streams and there is plethora of saints coming from low caste. Bhakti "opposed the institutionalisation of religion, tried to decentralise it, and declared that it is a private matter. It gave respectability to the separation of state power and religion and merged the concept of God worship with the process of getting knowledge." (Bhadu, 2003, 33) Warkari tradition in Maharashtra is one important trend of this. Chokhamela a poet saint coming from low caste, articulates the sorrow of poor in his poems. Reprimanding God for the condition of the society where there is such huge inequality complains to him about his world system for its cruelty to the poor. The devotion in this trend is away from Vedic rituals and its teaching is away from the Vedas and Upanishads. Chokhamela in one of his Abhang, folk form of poetry, says, "We have not read the Holy tomes, we are not experts in the interpretation of Vedant-Dharma but the core of religious teachings, the formless god is standing for us in the form of Vithoba. (God standing on the brick) and so is accessible to us." (Sardar, 1999, p. 64)

Tukaram is one of the most popular saints of Maharashtra. "His literature is free from the Sanskrit rich

Brahminical literature, which keeps the average reader at distance. Free from Brahminical elitism, Tukaram's literature has a force to assess the world from humanistic angle. The deep sympathies which his literature displays for the poor, contributes to enhancing his literary prestige." (Nemade, 1983, 9) Travails of poor people are the focus of his work. This Bhakti based tradition gave respectability to many low castes and also to Muslims. And thereby it was able to pose a challenge to Brahmanism.

Bhakti tradition had specific features. These were to oppose the hegemony of Brahminism, opposed the rituals, and opposed the Vedic Monopoly of educated elite of society. They uniformly opposed Sanskrit and adopted the languages more popular with the masses. Also they opposed the prevalent polytheism and talked of one God. In India, in particular, Hindu-Muslim unity has been one of the concerns expressed by most of the saints. Tukaram's literature shows that "There was prevalence of blind faith and rational thought was rejected by the dominant streams of society. Brahmins had a total hegemony on the faith, worship and knowledge... Bhakti tradition (Nath, Mahanubhav, Gosavi, Warkari and Dattasam-pradayi) saints challenged and opposed this Brahminical exploitation. The inequality in the field of spiritual attainments, which were opposed to the Shudras and women, had religious sanctions. Brahmins had vested interests in maintaining their own monopoly in religious arena... These Brahmins had no problem in serving loyally the Muslim rulers as Diwan, Deshpande and Kulkarni." (Nemade, 18)

In a way the streams of bhakti were not merely religious movements. They were targeted at the social evils and opposed the landlord Brahmin alliance. They propagated social equality and brotherhood.

Sufi saints also played similar role in the social sphere. They opposed the tyranny of the powerful and projected the popular elements of religion. Breaking the barriers of social inequality they also united the people and struggled against the prevalent orthodoxy, and blind faith. There following comes from the lower strata of society, irrespective of the religion of the people. Miyan Mir, Baba Farid, Gesudraj, Sheikh Salim Chishti and Nizamuddin Auliya were the revered by all for their humanistic preaching.

The Brahminical stream had its grip on the whole society, fully backed by those in power. This had its expression in the Vedic Rituals, in contrast the subaltern Bhakti, developed its own forms of worship away from the Brahminic norms, "The reduction in the emphasis on priest compared to his role in the sacrificial ritual of Vedic Brahmanism gradually led to devotional worship-bhakti-becoming most widespread form of puranic religion. The Vedic religion had well-defined rituals and was exclusive to the upper castes. The Puranic religion had a far wider appeal." (Thapar, 2002, 318). Bhakti tradition manifested in India in diverse forms, "As a broad based tradition...for the majority religion (Bhakti) remained an area of interplay, accommodation and contestation of a localised kind... (Thapar, p. 351)

Bhakti movement gave hope and awakening to the people. The section oppressed by the spiritual tyranny of the Brahmins got a feeling of their worth in the society. This movement rejected the *devbhasha* (Language of gods) Sanskrit and used the languages popular in the masse, like Marathi in Maharashtra. Avadhi in UP. It came as a whip of air liberating the people from the stranglehold of Brahmanism. "The rise of Bhakti movement was a rebellion against the idol worship, the oppression of caste system getting manifested through the rigid rituals."

(Mukherji, 1999, 70) "These movements were opposed to the Vedanitist concept of Sanyas, which involves no work. They bridged the gap between Hindus and Muslims." (Mantri, 70) These were also having very progressive attitudes on most of the matters related to the position of women in society.

The scholars of Syncretism have pointed out that many a subaltern traditions defy the rigid classification into Hindu or Muslim in the continent, so thoroughly intermixed they are in their social expression. The ordinary people have imbibed the prevalent traditions irrespective of their source, so far as they appeal to them in a spiritual and social way. "Scores of communities scattered across this vast subcontinent still refuse to be neatly categorised as 'Hindu' or 'Muslim' or whatever, freely borrowing from diverse traditions to create their own way of understanding the world." (Sikand, 2003, 3)

Kabir: Nanak

Kabir and Nanak stand tall as those challenging the authority of the clergy and in turn those in power. Their attempts to explore the religious language which can express the woes of the masses led them away from the power centred Brahmins and Mullahs. Kabir the medieval saint developed the set of values which were against the dominating of elite and tried to unite the people cutting across both the religions. He denounced caste system and was against untouchability in particular. "He upheld fundamental unity of man, and was opposed to all kinds of discrimination between human beings, whether on the basis of caste or religion, race, family or wealth. His sympathies were with the poor man with whom he identified himself." (Chandra, 1990, 127)

Nanak had a mystic bent of mind and he composed verses and sang them with the accompaniment of rabab, a string instrument played by his follower Mardan. He visited Mecca, Medina, Sri Lanka and other places searching for knowledge, like Kabir he also denounced the rituals Idol worship and formal observances. He aimed at bridging distinctions between the Hindus and the Muslims, in order to create an atmosphere of peace goodwill and mutual interaction. "Nanak and Kabir both insisted that they were neither Hindu nor Muslim, along with other similar iconoclasts, and defied the might of Brahmans and Mullahs." (Sikand, p. 9) The following of both these major saints of Indian tradition was more amongst the poor and oppressed sections of society. The story of Nanak in which, he preferred to have meals at the house of a weaver Bhago, in preference to accepting the hospitality of the landlord is fairly symbolic of their social affiliation. The story in a symbolic way shows Nanak's opposition to the landlords as their income is laced with the blood of oppressed.

The Sufi tradition is basically deriving from the teachings of Islam. The Sufis have a mystical bent of mind and they were having a deep devotion to spiritualism. They were disgusted by the vulgar display of wealth and power. Hence they kept aloof from the state. There were many similarities between the ideas of Sufi saints and Hindu Bhakti saints. They chose the Hindavi or Hindi language to converse with the people and many of their verses are composed in Hindi.

Current Times

In India alone if we see, there are plethora of Godmen, who are a category of their own. They come from the parallel authority structure of clergy and built their own following while reiterating status quo a la the clergy. The unique features of these Godmen, their novelty in picking up some issues, which may appeal to large section, be it spiritual, be it profane, from addressing the stress of present society, to the habits of addiction. What unites them is their huge estates and plush material gains in the process, their silence on social ills and their ignoring the material issues of the poor. In today's context they will not talk of evils of caste, dowry and female infanticide, instead they will talk about peace of mind and need to be calm.

This new set of Gurus and Acharyas, Sri Sri Ravishankar, Asaram Bapu, Pandurang Shastri Athwale, Sudhanshu Maharaj, Aniruddh Bapu, Narayan Maharaj and the like, are the nerve soothers for the existential tensions of the middle class, and upholders of status quo of caste and gender. These Gurus are pushing the Manusmriti and the feudal values of caste and gender hierarchies in a new language, the language laced with modernity, so to say. Similarly one notices the presence of Muslim Ulama, Mullahs and the likes of Shahi Imam who have been promoting obscurantism in the Muslim community. Starting from their role in putting pressure to reverse the Shah Bano judgment to their opposition to abolition of triple talaq and polygamy amongst Muslims, their retrograde role is a bane of Muslim community in India. Deriving from Christian tradition, Benny Hinn has been doing public hypnosis exercise to cure diseases; Ramdev Baba has a more permanent set up and strong rooting in the elite of the society. We will take two typical cases of Godmen for our understanding.

Shankaracharya

Shankaracharya Jayendra Saraswati, the pontiff of Kanchi Kamkoti Peetham, was arrested as the main accused in the murder of a Shankar Raman, a manager in the *math* (place of the holy seer) (Nov. 12, 2004) came as a big surprise to many. He was the one who was in the media for his role in the resolution of Babri masjid dispute. While many observers said that it is a police case and should be dealt with like that, Vishwa Hindu Parishad went hammer and tongs against the government. Also that it is a humiliation to the Hindu society and in retaliation they will protest and the ministers will not be blessed in the Hindu temples for the next day. He also threatened to launch an agitation against the arrest of Holy seer. While Mr Modi the Chief Minister of Gujarat talked to the Prime Minister saying that government should think of the sentiments of the people before arresting such holy people.

One is not sure as to how much religious following Shankaracharya has amongst the Hindus. It seems it is only amongst a section of Hindu. Does he represent the Hindus of the country? Surely this is not an elected post and it is through the inheritance of the *Maths* that the likes of him come to occupy these seats of power and pelf. The views of Shakaracharya about dalits and women may not be heartening to them and to large section of India's Hindus. Talking of such *maths* these are the places dime a dozen, though Shakaracharya does have an exalted position amongst that. This *maths* have great amount of wealth, which comes through donations of the people. Since most of the chiefs of this maths are bachelors, many a times there is a power struggle after the demise of the chiefs and in that there are serious clashes not Tantamounting to even the most serious crimes. This is a whole world by itself full of all the dimensions of human life, quest for power, jealousy, money and all that. But of course all this is in the name of religion.

Can these Holy seers be above the law? Can they be law unto themselves?

Baba Ramdev

It is not for the first time that the followers of Godmen rampaged when their Guru was asked questions or doubts on the grounds of laws of the land. Brinda Karat, CPI (M) leader and MP pointed out (Jan 04, 2006) that the medicines produced in Baba Ramdev's factory in Haridwar contained animal and human parts. She stated this on the basis of the version of the workers sacked from the factory. In response hell was let loose and the supporters of Ramdev attacked the office of CPI (M) leading to the skirmish between the followers of CPI (M) and Ramdev.

Ramdev said that CPI (M) is not nationalist, that it is a ploy of multinationals and that he is being defamed. His strong support came from the Sangh Parivar followers, the hooligans of VHP and Bajrang dal joined the attack on the office of CPM, while the BJP leaders came out strongly to condemn CPI (M) for its insult of India's culture. One of them went to the extent of saying that whenever Indian (read Brahminic Hinduism) culture is gaining prominence CPI (M) feels threatened. Many leaders from other parties kept quiet or 'supported' Ramdev.

The story, which has been undermined in the din of hysteria, began with factory owned by Ramdev where many a women employees were exploited heavily and 133 women were sacked for demanding the implementation of work norms in the factory. That's how Brinda Karat, who wanted to defend the rights of women employees, got to know about the factory and got the samples analysed. The issue was raised by her as a citizen and as an MP. According the prevalent laws, the Ayurvedic medicines cannot put any human or animal extract in the medicines. The basic issue of workers right and the ethics of production of Ayurvedic medicines both have been swamped by the emotions roused because the owner of the factory has the halo of a Godman, conducting shows of Yoga on TV.

The cover of Baba-dom is the best to hide the things or to avoid following the laws relating to business and industry. It is not too far back in the time that one Narendra Maharaj was not allowed to violate the norms of security of air travel, as he was prevented from carrying his dandam (Holy staff) along with him while traveling. The whole hell was let loose; his followers were on the streets, rampage and the usual venting of ire. It is touted that the Godmen teach religious values of tolerance, peace and non-violence! Most of the occasions these followers go on rampage when their Guru is not allowed to flout the laws with impunity, or an uncomfortable question is raised about their activities. It is no different in other religions. Once Asghar Ali Engineer, human rights activist of great repute, questioned the delay in the flight due to late coming of Bohra High Priest Syedna, this mild questioning was followed by the ransacking of his house and office and he himself was beaten up mercilessly.

While nobody in the political circles is picking up courage to raise the question regarding Ramdev, can one presume that those in the electoral politics believe that there are two sets of laws, one for the ordinary mortals and another for the 'divinely ordained'. The association of saffron Godmen with Hindu right is close and overt/ subtle, both at the same time. Recently Ramdev attended the annual convention of Rashtra Sevika Samiti a subordinate organisation of RSS (incidentally RSS does not permit women to be its members). When Shankaracharya was arrested in the Shankar Raman murder case, Vajpayee and Aasaram Bapu rubbed shoulders, to protest against the arrest of the 'holy seer'. The argument put forward was that Shankaracharya represents Hindus and is revered by Hindus, so he should be treated differently.

Godmen

One has some general observations about the Godmen. During last several years they have been flourishing at exponential rate. Most of them have done very well by the profane standards of accumulation of wealth, chain of plush Ashrams, lakhs of devotees, infinite money, foreign junkets and all the luxuries possible. You renounce the world to get the best of it! Their prefixes also are very diverse and keep on getting better and better with time. They do choose their prefixes and suffixes. While other Godmen do it in their own way, Rajneesh had an interesting trajectory of these. He began as Acharya, went on to become Bhagwan (God!) and finally gave himself the title of Osho before he left this planet. All of them have different strengths and weaknesses), someone is more for diamonds, someone likes cars and expensive clothes and yet another one prefers videos of dubious distinction.

While many other politicians are bowing to the popular pressure and defending Ramdev, Sangh Parivar regards them as the representatives of Hindu culture. What is

Hindu about their culture needs another investigation. One has seen the Spartan life of Buddha, Kabir, Nanak and Gandhi. Buddha in fact renounced his palace to take to jungle and merge with all and sundry in their deprivations. The many from the current genre, which in fact is a blot on the humane traditions of saints, are also close to centres of power, Dhirendra Brahmachari, Satya Sai Baba, Chandraswami and Jayendra Saraswati being some notorious examples.

Ayurveda is being linked to Indian Traditions. As such the development of the Ayurveda was halted, mainly by Brahminical dictates. Ayurveda has lot of elements, which can be put on the scientific foundations to make it more suitable to the human kind. The proper research where critical reason is employed to make it better is not employed in the Ayurveda as it is strongly linked to faith. No doubt multinationals may have their own axe to grind in the whole story, but we need to look at the proper investigation of facts and laws before the medicines produced by any Baba, Acharya and Mahant, can be put to public use. Karat has just raised a simple question, why is Ramdev's factory violating the laws of the land? It is a simple matter to investigate and set right. But since here the factory owner has the hallow of Godmen, radiating in the reflected glory of God almighty how dare we the mortals raise such questions. The Godmen are above the law is the premise of their followers and supporters, whoever they be! So in a single stroke Brinda Karat and her party are dubbed anti-Hindu (Anti-National, against Hindu Nation) so how is nationalism defined? If you blindly submit to the self-proclaimed Godmen, you are a nationalist else! Is one against the indigenous system of practices? No way. The only demand is for ethical and rational implementation of the therapies to avoid any one coming up and putting in market medicines or methods which can be injurious to the health. Social scrutiny of anything and everything is called for. The cloak of Holiness does not exempt one from the laws of the land and being subject to the critical questioning of peers and others from raising questions about the composition and techniques being put forward. The claims related to the efficacy of the medicines and techniques have to be evaluated on the basis of the criterion already developed by rational techniques. Subjecting traditional systems to these rigorous methods will only make them more effective, meaningful and will prune out the grain from the chaff. It will make them above the subjective claims of those promoting it.

If Ramdev has done no wrong; why this emotional outburst, and why this misuse of label 'anti-National' against Karat is being bandied? If he has things to hide than this angry outburst is understandable, as it will harm the proliferating business built up with such a meticulous mix of some knowledge sprinkled with generous helping of emotions and faith which are wonderful smokescreen for hiding one's wrongs. This 'faith' can surely act as opium, the frenzied followers of Baba's rampaging shows that time and over again!

Saints

The rise in the religion based politics, the increase in religio-sity and the prominence of these Godmen is running hand in hand. Many of them are supporters of VHP and others have their own agenda in strengthening the traditional Hindu social order. Some of them are working in tandem with RSS's Vanvasi Kalyan Ashram, Lakkhanand Sarswati (Orissa) Aseemananad (Dangs, Gujarat) and followers of Asaram Bapu in Jhabua area (Madhya Pradesh). Recently Narayan maharaj came in support of VHP and organised the *ghar vapasi* (return home, a euphemism for conversion to Hinduism) of Adivasis.

None of them talks of social ills, and it seems most of these are the religious platform for the politics of RSS combine. Assuming the babadom gives them a halo and immunity from the rules of the land. They are the religious face of the religious face of the politics of Hindu right.

Conclusion

More work needs to be done to draw out the deeper connection between global economic and political changes, the rise of deprivation and aggravation of worldly problems during last few decades and the rising clout of Godmen. How these Godmen play a role in neutralizing the people's dissatisfaction and help in perpetuation of status quo is an interesting exercise to grapple with. Why the expressions of deprived people's problems is not finding expression in the language of religion as in medieval times is a matter of great concern and investigation. While one does not subscribe to the conspiracy theory of conscious planning there is a deeper connection between unjust economic system and its beneficiaries encouraging such trends is a wee bit obvious. Why the other less privileged fall into this addiction of Godmen's tricks is another fascinating aspect of the whole phenomenon.

References

Bhalchandra Nemade, Tukaram, Sahitya Academy Delhi, 1983, p. 9.

Debiprasad Chattopadhyay, Religion and Society, Ma Le Publishers, Banglore, 1987.

Engel's, The Peasant War in Germany, from Marx Engel's, On Religion, p. 88.

Engel's, "On Religion, Progress Publishers Moscow, 1972.

Peter van der Veer, Religious Nationalism, OUP, New Delhi 1998, p.

Progress Publishers, A Dictionary of believers and non believers, Moscow, 1985.

Rajaram Bhadu, *Dharmasatta Aur Pritirodh ki Sanskriti,* Rajkamal, New Delhi, 2003, p. 33.

Romila Thapar, The Penguin History of early India, Penguin, Delhi 2002, pp. 318-319.

Satish Chandra, Medieval India, National Council of Education Research and Training, Delhi, 1990, p. 127.

Uday Mehta, Modern Godman in India, Popular Prakashan Mumbai.

Uday Mehta, Secularism, Secularisation and Modernity, S Sand R, Ajanta, 1998, 22.

Yoginder Sikand, Sacred Spaces: Exploring Traditions of Shared faith in India, Penguin, Delhi, 2003, p. 3.

Section - B
RELIGION IN INDIA

5

Religion, Ideology and Society

Krishna Mohan Shrimali

The problems I refer to, concern what Friedrich Max Muller called *Religionswissenchaft* or 'science of religions' as early as 1867.[1] Although my own research output is minimal, I have nevertheless ventured to undertake the subject because having taught the subject at the postgraduate classes for nearly two decades, I have often felt there is a paramount need for developing the discipline along scientific lines. I propose to undertake a world view with the objective of placing studies on Indian religions in proper perspective.[2]

We shall not attempt any definition of religion and prefer to take its multi-dimensional character as a convenient starting point.[3] Briefly, it may be mentioned that myths, rituals, doctrines, theology, mystic experience, socio-ethical content, etc., constitute some of the major dimensions of the religious phenomenon.[4] Similarly, *Religionswissenschaft* has been variously defined but one of the best known classifications takes cognizance of the psychology, history, sociology and phenomenology of religion.[5] A bird's-eye view of the major phases in the creation of a 'science of religions' as an important discipline is desirable to understand the Indian scene. Surely, one can easily identify the methodological transformations between Max Muller's writings on comparative mythology with an accent on philology in the latter half of the nineteenth century and Bruce Lincoln's analysis of the Rigvedic religion published about a hundred years later.[6] From the rather simplistic, though not uncritical, presentation of A. Barth[7] to recent writings with pronounced influences of Levi-Strauss' structuralism and Freud's psychoanalysis represents a *very* long trek.[8]

Lewis Henry Morgan in his classic work *Ancient Society*[9] published in 1877 wrote Religion deals so largely with imaginative and emotional nature, and consequently with such uncertain elements of knowledge, *that all primitive religions are grotesque and to some extent unintelligible'* (emphasis added).[10] More than half a century before this, August Comte, in his famous *Cours de philosophic positive* (based on his lectures of the 1820s) had pronounced his theory of the Law of Three Stages' with the theological as the 'lowest' state of development. 'Positivism', the creed of Comte, tended to regard religion as 'merely a survival from Man's primitive past, and doomed to disappear in an era of science and general enlightenment.[11] Even a synoptic survey of the growth of the science of religion in the last one hundred and fifty years is sufficient to show how wrong both these savants were. Religion is with us all even in the most scientifically advanced societies. Nor is it (not even 'primitive religion') 'grotesque and ... unintelligible' any more.

It is generally accepted that the *Religionswissenschaft* was largely a child of the Enlightenment which is characterised as rejecting religion in the light of scientific and intellectual progress.[12] It is in this background that an attempt can be made to delineate the broad course and framework of the methodology of studying religions.

Methodology of the 'Science of Religion'

The major trends in the growth of the methodology of

the 'science of religions' can be broadly studied under four phases:[13]

(a) Up to the end of the first decade of the twentieth century, the pre-Durkheim-Weber phase.

(b) 1910 to the 1920s when the sociology of religion took off with the thought-provoking contributions of Emile Durkheim and Max Weber.

(c) The three decades between the 1920s and 1950s when the anthropological perspective with an accent on field work giving birth to social anthropology was developed by the Functionalists, such as A.R. Radcliffe-Brown (1881-1955) and Bronislaw Malinowski (1884-1942).

Writings since the 1950s, where one of the most dominant influences has been that of Claude Levi-Strauss' Structuralism.

Phase I: Upto c. 1910

In the sphere of *Religionswissenschaft* the nineteenth century was essentially dominated by philologists and ethnologists, focusing largely on myths. The scientific study of myths did not begin until Karl O. Muller's *Introduction to a Scientific Mythology* published in 1825.[14] Needless to mention, however, the peer in the field of studies on myths is Max Muller, for whom the 'key' to comprehend the essence of religion was 'Comparative Mythology,' and this in turn could only be understood by a method of philological analysis.[15] More specifically, he was an exponent of the 'nature-myth school' for which the 'key' was solar mythology.[16] For him the whole supernatural world arose from the limitations, ambiguity and 'illusion of language'.[17]

Shortly after the birth of language-based comparative mythology, ethnologists came to the scene and laid the foundations of the anthropological approach to the study of religion. Apparently influenced by Darwinian Evolution, ethnologists such as E.B. Tylor, Andrew Lang, Robertson

Smith, R.R. Marett, Sir James Frazer, etc. tended to combine their 'positivistic' approach with religious facts. Tylor described the unilinear, evolution of religion from animism through polytheism and finally, to the monotheism of more 'civilised' cultures.[18] Tylor's animism as 'minimum definition of religion' evoked tremendous reaction and pre-animistic evolutionary and anti-evolutionary theories focusing on *mana,*[19] *taboo,*[20] magic,[21] High God[22], etc. were formulated. Regrettably, these reactions shared most of the assumptions of Tylor, particularly his 'negative' view of religion in which *homo-religiosus* was placed at the origin of the evolutionary process.[23]

To sum up, the philologists and ethnologists of the first phase of our survey claimed to have established an 'autonomous' discipline for the 'scientific' study of religion. It was, however, far from being so. Nevertheless, by accumulating 'religious facts' and looking for common elements or 'parallels', by locating and translating the 'original sources' and by assuming a critically 'rationalistic' attitude marked by personal detachment, they had certainly taken the first step in that direction.[24]

Phase II: 1910-1920s

It is remarkable how a short span of less than two decades unleashed such forces in Western Europe as gave birth to a distinctive approach to the study of religion. These years of the early twentieth century saw the emergence of what has now come to be known as the 'Sociology of Religion'. Emile Durkheim (1858-1917) in France and Max Weber (1864-1920) in Germany were the real harbingers of this current. Both shared many common interests, though their raw materials and methods differed a great deal, Weber's emphasis on the importance bureaucratic organisations and rational legal authority relationships \ his understanding of charismatic leadership, his analysis 'disenchantment' of the modern world, his explanation of the 'Problem' of Meaning' are such elements as easily enable us to draw parallels with Durkheim. The latter's concern with such themes as the Major processes of social, economic and political specialisation relating to the division of labour; his notions of 'sacred' and 'profane' and his search for modern equivalents of the sacred beliefs and symbols and above all, his deep-rooted interests in the problems of group cohesion provide links with the German doctrinaire. It may, however, be pointed out that while both savants grappled with the problem of societies' management without religion, their ways of analysing it were dissimilar. While Weber was primarily interested in establishing links between *specific* social stratum distinctions and modes of religious expression, Durkheim concentrated upon *general* social significance of religious experience and belief. Both were, however, concerned with problems of how individuals and groups identify themselves in the world not only in relation to each other but to the social, cultural and natural conditions of their existence as well.

Les formes elementaires de la vie religieuse (The Elementary Forms of the Religious Life) of Durkheim was published in 1912. Arguing that religion does not rest upon an 'illusion,' as the positivists had thought, but rather upon a 'basic fact of experience', Durkheim defined it as follows:

> A religion is a unified system of belief and practices relative to sacred things i.e. things set apart and forbidden—beliefs and practices which unite into one single moral community called a Church, all those who adhere to them. The second element which finds a place in our definition is no less essential than the first; for by showing that the idea of religion is inseparable from that of the Church, it makes it clear that religion should be an eminently collective thing.

Durkheim had occasionally used the existing writings on Indian civilisation to highlight his general framework of religion. That religion cannot be defined as belief in gods was sought to be established [by alluding to the early Buddhism, which had no place for gods but was regarded as religion.[25] He said rather emphatically, that which human beings have meant by God and that which has served as the object of their religious emotions and practices is society. Society has deified itself; religion is the means of symbolically expressing the total collective life.[26]

Durkheim also speculated on the origin of religion and sought to argue on the basis of the Arunta and Central Australia that totemism was the primordial from of religion.[27]

Durkheim's approach has been vulnerable on many counts. By emphasising only the sociological dimension of religious experiences, *the* failed to realise that the manifestation of the sacred as social 'does not exhaust the manifestation of sacrality.'[28] Another Durkheimian notion that has not gone unchallenged is that society is necessarily anterior to religion[29] or that cognition is socially determined.[30]

Notwithstanding these criticisms, Durkheim's contribution had potential openings for more fruitful interpretations. He challenged many of the 'negative' assumptions of the first phase. Further, by emphasising the importance of religious symbolism, he had sown the 11 seeds of structuralism of Claude Levi-Strauss. His impact, from the point of view of India, is apparent in the works of Marcel Mauss and Henri Hubert. Indologists such as G. Held, Georges Dumezil and P. Masson-Oursel also show influences of Durkheim. Mauss-Hubert's pioneering study on the ritual of sacrifice,[31] G. Held's ethnological study of the *Mahabharata*[32] and Dumezil's numerous works on Indo-European society and mythology are some of the indicators of Durkheim's influence on Indian religious studies. Even Masson-Oursel's attempt to separate the magical elements from the rational in the structure of early Hinduism can be linked with the French sociologist.[33]

Max Weber, a junior contemporary of Durkheim and a product of Bismarckian Germany, is known for his numerous writings not only on religions of specific countries such as India[34] and China[35] but also on specific religions as well as the sociology of religion.[36] His *The Protestant Ethic and the Spirit of Capitalism*[37] is a great classic.

Weber was deeply interested in distinguishing traits of world religions but not from any theological point of view. Instead, he looked for perceptive and meaningful consequences of theological doctrines for the orientation that men bring to their economic activities. Weber wanted to go beyond a narrow focus on the indirect impact of ideas on behaviour by examining in detail the 'anchorage' of religious ideas in social organisation. From the perspective of sociology of religion he highlighted the following three forms of relationship between social organisation and religious ideas:

(a) Social groups with particular economic interests often show themselves to be more receptive to some religious ideas than to others. Where they were chivalrous warrior heroes, political officials, economically acquisitive classes or finally, where an organised hierocracy dominated religion, the results were different than from where genteel intellectuals were decisive. The social stratum including artisans, traders, entrepreneurs engaged in industry are attracted by all sorts of individual pursuits of salvation. Everywhere the hierocracy has sought to monopolise the administration of religious values. The individual's quest for salvation or the quest of free communities by means of contemplation, orgies or asceticism has been considered highly suspect and has had to be regulated ritually and controlled hierocratically.

From the standpoint of the interests of the priesthood in power, this was considered natural.

(b) Religious ideas lead to the formation of certain groups, such as monastic orders, guilds of magicians, or a clergy and these groups may develop quite extensive economic activities.

(c) The gap between the elite and the masses poses a problem with which each of the great religions of the world has had to cope with. With specific references to religion in China, particularly Confucianism and Taoism, Weber shows how the former remained confined to the Emperor and the bureaucratic order but broadly excluded the masses. In contrast, the *brahmanas* in India, who were royal chaplains, spiritual advisers, theologians and authorities on questions of ritual propriety, achieved a 'systematic rationalisation of magic' and effected a compromise between their own elite interests in a dignified way of life and their need to provide for the release of the masses from the misfortunes that were their lot.

One aspect of Weber's writings having a far-reaching; consequence and an ideological tilt as well is the *antireductionist* tendency.[38] It is argued that this is sociology of religion *sensu stricto*. Throughout his writings, Weber assumes that the specific religious features are at least partially independent of the relevant social and economic conditions and tries to emphasise the 'religious anchorage" of economic, political, social and cultural institutions. Undoubtedly, the most famous illustration of Weber's anti-reductionism appears in *The Protestant Ethic and the Spirit of Capitalism,* where the religious determination of life conduct and 'economic ethic' has been the dominant strain—an idea which is underlined in his analysis of Hinduism and Buddhism as well.[39]

Weber's reference to 'ideal interests' and 'material interests' enable us to recall Marx's sharp contrast between 'base/infrastructure' and 'superstructure'. Which is *the determinant* in the last analysis-religion or economy? An answer to the question is rather crucial to our understanding of the role of religion in society. Did religion serve as an ideology? The issue is discussed later.

Weber was bound to draw great attention in view of his specific application of the 'economic ethic' conception to Hinduism and Buddhism. No wonder, after the appearance of the English translation of *The Religion of India,* the National Institute of Community Development, Hyderabad organised a symposium in 1966 with the key paper entitled 'Socio-Economic Change and the Religious Factor in India' focusing on Max Weber's views.[40] Weber's contentions have been convincingly questioned, largely because despite his many divergences from Marx, he does share the latter's enthusiasm for what has come to be known as the Asiatic Mode of Production (AMP) based on, amongst many other features, the absence of private ownership of land in Asian civilisations.[41] We would also do well to keep in mind Weber's racial framework as well as the limitation inherent in the sources used by him.[42] Not being a professional Indologist, Weber had to rely on translations little realising that even Sanskritists of the reputation of Monier-Williams had faltered a great deal in giving English equivalents of crucial Sanskrit terms. Further, Buddhist texts in Pali ere regarded as somewhat less reliable than brahminical Sanskrit tings. This was obviously far from being justified. If, however, we out Weberian notion of the 'economic ethic' and its 'anchorage' in religion, the three broad relationships between social organisation and Religious ideas mentioned above do offer useful vistas for enquiries into the religious domain.

The decades when Durkheim and Weber were laying the foundations of the sociology of religion, Sigmund Freud was opening up the psychological approach to the study of religion. In 1913, he published *Totem and Taboo* postulating that 'the beginnings of religion, ethics, society, and art meet in the Oedipus Complex'—religion originated with the 'first patricide,' a 'primordial murder' which is ritually repeated in the 'totemic sacrifices'. Freud's interpretation of religion has been convincingly refuted by ethnologists of all shades—Marxian and non-Marxian,[43] but his discovery of the unconscious and the method of psychoanalysis are important contributions to the history of religions. In fact, a little later, Jung broadened his analysis by declaring that there are universal structures of the unconscious that keep reappearing in dreams, hallucinations, art, myth, etc. Much of the interest in symbols and myths and in archaic and oriental religions can be traced back to the impact of Freud's writings. Specific mention in this context can be made of Zimmer's writings on Indian art and philosophy.[44]

Phase III: 1920s-1950s

For almost three decades following the First World War, the sociology of religion languished for want of theoretical sophistication. In contrast, social anthropology really took off in a big way. With phenomenal field workers of the calibre of Malinowski and Radcliffe-Brown, not only social anthropology took roots, religious studies also got a fresh orientation. To them we owe the rise of Functionalism—a point of view which has left a distinctive stamp on the studies of religion in general and that of the so-called primitive religion in particular. The tone set by Brown and Malinowski was further sophisticated by Evans-Pritchard, Raymond Firth Lienhardt and Worsely.[45]

One of the major areas in which the Functionalists have further refined earlier understandings of religion is the relationship between magic and religion.[46] Both Brown and Malinowski are ultimately concerned with the role of religion and magic in social survival.[47] While Radcliffe-Brown's reconstruction of the content of the sacred symbols from the point of view of its 'ritual/social value' and 'utilitarianism' took him away from Durkheim, it also questioned the premises on which Levy-Bruhl had diagnosed the 'primitive mentality'.[48] The stage was now set for the next phase when the concern with the symbolic form was initiated by Claude Levi-Strauss.

Phase IV: 1950s to date

The post-Second World War studies on religion have been deeply influenced by *Structural Anthropology* of Claude Levi-Strauss.[49] He is concerned with the systems of classification, the 'home-made' taxonomies employed by tribal people to order the objects and events of their world. In this, he follows in the footsteps of Durkheim and Mauss. But rather than looking, as they did, to social forms for the origins and explanations of such categorical systems, he looks to the symbolic structures in terms of which they are formulated, expressed and applied. Myth and in slightly different ways rite, are systems of signs that fix and organise abstract conceptual relationships in terms of concrete images and thus make speculative thought possible. The objects rendered sacred are selected not because of their utilitarian qualities, nor because they are projections of repressed emotions, nor yet because they reflect the moral force of social organisation ritualistically impressed upon the mind. Rather, they are selected because they permit the embodiment of general ideas in terms of the immediately perceptible realities—the turtles, trees, springs and caves—of everyday experience, not because they are 'good to eat' apropos of Radcliffe-Brown's view of totem) but because they are 'good to think'. Strauss contends that primitive religions are, like symbolic systems, fundamentally communications systems. They can be understood as an integrated system of thought, logically sound, epistemologically valid and as flourishing in France as in Tahiti. Having combined in himself the traditions of French sociology and American cultural anthropology, Strauss also transformed the tenuous link between the nineteenth century comparative philology and anthropology and raised it to the sophisticated level of linguistic and semantic anthropology—a trend which is rather conspicuous in the realm of anthropology. As the recent work of such diverse students as W.E.H. Stanner, Victor Turner, E.R. Leach, Rodney Needham and Susan A. Langer demonstrates, the analysis of symbolic forms is becoming a major tradition in the study of religion in general and primitive religion in particular. This is despite certain reservations being expressed against what has been called 'extreme intellectualism which cerebralises religion.'[50]

The post-Second World War hermeneutical situation in the *Religionswissenschaft* would be incomplete without a reference to the ecological approach to religion and the emphasis being put on phenomenology of religion. In what seems to be an exaggerated outburst, it is claimed that until today every historian of religions is a phenomenologist.'[51] There is no agreement as to the nature and task of the phenomenology of religion.[52] However, more than any other approach, phenomenologists have emphasised the experiential basis of religion and have "attempted to describe and to systematise the basic structures of religious experience. In describing such structures, phenomenologists of religion have attempted to approach their data in a specific *antireductionist* manner, insisting upon the irreducibility and uniqueness of the religious dimensions of experience. Though Rudolf Otto's concept of the Holy[53] as the *sui generis* numinous experience characterised as *ganz Andere* ('wholly other'), transcendent and *mysterium tremendum et fascinosum* (the 'ambivalent' structure of the sacred) and the non-rational and even G.Van der Leeuw's religious aspects of power formulated in his *Religion in Essence and Manifestation*[54] are considered to be major expositions, it is in the writings of W. Brede Kristensen[55] and Mircea Eliade[56] that the phenomenological approach to religion has been underlined rather emphatically. It is the contention of these phenomenologists that religion must be approached *on its own 'plane of reference'* thereby making it an 'autonomous' discipline. Though an attempt has been made to dilute such contentions by arguing that (a) 'autonomy' does not mean that *Religionswissenschaft* is a 'self-sufficient' discipline and (b) 'irreducible' does not mean 'purely religious' phenomenon,[57] we feel very strongly that the phenomenologists are methodologically close to Weberian religious 'anchorage' and, therefore, raise similar issues regarding the role of religion in society.

Studies on Indian Religions

We shall now devote attention to studies on Indian religions by both Indian and foreign scholars in order to underline major trends. However, we shall try to go beyond two useful surveys of writings on various religions published in 1967[58] and 1981[59] and undertake a thematic survey from the prehistoric to the early medieval centuries.

The study of the prehistoric period of Indian history has taken significant strides in the post-Independence decades, particularly since the 1960s. Fascinating monographs on tool-types, pattern of shelters, ecological setting and rock paintings are not unknown[60] and a recent Presidential Address delivered at the Ninth Annual Congress of the Indian Society for Prehistoric and Quaternary Studies in 1982 even focused attention on 'Eco-Functional Frame of Early Man'.[61] In spite of their familiarity with the 'New Archaeology'[62] and 'Analytical Archaeology'[63] Indian archaeologists have not been so much influenced by cultural-social anthropology as to take interest in such areas as prehistoric religion.[64] When we take cognizance of the brilliant theoretical and conceptual studies being brought out under the 'New Directions in Archaeology Series' from Cambridge,[65] the utter poverty of Indian prehistoric studies in the realm of religion becomes all the more conspicuous. A few exceptions to this generally lamentable situation include studies on the Mother Goddess. None of these are products of professional archaeologists but the works of both D.D. Kosambi and

N.N. Bhattacharyya[66] need to be singled out for their wealth of data and scientific conceptual framework. Kosambi's study of the Mother Goddess cult-sites is particularly remarkable for the fieldwork in Maharashtra along prehistoric trade tracks. Otherwise one is forced to rely on writings on prehistoric religion in the world context.[67]

As distinct from prehistoric religion, interest in Harappan religion has been somewhat greater. There has been a major theoretical formulation on the role of religion in the process of urbanisation in all major centres of ancient civilisations including the Harappan.[68] Paul Wheatley stresses the sacred, symbolic character of the early city[69] much more than this had been stressed by the older theories—not even by Weber for whom religion was an important 'anchorage'.[70] Some recent writings dealing with the growth of the Harappans specifically have described religion as an 'intensifying factor' and a 'catalyst' for the urban process.[71]

Religion as Ideology

The issue has wider ideological ramifications and concerns the role of religion as an ideology. Though a prominent role was attributed to religion in the Harappan set-up long before Wheatley's work,[72] the theorising is based more on negative evidence, notwithstanding the highly speculative suggestion of Kosambi regarding the Great Bath at Mohenjodaro being a ritual complex of fertility rites.[73] Fairservis' reference[74] to religion as an 'intensifying factor' suffers from internal contradictions. Apart from strong diffusionist influences in his reconstruction, one finds very little evidence regarding the form(s) of religious manifestations amongst the rural folk. It is now being realised by historians and archaeologists alike that the mature Harappan phase was a product of strong rural hinterland[75] and village communities. Have we got enough empirical evidence of religious beliefs and practices of these people? Further, though Fairservis talks about five stages of the origin, growth and decline of this culture,[76] he insists on looking for a 'static civilisation' because he has to rationalise his understanding of religion as an 'intensifying factor'— this perhaps seems to be a hangover of colonialist-imperialist historiography. Finally, his references to 'different kinds' of civilisations of the world with different emphases in their organisation also run counter to Wheatley's hypothesis mentioned above.

There are very convicing studies on the conspicuous role of religion in the set-up of some ancient civilisations in Mesoamerica[77] and of the Aztecs and Incas.[78] The empirical data from the Harappan civilisation, however, still needs to be probed from the point of view of scientific conceptualisation of the problem. The two recent studies on Harappan religion either do not even raise the issues or run counter to some of the assessments mentioned above.[79] Ildiko Puskas' mention of the 'Empire phase' of the Harappan society, for example, is not in keeping with the distribution of economic resources and the mechanism of their harnessing.[80] However, Shubhangana Atre's doctoral thesis on the Harappan Mother Goddess, *The Archetypal Mother,*[81] offers provocative rethinking on:

(a) The so-called Pashupati seal, which has hitherto been regarded as proto-Shiva is in fact 'Lady of Beasts' and fire and water formed the main elements of her cult.[82]

(b) The famous depictions of the 'unicorn'[83] had phallic importance and, therefore, fertility associations.

(c) Use of antlers as hand plough or ploughshares.

Atre concludes that 'the cult of the primitive goddess who rules the world of wild animals was modified to suit a prospering society, sustained basically by a combination of agriculture, animal husbandry and trade.'[84] While all this is very fascinating rationalisation of the important features of Harappan religion in terms of the material base and is welcome as a useful contribution, the issue of religion as an ideology remains unanswered. On the contrary, her references to 'regional variations' of Harapan cults only raise certain question marks against hypotheses of the type of Wheatley's. Even Possehl's recent work on Kulli discusses the problem of Indus urbanisation exclusively in the light of Mesopotanian trade with the Indus[85] without any allusion to the so-called 'catalytic' role of religion in it. Further, it would require a more rigorous integration of the Harappan economic subsistence base with the religious phenomenon. This has become particularly necessary in view of the complex functioning of economic activities in the region as shown by some recent writings.[86] In the absence of the integration mentioned above, attempts such as those of Atre look rather simplistic.

Max Muller's Influence

For almost half a century before Max Muller laid the foundations of *Religionswissenschaft,* there had already developed keen interest in Vedic studies, even though specific notices on religion and mythology had been very few. In fact, when Henry Thomas Colebrook published his essay, 'On the Vedas, or Sacred Writings of the Hindus'[87] in 1805, he became the first western scholar ever to write about the Veda. Since then, many European scholars have contributed to a very considerable extent to the knowledge of Vedic religion. The names of Eugene Burnout (1801-52) and his pupils such as Roth, Adolphe Regnier and Felix Neve deserve special mention. In his work *Die Herabkunft des Feuers und des Gottertranks* (1859), Kuhn has studied, among others, the legend of Pururavas and Urvashi[88] and of Chyavana from the point of view of comparative mythology.[89] As early as 1850 Albrecht Weber published in the first volume of his journal *Indische Studien,* a paper on the two legends from the *Shatapatha Brahmana,* viz., the flood legend involving Manu and that of Videgha Mathava.[90] Some other scholars who were influenced by Max Muller's parameters of 'science of religion' were

Gubernatis,[91] Abel Bergaigne[92] and to a very limited extent John Muir.[93] Barth's reconstruction of the Vedic religions[94] provides some useful insights, which have been utilised by subsequent scholars, for example, his reference to popular religious cults existing along with hierarchical Vedic religion giving rise to Vishnuism and Shivaism later.[95] However, his suggestion that Varuna in the *Rigveda* can by no means be said to appear in 'a state of decadence' or 'god on the wane'[96] still needs to be pursued.[97]

Philological and comparative mythology as bases for the study of religion had influenced Russian writings as well.[98] However, two scholars need to be mentioned at some length for their different but scientific approach. Dmitry Ovsyaniko-Kulikovsky (1853-1920) published *The Cult of the God Soma in Ancient India in the Vedic Age*[99] in 1884 and another work entitled *On the History of the Cult of Fire Among the Indians in the Vedic Age* only three years later (1887). He highlights the fact that the development of cults and religious concepts kept pace with the social developments of the Aryans. Such an orientation of Kulikovsky was perhaps the result of his exposure to the works of Karl Marx and his followers and contemporary French ethnologists. Like Kulikovsky, Dmitry Kudryavsky's (1867-1920) monograph on domestic rituals was also inspired by similar influences. He analysed the essence of rites and social institutions in the context of ethnographic material and stated that the ashrama system was based on the age-group principle.

Barring a very few works influenced by the French sociologists and anthropologists, a great majority of writings on Vedic religion continue to be influenced by the approach of Max Muller. This is true of even such giants of Vedic studies as Macdonell, Jan Gonda and R.N. Dandekar.[100] Broadly, A.B. Keith's otherwise monumental work *The Religion and Philosophy of the Veda and Upanishads*[101] would also fall in the same category. It is regretted that he did not find Durkheim of much use[102] while his slightly junior contemporary in France, viz., Dumezil was so inspired by the French master.[103] Equally surprising is his inability to harness his data along Weberian lines on the issue of the gap between 'priests and populace'. Instead, he prefers to emphasise that 'it is to those only who deeply busy themselves with religion (Priests) that, for good or bad, changes in popular views are ultimately due.'[104] There are also some veiled echoes of racial bias, as for instance, in his note on "The Dravidian Element in Indian Thought.'[105] Notwithstanding these criticisms, there is plenty of data in the volumes, which could still be harnessed into a scientific conceptual framework.

Amongst more recent writings, one can safely include J.C. Heestermann's study of the *rajasuya* sacrifice[106] for its healthy combination of Gonda's linguistics and Durkheim's sociology. Some refreshing orientation is also available in Naama Drury's study of the *agnishtoma, ashvamedha* and the *agnichayana* sacrifices on the basis of the *Shatapatha Brahmana* which has drawn upon the 'insights of Jungian psychology in the field of archetypes and symbols'.[107] This unfortunately cannot be said about a few recent works on Vedic religion, which, though rich in data, suffer from absence of any meaningful conceptual frame.[108]

From amongst recent- writings on Vedic religion which can be regarded as approximating a 'science of religion', special mention should be made of Bruce Lincoln's meticulous work on Indo-Iranian religion with a distinct focus on the *Rigveda.*[109] While Lincoln is relying considerably on linguistics and comparative mythology, the tools of Max Muller, it is more than obvious that the overall orientation does take cognizance of sociological, anthropological and Marxian formulations on religion. In addition, its emphasis on the ecological approach to the study of the religious phenomenon is a novel feature which will be discussed at length later. Though we do not share some of the formulations of Lincoln, e.g. the reservations expressed on the use of archaeology in the reconstruction of Indo-Iranian religion,[110] or the assumption of neat priestly and warrior classes in the context of the Rigvedic social v organisation;[111] it goes without saying that the work does present a refreshing departure from the model set by Max Muller.

A Perspective

Finally, I turn to the perspective on Vedic religion. Simply put, there is an absence of intensive study of Vedic religion in the total perspective of its material setting. Scholars such as R.S. Sharma[112] and Romila Thapar[113] have already laid the foundation with studies of the socio-economic and political structure of early and later Vedic times. We are, as a consequence of these seminal writings, now in a position to comprehend the dynamics of the life of the contemporary populace, their transformation from the largely pastoral to agrarian economic base; from relatively undifferentiated to class society and from lineage to state political apparatus. How did these material changes affect religious manifestations? Postulations such as Varuna religion *versus* Indra religion[114] or Indra-Usha tussle being an Aryan-non-Aryan conflict[115] are rather simplistic formulations. Manifestations of fetishism, totemism, magic, ancestor worship, beliefs in ghosts, spirits, demons, goblins, etc., which are in sociological and anthropological terms, associated with tribal religion, are found in plenty in the *Rigveda* and *Atharvaveda.* Totemistic origins of tribes such as the Matsyas, Ajas, Shigrus; priests being named after Gotama, Vatsa (calf), Shunaka (dog), Kaushika (owl), Mandukya (frog); Kurus tracing their descent from Riksha (bear) are examples of totemistic influences. Malevolent deities such as Kritya, Nirrti and Yatudhana haunting funeral places; Vishvamitra vanquishing his rivals with the help of an evil spirit called Sasarpari; sorcerers such as Rakshasvin, Yatumavan and Yatuman and even female sorcerer Yaturmati; ghosts, spirits, goblins, etc. such as Nihsala, Dhishana, Ekavadya, Magundi; *apsaras* residing in tree and water resorts—one such *apsara* is even called *rashtrabhrita* (sustainer of the kingdom) in the *Atharvaveda;* bad dreams occurring due to Grahi, Nirbhuti, Abhuti, etc. are some of the manifestations of religion at the popular level.[116] A recent study has convincingly rationalised the well-known Rigvedic concept of *Rta* in terms of tribal influences and its decline as a product of class differences.[117] Similarly, intensive studies need to be undertaken on major Vedic sacrifices such as *vajapeya, ashvamedha, purushamedha, agnichayana,* etc. to rationalise them in terms of agrarian growth and the emergence of the idea of territoriality.[118] Further, work needs to be done on Indra to explain his transformation from *gopati* to *shunasira* (lord of cattle to the wielder of the plough). Nor can one be content with abstract philosophic discussions of the monistic philosophy of the Upanishads.[119] We have already tried to explain it as a product of the brahmana-kshatriya rivalry for the acquisition of agricultural surplus.[120] Elsewhere, it has been rationalised as man's urge to overcome alienation consequent upon the emergence of *varna* divisions in the pastoral tribal society of the early Aryans.[121] There has even been a suggestion that the Upanishadic philosophy, a *kshatriya vidya,* had the force of a new ideology.[122]

Studies on Vishnuism and Shaivaism[123] have already conformed to a common pattern.[124] Broadly speaking, works on these subjects generally delineate the growth of Vishnu and Shiva from the Rigvedic[125] to Puranic accounts.[126] Occasionally, they also take cognizance of archaeological remains.[127] By and large they tend to be rather descriptive accounts—sometimes even degenerating to a rehash of existing knowledge.[128]

There has been some refreshing writing in the last three decades, beginning perhaps with Jan Gonda's *Aspects of Early Vishnuism*[129] where the ideas of Vishnu's link with the fertility cult specially through Lakshmi, and his links with Indra were mooted. His later work, a comparative study of Vishnuism and Shivaism[130] was an equally fascinating and incisive study. Perhaps even more perceptive land path-breaking are the contributions of D.D. Kosambi on the cults of Krishna, Shiva and on the social and economic aspects of the *Bhagavadgita.*[131] These are based on not only a profound study of literary sources but also on carefully planned field-work—a unique combination not to be found elsewhere. Sukumari Bhattacharji's work[132] on a comparative analysis of the historical growth of both Vishnu and Shiva delineates the transformation of these deities through the millennia—from the Vedas to the Puranas, and convincingly puts forward the case of dynamism of Indian mythology. However, the works of Suvira Jaiswal and Wendy Doniger O'Flaherty, invoke multi-disciplinary tools of analysis. Jaiswal's *The Origin and Development of Vaishnavism*[133] deserves our attention for its scientific approach_which never loses historical perspective. The entire growth of Vishnuism has been unfolded in terms of cultic integration of diverse autochthonous elements,[134] particularly in the form of Narayana, Samkarshana-Balarama, Ekanamsha, etc. The work is further noticeable for its utilisation of untapped literary epigraphic and numismatic data, e.g. Jain and Buddhist works. This has enabled her to trace the regional extent and popularity of Vishnuism in detail which had been hitherto overlooked or unknown. The fact that the entire work purports to study the religious phenomenon in the overall context of its material setting makes it a pioneering effort. W.D. O'Flaherty's study on the mythology of Shiva[135] belongs to a different class. A wide range of Indian texts (Vedic, Puranic, Classical and modern) is examined in the light of a dialectic pattern of inter-locking motifs which centre upon the myths of the great ascetic Shiva and his erotic *alter ego,* Kama, to explain an enduring human dilemma: the conflict between spiritual aspirations and human desires. It is a painstaking effort to apply Levi-Strauss' Structuralism but lacks any historical perspective.[136]

Of late there has been growing realisation that the epigraphic material has the potential of yielding useful results from the point of view of religious developments. Two studies may be mentioned in passing, in this connection, not for their theoretical or conceptual brilliance but for the richness of their data. V.S. Pathak's *Shaiva Cults in Northern India (A.D.* 700-1200)[137] and Urmila Bhagowalia's *Vaishnavism and Society in Northern India (A.D. 700-1200)*[138] fall in this genre.

The Role of Bhakti

Since the late sixties there has been a very noticeable tendency to undertake indepth analyses of the role of Bakti in Vishnuism and Shivaism. We shall even go to the extent of saying that a great majority of these writings tend to focus on the rationale of religious developments in terms of their material milieu. R.S. Sharma's epoch making work *Indian Feudalism*[139] based on the practice of land grants, unleashed a force of tremendous magnitude, which has provoked historians to think afresh on practically every sphere of people's activities, whether they be in the realm of economy, polity or society or even in ideas. Our assessment is that the post-Gupta scene in the entire subcontinent is marked by two distinctive strains in the domain of religion, viz., the growth of *bhakti* and the all-pervasive influence of tantric practices. It is possible to explain their widespread dispersal in terms of the growth of the feudal mode of production,[140] which had become almost a pan-Indian phenomenon.[141]

For about half a millennium from the mid-sixth century, Shaiva and Vaishnava saints (Nayanars and Alvars respectively) and their followers practised and propagated *bhakti* in the countryside and went to pilgrim centres singing and dancing. The overall pattern is that of consolidation of classical brahmanical society in early medieval India.[142] Originating in the sixth century Kanchipuram area under the Pallavas, it had traversed the full length of Tamilakam by the end of the ninth century and engulfed all the major kingdoms of the Cholas Pandyas and Cheras. If we are to believe in recent analysis, the spread of the *bhakti* movement in the north, epitomised in such a popular work as the *Bhagavata Purana,* was also the result of the impetus given by the Tamil saints.[143] The spread of the movement is intimately associated with the temple base, which in turn derived its *raison d 'etre* and economic sustenance through land grants received from not only kings and men at the helm of political affairs but even from other influential members of society.[144]

To conclude our presentation of Vishnuism and Shaivaism, a few more recent studies may be mentioned for the freshness of their approaches. G.S. Ghurye's *Gods and Men* (1962) deserves our attention for its delineation of the growth of these religions with a sociological and anthropological perspective. Hitherto, iconographic studies have remained confined to the identification, description and interpretation of divine images and their attributes. Largely forming a part of art history, these works have rarely been looked at as an index to socio-religious changes at macro and micro levels. Treating iconography as an integral part of the history of religions as well, R. Champakalakshmi's *Vaishnava Iconography in the Tamil Country* (1981) is a slightly different work. It tries to trace the evolution of the concerned subject through folk movements and integration of tribal cults of pre-Pallavan centuries. Yet another work which undertakes a micro study of the process of cultural coalescence and agencies of acculturation is Fred W. Clothey's perceptive study of Murugan.[145] The growth of this significant deity of the Shiva pantheon is presented as a convergence of two cultural streams, 'Sanskrit' and 'Tamil', without taking any of them as 'monolithic or unidimensional'.[146] David Dean Shulman also analyses sacrifice and divine marriage in the south Indian Shaiva tradition[147] in the light of the many traditions that have contributed to their formation, including Vedic, epic, puranic, classical Tamil and southern folk traditions. Studying the religious meaning of myths contained in these traditions, Shulman uncovers two persistent themes: the approach to power in all its manifestations, and the attempt to reconcile contact with power with the desire for purity. Broadly following O'Flaherty's modifications of Levi-Strauss' Structuralism as his key method, on which we have already expressed our reservations,[148] Shulman's conclusions about the Shaiva myths in terms of the aforesaid two themes seem to be influenced by Louis Dumont's *Homo Hierarchichus.* Though we share the reservations expressed regarding Dumont's assumptions, notions and methods,[149] we do not hesitate to say that Shulman's work is one of the very few stimulating monographs of the last decade.

Tantricism, like *bhakti,* permeates all religions in the post-Gupta centuries, not excluding even the so-called puritanical non-brahmanical religious systems. A recent survey of tantric religion,[150] though fairly comprehensive, is surprisingly unfamiliar with very important contributions on the subject. R.S. Sharma has rationalised it in terms of the preponderance of the cult of the Mother Goddess consequent upon the spread of agriculture as a result of land grants.[151] A fascinating dimension of this analysis is the process of cultural interaction of priestly Sanskritic and tribal elements. A recent study, based entirely on literary data, argues that the *Devi Mahatmya* of the *Markandeya Purana* (c. sixth century AD) is the first comprehensive account of the goddess to appear in Sanskrit—the explanation is sought in terms of Sanskritisation. It is underlined that the basic impulse behind the worship of the goddess is of non-Aryan and non-Sanskritic origin.[152] A survey of Shakti sculptures in Madhya Pradesh alone refers to as many as 400 images.[153] A great majority of their names such as Charchika, Umarimata, Bijasanidevi, Behamata, Birasanidevi, etc. link them with popular tribal deities.[154]

The few writings which have inspired us to study Buddhism and Jainism in the socio-economic milieu include R.S. Sharma's analysis of the origin of Buddhism,[155] A.K. Warder's rationalisation of Mahayana[156] and N.R. Guseva's presentation of the historical and ethnic roots of Jainism.[157]

The Material Milieu

A few general works not restricting themselves to any specific religion but distinctly focusing on the need to study it in its material milieu may now be mentioned. The most striking works falling under this category are of course, D.D. Kosambi's pioneering, provocative and very often even iconoclastic and unconventional studies. Apart from his numerous perceptive comments lying scattered in two path-breaking brilliant surveys on ancient India,[158] the collection of his essays entitled *Myth and Reality* (1962) has inspired the imagination of a generation of historians. The work is extremely refreshing in its range of new material presented and an impressive use of scientific methods in many fields: archaeology, ethnography and philology, without losing an overall historical perspective. Apart from his reflections on the cult sites of the Mother Goddess, the symbolism and meaning of the legend of Urvashi and Pururavas and the social and economic aspects of the *Bhagavadgita* mentioned above, one may also cite insights provided by him on Shiva's household, fertility rites enacted through primitive dancers and parallels between European Ice-Age drawings and modern Indian representations of certain deities. His masterly analysis is logically consistent and enormously stimulating. The conclusions, though startling, are most often convincing. The work is unquestionably a landmark in the study of the Indian religious tradition.[159]

The writings of Debiprasad Chattopadhyaya are also quite iconoclastic. With an orthodox Marxist framework and a passion for historical materialism, he has consistently tried to explode the myth of the other-worldliness of the Indians. Of the rare absurdities of our times, none is so prevalent and sacrosanct as the belief that mundane or this-wordly matters never entered the hallowed precincts of India. Chattopadhyaya has, through his studies on ancient Indian materialism and atheism[160] been raising his voice against such a naive view of the Indian religio-philosophic ethos for more than three decades. Recently, while delivering the famous Stephanos Nirmalendu Ghosh Lectures of 1981 at the Calcutta University, he struck another blow to Indian chauvinists when he argued, Vedic religion in its strict sense, in the sence of being the direct outcome of the Vedic literature and as produced by the Vedic people themselves, is really a misnomer,' and 'the great Vedic gods—Indra, Varuna, Mitra, Soma—have simply no place in the actual religious beliefs and practices of the vast Indian people—the word Veda became only a political tool rather than the source of any genuine religious sentiment.'[161]

The role of productive forces in determining the forms of religious expression has attracted attention of R.N. Nandi as well. He too has in the last two decades, made numerous contributions to the study of ancient Indian religions in the perspective of material developments covering a millennium from the third to the twelfth century AD. Apart from his doctoral study on *Religious Institutions and Cults in the Deccan,* his latest work *Social Roots of Religion in Ancient India* (1986) also takes up many issues and rationalises them from such a perspective. He has admirably focused attention on the impact of decaying towns, the disintegration of market economy, feudal mode of production and revival of market economy on such developments in the religious sphere as the brahmana-*jajamana* relations,[162] dispersal of *jajamani* brahmanas, the beginnings of *tirthayatras* (pilgrimages), the medieval gift exchange system, the origin of Shaivite monasticism, the occult in Jaina liturgy and the origin of the Virashaiva movement.

Amongst other recent works which investigate the religious phenomenon in the material setting, the important ones are: Francois Houtart and Genevieve Limercinier's. The *Great Asiatic Religions and their Social Functions*[163] and Vijay Nath's *Dana: Gift System in Ancient India* (1987). Though a sketchy and skimpy work, the former presents the important phases of the Asian religions down to present the times in an overall framework of historical materialism. The latter adopts a multi-disciplinary approach and presents an exhaustive study of the complex mechanics of the unique institution of *dana* between c. 600 BC and c. 300 AD from a socio-economic perspective. Recently, we had surveyed the changing perspective of contributions on religion presented during the last fifty years of the Indian History Congress to underline that there is, in the last fifteen years, a growing realisation of the necessity to study the religious phenomenon as an integral part of social formations and product of material conditions.[164]

Ecological Approach to Religion

More than two decades ago, the Swedish ethnologist and historian of religions, Ake Hultkrantz, proposed a daring new means of attack on the problem of comparing religions rooted in similar cultures.[165] Starting with the insight that religion is rooted in culture and following Julian Haynes Steward in seeing culture rooted in environment,[166] Hultkrantz has argued for what he calls 'an ecological approach to religion.' Just as there are 'types of culture' commonly recognised by anthropologists such as desert, nomad and arctic hunting, so also are there types of religion[1] that are intimately related to and in fact formed by the culture type in which they are found. 'The type of religion is in its essence timeless: in principle it should occur wherever ecological and technological conditions of a similar level and integration appear.' His goal is to establish these types of religion and to describe their essential features, drawing comparisons between cultures that may have no geographical or historical relation to one another but whose ecologies, technology and subsistence pattern are similar.

The study of the environmental integration of a religion and its implications is the crux of the ecology of religion. It is concerned with forms of religious expression and specific religious contents motivated by these forms, but not with the communication of ultimate meaning and value. 'In my understanding, at least, conclusions as to the latter are not allowed by the ecological approach.'[167] The religio-ecological approach investigates religion in its general environmental framing and should not be evaluated as a tool for economic determinism.[168]

Hultkrantz recognises three different levels of integration of religion and environment:

Primary integration, i.e. the environmental adaptation of basic cultural features, such as subsistence and productive arrangements, technology, etc. and behaviour patterns associated with these features, such as social and religious attitudes.

Secondary adaptation is an indirect adaptation of religious beliefs and rituals. These are organised into a framework that takes its forms from the social structure, which is in its turn a model suggested by the economic and technological adaptation to the environment.

The third possibility is *morphological adaptation,* the covering of religious features with forms taken from the physical and biological environment. 'Since religion has a conservative tendency, religious features that were adjusted to earlier ecological patterns often remain in later religious constellations. For instance, in agrarian cultures the spirits of the field appear in animal disguise, most certainly a left-over from the hunting cultures.' Although religious concepts are traditional, they borrow their formal appearance from forms within the immediate biotope and this choice of forms is not arbitrary, but is related to the symbolism that is inherent in them.[169] Obviously, Hultkrantz implies that religion is not something made up of environmental influences. He mentions four ways of handling religious forms: (1) to look at the pattern and functioning of a religion through ecological analysis, not as a reductionist approach, but as a study of its functional interweaving with the forms of nature; (2) comparison between religions and between religious traits, and thus also a phenomenological approach; (3) arrangement of types of religion into historical strata, i.e. to bring different historical or archaeological strata, such as gatherers, hunters, cultivators, nomads, etc.;[170] and (4) ecology could indicate an imminent process of religious change; for if the holistic thesis holds good, i.e. that phases of religious expression belong to the primary ecological integration of culture, then changes in the basic structure of the 'culture core', to use Steward's term, should be expected to affect the structure of religion.

The research strategy which postulates that similar technologies applied to similar natural environments tend to produce similar economic and social systems and further, similar systems of religion is what Marvin Harris had called cultural materialism—the anthropological counterpart to historical materialism.[171] This position does not deny that changes in social organisation or religious innovations can bring about changes in technology and thus change the ecological adaptation, but only states that these in general tend to be dependent factors. The distinction drawn by Marx between *base* and *superstructure* is theoretically more fruitful than Steward's distinction between 'cultural core' and 'secondary cultural features'.[172]

That the ecological approach to religion has many vulnerable spots and even an 'ecological fallacy' has been recognised by the exponent himself.[173] The very conception of 'environment' requires clarification. It is not immutable.

The identification of environment with nature was correct at some stage but cannot be true of the present times. We are a witness to the process of transition—from the phase of the struggle to master nature, from the phase directed *against* nature to the phase of struggle *for* nature and for its preservation *from* and *for* man. The wasteland landscape of the large mining and steel centres clearly indicates that the 'technical environment' is gradually becoming man's 'ecological' and 'natural' environment.[174] In defence of Hultkrantz, however, it may be stated that he has not argued in terms of a direct link between environment and religion; on the contrary he has repeatedly stressed the middle term in the relation, i.e. technology and the subsistence pattern. Further, it has been argued by some[175] that the ecology of religion deals with religion as a cultural rather than a religious phenomenon. Religion as such eludes the ecologist of religion, 'we need a method of inquiry, a science, which can and will cope with religion religiously, i.e. with religion as religion ...' But the precision with which Hultkrantz has defined his field, not as religiosity of the individual, nor as religion itself, but as the environmental conditioning patterns of religion needs to be recalled here. What was important was not religiosity of individuals within a social system, but the religious qualities of the social system itself. Finally, it aught to be kept in view that a similar ecological setting giving rise to different religious forms or similar religious forms arising in varied ecological conditions are not unknown. The field work amongst Indian tribes such as the Andamanese, Todas, Birhors, Saoras and tribes of Chota Nagpur raises certain doubts about the approach under consideration.

While issues raised by the ecological approach to religion are still being debated, it may be underlined that this approach is not proposed as an alternative *to* other methods, it never supplants other methods; it is a way of securing new information for other approaches, it offers more solutions and fresh insights.

One recent study, particularly in the context of early India, which highlights the potentialities of the ecological *approach* to religion is Brace Lincoln's *Priests, Warriors, and Cattle* (1981) dealing with Indo-Iranian religion, specially the Rigvedic phase. Do cultures which have similar socio-economic and ecological bases also have similar religious systems? Is religion primarily directed towards abstract universal concerns, or are practical and temporal matters a fundamental part of religious thought? Two cultures, historically and geographically quite separate but ecologically and socio-economically quite similar are taken up as a test case to answer the above queries. The present-day Nilotic people of East Africa (Nuer, Dinka and Masai) and Proto-Indo-Iranian, who flourished around 2000 BC were selected for the purpose because both were 'semi-settled pastoral groups whose livelihood depends on herding of cattle'.[176] The religion of each group is examined in detail, with special emphasis being placed on the myths they recount, the rituals they practise, and the ways in which their societies are organised, as well as on the deities they worship. Strong similarities of detail are readily apparent. Both cultures perform cattle sacrifice as their foremost ritual act; both possess elaborate myths of the first sacrifice and the first cattle raid; both worship celestial sovereigns; and both suffer serious tensions between priests and warriors. More important than these resemblances of detail, however, is the overwhelming similarity of the religious systems taken as a whole. These systems are shown to centre on what Lincoln calls the 'cattle cycle', a pattern in which religious activity and speculation are focused on the acquisition and disposition of cattle, all such thought and action being seen as sacred, chartered by the gods, and established in the acts of creation as recounted in myth. On the strength of these pieces of evidence, the author suggests that cultures with similar socio-economic bases do exhibit similar religious forms, and that religion must be studied as an eminently practical matter being firmly rooted in culture, and culture in turn being rooted in ecology.

The Geography of Religion

Any discussion of the ecology of religion would remain incomplete if it does not take cognizance of the geography of religion, for the two share common frontiers and are complementary to each other. The impression is sometimes created that since the ecological approach highlights the impact of environment on religion while the focus of the geography of religion is to work out its impact on the landscape, the two are antagonistic. Far from being so. It is not the task of the geographer to evaluate religious experience and neither is he concerned with assessing the validity or otherwise of religious claims and beliefs. This brings him closer to the ecologist interested in religion. The relationship under reference has varied nuances. To illustrate, Biblical geography was an early form of historical geography although today it is left to the archaeologist. Ecclesiastical geography is specifically concerned with mapping out the spatial advance of the Church in terms of its own institutions and the political territories allocated to it.

Though the religious conception forming the central core of the world view or the notions of universe have been known from very early times and perhaps in most of the centres of ancient civilisations,[177] geography of religion' as a concept can be traced to Kasche's work of 1795. As a distinctive approach to religion, it owes a great deal to the works of P. Fickeler and P. Deffontaines in the 1940s and more recently to D.E. Sopher's *Geography of Religions* published in 1967.[178]

We would like to make a fervent plea for a geography of Indian religions, but with an extended scope than had been visualised by Deffontaines and Sopher. It would also take cognizance of Hultkrantz's 'types of religions' and what has been called the 'anthropology of the sacred'.[179] Broadly speaking, ours is a plea for an atlas of Indian religions in which mapping *per se* must have the objective of grappling with some problems of the growth of Indian religions. Perhaps certain specific illustrations can help us in identifying the directions of our plea.

D.D. Kosambi's fieldwork in Maharashtra along what he has called microlith trade tracks suggested such variables as 'highland' and 'lowland' cultures affecting their cultic practices.[180] His perceptive* insights about Mother Goddess cult sites in association with 'crossroad' provide fascinating clues to work out Hultkrantz' 'types of religion'. The phenomenon of the Mother Goddess has persisted in India through the millennia, almost as a pan-Indian feature. This is obviously a generalisation that would require considerable particularisation in terms of time, space, type and, of course, the material milieu. What type of mother goddesses prevail in a particular geographical-ecological setting and at what point of time? Mapping of such data may enable us to weave a pattern. We have already referred to the problem of religion as a 'catalyst' for the urban growth of the Harappans.[181] It is possible that some light may be thrown by the cartographic delineation of the settlement pattern superimposed on the geographical distribution of antiquities unearthed at various centres of the civilisation—particularly different types of seals and sealings and terracotta objects with their quantitative data. This delineation must also include the so-called copper-bronze implements in view of the often repeated contention that since the Harappan state does not appear to be war oriented, religion must have provided the ideological support for policing the 'empire'.[182] The cartographic delineation of antiquities we propose, when seen in relation to the landscape and material base of multifarious centres of the civilisation, is likely ftp enable us to understand processes of 'uniformity' or otherwise of the civilisation.

Another problem-oriented approach to the geography of Indian religions may be considered. This relates to the origin and dispersal of Shaivaism in north and south India in the centuries up to the reign of the Guptas, i.e. mid-sixth century. It is rather simplistic to argue that Shaivaism had '*non*-Aryan' origins. It has struck us very often that the pattern *of* growth of Vaishnavism and Shivaism was, in some respects, very dissimilar. While both the deities were endeavouring to amalgamate diverse cultic deities, many of whom were of the so-called 'non-Aryan'[183] strain, a concept of *avatara* did not develop within the Shaiva fold; the integration of Ganesha, Karttikeya, Manasa, Ganga, Sarasvati, etc., assumes the form of a family—sons, daughters, wife, etc. In other words, there is a perceptible emphasis on kinship relations. Could we juxtapose this with the *avataras?* Is it possible to argue that the appeal of Shaivaism was relatively greater in those areas which retained their tribal moorings and had not been adequately brahmanised? An hypothesis of this nature can be tested if a micro analysis of the Shaiva antiquities, cults, cult-sites is undertaken regionwise along the horizontal axis and in point of time along the vertical axis. As a second stage of such an analysis, one can legitimately juxtapose the post-sixth century Indian scene of the Shiva followers. The little work done on the geographical distribution of temples and monasteries in the Deccan in general and Karnataka in particular between c. AD 500-1200[184] brings out fascinating details of the mutual relationships of brahmanical and non-brahmanical religions. There is obviously a great deal that needs to be done in this context: an intensive mapping of different sects *in relation to land grants* as well as the geographical distribution of other related antiquities is desirable. A close scrutiny of the epigraphical material from present-day Karnataka, Tamil Nadu and Kerala has been quite revealing from the point of view of the Shri-Vaishnava settlements and has enabled us to undertake a fresh look at the role of the Cholas vis-à-vis this important sect of the early medieval south India.[185] Charting of this data would be an equally rewarding experience.

A recent attempt to reconstruct the geography of Indian religion along some of the lines being suggested here may be seen in the meticulous presentation of the movement of the Alvars.[186] Delineating more than ninety temples mentioned in the writings of these Vaishnava saints, it not only sketches the general spatial movement of the *bhakti* cult but also endeavours to indicate possible regional variations by showing the data for important individual Alvars separately. Interestingly, it has also been possible to show the correspondence between geographical distribution and the religious and poetic variations in what has been designated as 'temple poetry' by invoking the imagery of landscape.[187] Some of the major findings of this cartographic depiction having a distinctive bearing on our understanding of the developments in the *bhakti* movement in the south are:

(a) Venkatam Kanchi is the oldest Alvar environment.

(b) The Alvar movement spread further south from Kanchi; already the attention of the early Alvars was directed to the other part of the Tamil country and not to the regions north of Venkatam.

(c) The writings of Nammalvar enable us to comprehend the shifting focus—he knew Venkatam rather indirectly, isolates completely and the southernmost points of Tamil Nadu art southern Kerala emerge as the new focal points of the Vaishnava saints of c. AD 700.

(d) The mid-eighth century scene of the time of Tirumangai, the most 'temple oriented' of the 'sages' shows, the emergence of the south Indian temple culture as a complex system. The large number of temples and the systematic arrangements based on a *tirthayatra* in *pradakshina* fashion shows that the pilgrimage started with Venkatam in the north, proceeded towards the south via the large temple complexes in the Thanjavur area, and in Kurukuti, its southernmost point, turned clockwise to the west and then returned to the north to end at Kottiyur.

(e) Tirumangai attempted to compile a comprehensive and systematic 'temple geography', but a different trend is noticeable in the later Alvars (c. AD 750-850) such as Periya, Andal, Tiruppan, Kulashekhara, etc. when the Srirangam temple becomes the focal point. The concentration on this temple corresponds to the situation found in early Shrivaishnavism.

Though creditable, fascinating and illuminating, Hardy's exercise in the geography of the Alvars could perhaps also do well to incorporate the data on the material base. Some recent writings on the Pallavas, the Cholas and the Alvars as well as the Nayanars (the Shaiva saints, particularly the Tevaram trio of Appar, Sambandhar and Sundarar),[188] have been able to show the gradual importance of paddy cultivation in the Kaveri valley and the resultant pattern of brahmanical settlements, which in turn contributed to the growth of Chola power.

On the Notions of Death

In recent years there have been some very refreshing and stimulating writings on the notions of Death—in terms of rituals, religious beliefs and practices, art forms and above all, in association with socio-economic developments. These have resulted in a special genre of literature on an obscure field of religious history of the subcontinent. These studies centre round the hero-stones, which are littered over most parts of the Indian subcontinent! There has been a long and almost continuous history of these relics for more than 1500 years and extends to both brahmanical and non-brahmanical religions. Locally called *viragats, paliyas, govardhana stambhas, kirti-stambhas, chhaya-stambhas,* or merely, *chhatris, stambhas, devallis,* etc., these tablets or pillars fall into several groups originating in ritual or cult practices as well as religious or social customs of its patrons. The *chhaya-stambha* is among the earliest archaeological evidence, and it seems to be rooted in the social practices of the Buddhists. The *nisidhi* represents the ritual death practices exclusively by the Jains.[189] The *viragals,* or at least the currency of this term, cross-religious demarcations, if not the' conventional geographical limits of southern India. The *kirti-stambha, paliya, chhatri, devali* and *siambha* share the country between the Himalayas and the Vindhyas—mostly in Gujarat and Rajasthan.[190] The accumulation of these data can be of great help in undertaking an ecological and geographical analysis of religious belief patterns through the millennia. The change in the style of hero-stones seems to reflect a change in the status of the hero being memorialised. Many of the earlier stones from Tamil Nadu come from the North Arcot district which is known to have been at that time an area of livestock breeding, where cattle-raiding would be one method of increasing wealth. Later, elaborate stones commemorated heroes who claimed to belong to the upper caste groups, often claiming kshatriya status. The indication of the hero's religious sect may have been due to the influence of the *bhakti* sects.[191] It is suggested on an impressionistic basis: topographically and ecologically there is a frequency of such memorials in upland areas, in the vicinity of passes across hills, and in areas regarded traditionally as frontier zones which often included primarily pastoral regions, the outskirts of forests and the edges of what have come to be called the 'tribal areas of central India'. Hero-stones are relatively infrequent in the large agricultural tracts of the Indus and the Ganga valleys and in the agriculturally rich delta areas of the peninsula. Frontier zones were often maintained as buffer regions where political security was transient and where royal armies did not necessarily guarantee protection to local inhabitants. They would, therefore, inevitably have recourse to their own arrangement for protection, in which the village hero or the local chief played a major role. This would suggest a differentiation of military functions in a decentralised political system.[192] Obviously, substantiation of such a hypothesis would require a cartographic presentation of types and varieties of memorial stones in their ecological setting. Further, since these relics proliferated in the post-sixth century period, it would be worth finding out the correlation and correspondence, if any, between the distribution of land grants on the one hand and that of the memorial stones on the other. This is particularly desirable in view of several assumptions: (a) the phenomenon of land grants is associated with the expansion of agriculture, (b) both memorial stones and land grants are considered to be useful mechanisms of cultic integration,[193] and (c) both phenomena have also been instrumental in the processes of state formation. In view of these, the only way to establish a correspondence between memorial stones and land grants is to undertake extensive mapping. This may also have to be linked up with the geography of the *bhakti* cult mentioned earlier.

The geography of Indian religions must also include the 'anthropology of the sacred'.[194] How ecology and geography have interacted with religion has been shown in respect of many countries. The example of Waldensians in Italy has some bearing in the present context. Though traditionally farmers, members of this community commute to nearby industrial establishments for livelihood. They have not given up farming, which is undertaken on Sundays; this pricked their conscience as it violated the strict commandment about the observance of feast days. But pastors nowadays interpret the command to observe feast days differently.[195] Similarly, an emphatic plea has been made to analyse the expansion of the cult of Mary in nineteenth century France and the model of pilgrimage in the light of growing urbanisation. The specific methodology suggested for the purpose includes not only the study of old maps but the charting of chapels, oratories or crosses and cult sites to determine the 'rhythms of a sacred space'.[196] It is argued, for instance, 'old maps, place names, still vivid collective memories of cults, or other traces, may point to the existence of churches or chapels which have now disappeared.... This approach would necessarily limit one to by now well-established facts, such as the spread of the mendicant orders to the cities, the *intra muros* rivalry between the new congregations and the old religious families who had returned from the countryside, and the passions of the rich and powerful as they used the city as a stage upon which to fight for their own cult sites and for their glory.'[197]

The Study of Sacred Sites

As far as India is concerned, some anthropologists have tried to work out the methodology of studying sacred complexes in general and specific sacred sites in particular.[198] Though this methodology has been evolved, it is limited to brahmanical complexes and neglects the historical perspective. It is well known that brahmanical literature alone mentions more than 4000 *tirthas* in early medieval times and that the *Mahabharata* and the Puranas alone contain at least 40,000 verses on *tirthas, sub-tirthas* and legends connected with them.[199] To this, one can add not only numerous *sthalapuranas* but specific digests on *tirthas* dealing with brahmanical and non-brahmanical centres of pilgrimage. This raises various questions that need to be answered.[200] However, since we are broadly concerned here with the ecology and geography of Indian religions, it needs to be emphasised that there are at least two broad types of inquiries that can be carried out in the context of *tirthas* and sacred complexes:

(a) Micro studies of specific sites and temples. We have some very good works on individual temples, but most of them are concerned with architectural and iconographic details, though a few also take cognizance of their material setting and role in society and economy.[201] However, there is none which could fulfil the criteria laid down in our perspective of the geography of Indian religions. Recently, an intensive analysis of the Vishnupada at Gaya has been undertaken in the light of tradition and archaeology. The resultant picture is quite illuminating.[202] Such studies need to be carried out at many other complexes and it is hoped that these would enable *us* to evolve a 'sacred geography.'

(b) We require more extensive macro analysis of pilgrim centres at regional levels with a view to creating a pattern, if possible, of the types of these centres in terms of the nature of pilgrims, deities associated, extent of appeal, etc. Both lines of enquiry would have to take into account the socio-economic context.[203] Nor is ecology to be sidetracked. Places proclaimed as *tirthas* include crossroads, river-crossings, banks of rivers, hermitages in forests, mountain passes and important towns. Did *tirthayatras* typify medieval dana-oriented and agriculture-based gift exchange systems?[204] Did the land grants to monastic establishments and temples contribute to the rise of rural centres?[205] Did the *tirthas,* like the memorial stones, represent yet another manifestation of acculturation in the areas peripheral to the Madhyadesha? Such questions can perhaps be answered effectively if investigations based on ecology and geography are undertaken.

The Marxist Approach

Without identifying religion and ideology, it may be safely asserted that writings in the last three decades, particularly those of Marxists in varied disciplines, have considerably enriched the study of both as cultural forms and processes. While the older Marxists thought of religion and other cultural phenomena as mere epiphenomena, as part of a superstructure determined by the economic base, more recent Marxist-inspired debates, particularly in the last fifteen years, have postulated not only a higher degree of relative autonomy but even attributed a hegemonic position to such phenomena in the overall social framework.

Amongst the classic statements about the relations between religion and society one can mention scattered and unsystematic references to religion in Marx and Engels.[206] As early as 1844, young Marx reveals traces of Feuerbach's critique of religious alienation: 'The basis of irreligious criticism is: *Man makes religion,* religion does not make man. Religion is the self-consciousness and self-esteem of man who has either not yet found himself or has already lost himself again'.[207] Yet Marx goes further than Feuerbach. For Marx 'man is no abstract being encamped outside the world. The only way for man to rid himself of this illusion is to destroy the social world that produces it As Marx proposes: 'Religious distress is at the same time the expression of real distress and also the protest against real distress. Religion is the sigh of the oppressed creature.'[208] So the struggle against religion is necessarily a struggle against that world whose '*halo* is religion' and 'of which religion is the spiritual *aroma.'* It is in this context that religion becomes the 'opium of people'.[209] Here Marx anticipates one of the crucial elements of his concept of ideology, namely that religion compensates in the mind for a deficient reality; it reconstitutes in the imagination a coherent solution which goes beyond the real world in an attempt to resolve the contradictions of the real world. So Marx confirms his conviction that the ideological inversion responds to and derives from a real inversion. As he suggests: 'Man is *the world of man,* the state, society. This state, this society, produce religion, an *inverted world consciousness,* because they are an *inverted world.*'[210] This basic idea of a double inversion in consciousness and in reality is not only retained by Marx and Engels in their subsequent writings pinpointing the exact economic mechanisms in which this inversion originates and by which it is concealed but one can also see in this double inversion a precursor to the use of 'ideology' by them. The effect of the ideological inversions was also grasped from the very beginning when religion was described by Marx as compensating in the mind for the deficiencies of the world. These are considered to be 'critical and negative connotations of the concept of ideology.'[211]

It was the earliest exponent of the sociology of religion, Durkheim to begin with, who contributed to the discussion on religion as an ideology The Marx, Durkheim made clear that religion and ideology have a social basis, particularly in patterns of social relations and organisation, but they also have a degree of autonomy, following certain rules peculiar to culture.

Surely, it was Max Weber who produced one of the most sensitive and complex accounts of 'elective affinities' between social groups and sets of beliefs or ideologies. His perceptive discussions of the different ideological inclinations of various intellectual strata provide a link with contemporary Marxist insights, such as those of Gramsci on 'organic intellectuals ideologies.'[212] We have already mentioned Weber's notions of 'religious anchorage', his anti-reductionist approach and their ideological ramifications. Even when he showed interest in 'material interests', he could not resist the channelling effects of ideas in determining people's actions.

Recent developments in the analysis of ideology have been concerned 'with improving the explanation of how and why ideology takes a particular form and of how it works. Two important developments are discernible: first, more attention has been given to what Geertz has called 'autonomous process of symbolic formulation', which entails examining ideologies as systems of interesting symbols and the ways in which they provide plausible interpretations of a problematic social reality for particular groups.[213] This has helped us in appreciating the intricate and complex nature of symbolic processes, which cannot be differentiated simply in terms of false consciousness *versus* true consciousness.[214] Second, there is now an awareness of the field of ideology in relation to classes and groups as being one of contestation and a lived relationship', not a mechanical process.

Perhaps no discussion of ideology would be complete without reference to Gramsci's idea of the hegemony of the intellect.[215] From the point of view of our present discussion the major point of interest lies in Gramsci's concern for the autonomous functioning of ideology of which religion, folklore and philosophy constitute essential components—a notion which is shared by contemporary phenomenologists of religion.[216] A further sophistication of these notions having a direct bearing on the theoretical framework is to make ideology an ingredient of the mode of production and thereby a part of the base/infrastructure.[217] It is this latter proposition which needs to be contested.

The Base-Superstructure Relationship

The orthodox interpretation of Marx and Engels takes it more or less for granted that the founders identify ideology with an all-encompassing superstructural level determined by the economic base. There are three or four places in their writings where expressions such as 'ideological superstructure', 'idealistic superstructure' or 'ideological spheres' are used. Although the 1859 *Preface* seems to restrict the use of the term superstructure to the legal and political level, other texts such as *The German Ideology* (1845-46), which is considered to be the first formulation of the base-superstructure thesis and the *Eighteenth Brumaire of Louis Bonaparte* subsume both politics and consciousness under the term superstructure. The spatial image of base and superstructure intends to convey the idea that the forms of social consciousness are not autonomous and that they do not emerge out of themselves, but that they have a foundation in the social relations of production. It has been pointed out that this building-like simile (base-superstructure) was mainly directed against spiritualist metaphysics and idealism which confirmed a belief in the self-development of the idea.[218]

More recently, the French structuralist anthropologists, particularly Maurice Godelier, have tried to redefine the parameters of infrastructure/base-superstructure relationship by arguing that the distinction between the two is not a distinction between institutions but between functions. Accordingly, infrastructure is defined as a combination of sets of social and material conditions that enable a society's members to produce and reproduce the material conditions of their existence.[219]

These attempts to refine Marxian formulations of historical materialism tend to suggest that the base-superstructure distinction applies to capitalist societies,[220] which is borne out neither by Marx-Engels' writings on pre-capitalist socio-economic formations nor by empirical data collected by sociologists and anthropologists since the turn of the present century. More fundamentally, it is also an attempt to blur the distinction between forces of production and relations of production. Godelier, while recognising them as 'distinct phenomena', also argues, 'they never exist separately; they always exist together in some specific combination'. Relying on Radcliffe-Brown (on Australian aborigines), Dumont (on Indian caste system), E. Will (on politics in ancient Greece) and studies on ancient Sumerian religion (such as those of Frankfort, Oppenheim and Adams) he draws a distinction between 'determination' and 'dominance' by highlighting the 'dominance' of relations of production (supposedly 'superstructure') such as kinship, politics and religion. Marx's formulation regarding the determinant role of base/infrastructure 'in the last analysis' is construed in the sense of the 'universal existence of a *hierarchy of functions* to be assumed by social relations in order for a society to be able to exist *as such* and to carry on reproducing.'[221]

Our position in this theoretical debate about the base-superstructure and the place of religion and ideology therein is to reiterate the centrality of the mode of production and its role as *'determinant in the past analysis'*. Further, while we appreciate the considerable influence exercised by religion and ideology at a given point of time and perhaps even their functioning as material force due to passage of time,[222] the sort of autonomy-hegemony-dominance attributed to them from the days of Durkheim-Weber to Eliade-Gramsci and Godelier is exaggerated and unwarranted. Religion and ideology and their role in the society should be taken as the components of the 'superstructure' formulated by Marx and Engels. Let us illustrate this position with reference to certain phases of Indian religions through millennia.

Regarding one of the earliest phases, the question of religion being an 'intensifying factor' or 'catalyst' of the urban growth under the Harappans has already been raised.[223] That this role has been attributed to religion on negative evidence is rather apparent to be overlooked. Equally exaggerated is the enthusiasm with which it is treated like an ideology.[224] While it is possible to infer certain social divisions, it is not easy to share Kosambi's dogmatic assertion of the prototype of brahmana priesthood recognisable in the Harappan metropolis. Even if parallels from other contemporary centres of bronze age civilisations are invoked, one would do well to recall V. Gordon 'Childe's perceptive observation on the priest kings of Sumer, viz., it was the economic system 'that made the God (through his representative) a great capitalist and landlord, his temple into a city bank.'[225] It must have been the potentialities of the people to generate agricultural surplus necessitating huge granaries at Mohenjodaro, Harappa and possibly at Kalibangan too, coupled, with the extensive mechanism and network of internal as well as long-distance overland

and maritime trade symbolised in the Lothal 'warehouse', which must have been instrumental in giving shape to such forms of religious manifestations as we are able to speculate about.

Asoka's *dhamma,* which is anything but religion in the literal sense of the *term,* and is perhaps closer to ideology, offers yet another manifestation which could be looked into from the aforesaid perspective. If the imperatives of *dhamma* are to be understood, one will have to go beyond the zeal of the so-called 'philosopher-king' and the 'revolutionary' impact of the great event—the Kalinga War. To concede an autonomous-determinant role to ideas would, in the present case, entrap us in the noose of brahmanical chauvinists who have rarely taken to the non-brahmanical men at the helm of affairs with kind disposition. Recent studies on the concepts of state and empire striking a severe blow to the notions of 'centralised' Mauryan empire[226] enable us to highlight the compulsions of the economic logic of the set-up and comprehend the driving forces behind Asoka's *dhamma.*

In our references to the Upanishadic thought embodying monistic ideas, early Buddhism of the Buddha, the rise of *bhakti* and tantricism in the post-Gupta centuries,[227] the paramount necessity of seeing these phenomena in the light of material milieu has already been indicated. But how these religio-philosophic manifestations functioned as ideologies in their respective times needs investigation.

There are certain crucial questions which need to be raised before the specificities of early Indian religions are taken up for discussion. If ideology is considered to be subservient to the interests of ruling/dominant classes, do we simultaneously assume the existence of an ideology of the dominated classes? What is the *raison d'etre* of dominant ideas? Are they dominant because they are supposed to be widely shared by the dominated classes themselves? Under what conditions do the dominated groups come to share interpretations of the world that legitimise the existing social order not only in the eyes of the dominant group, but also in their own eyes? Do we say that the ideas of the dominated do not constitute an ideology since they do not legitimise the existing social order? The Indian scene may not enable us to answer all these questions. Nevertheless, it would be worth determining the parameters of religion functioning as ideology in early India.

The existence of primary producers and managers of production in the later Vedic period is generally recognised by scholars. We have elsewhere argued not only for an antagonism between the two but amongst the non-producing classes too (brahmanas and kshatriyas) and the latter struggle has been rationalised in terms of the fight for agricultural surplus.[228] But do the exalted sacrificial cult of the *Brahmanas* and the *atma-vidya* of the Upanishads constitute ideologies of brahmanas and kshatriyas respectively? It may be tempting to call both ideologies of the ruling class. It seems to us, however, that such characterisation is not only simplistic but also ignores the dialectics of the development of these religio-philosophic systems. That none of them is a monolithic uniform idea should be apparent from the minutae of various sacrifices. Just one of the numerous ceremonies of only one sacrifice, viz., the *ratnahavimshi* ceremony of the *rajasuya* shows how the tribal and Patriarchal elements and how priestly domination was being replaced by that of the kshatriyas.[229] That sacrifices aimed at the creation of large communities by transcending kinship considerations ought not to be overlooked in the present context. Elaborate rituals were prescribed for the admission of the Vratya chief of Magadha to Vedic society and the chief of the *nishadas* called *sthapati* finds a place in Vedic rituals meant for higher orders.

Again it is generally accepted that as opposed to brahmanical Sanskrit works, the Pali texts of the Buddhists provided a different rationale of the origin of kingship, and the new monarchs of the Ganga valley in the sixth-fifth centuries of the pre-Christian era were favourably disposed towards non-brahmanical religions. But it would again be an over-simplification to say that the Buddha's was an ideology of the kshatriyas. This is being suggested not only because all the concerned monarchies were certainly not in the hands of the kshatriyas but also because it would unjustifiedly restrict the social base of early Buddhism. Apart from the material sustenance received by the Buddha from peasants and traders who were certainly out of reckoning of upper class dominance, a fairly extensive popularity of the Master amongst brahmanas too is not unknown.

Finally, such prominent manifestations of the religio-philosophic outlook of people of the Indian subcontinent of the post-Gupta centuries as the rise of *bhakti*, tantricism, pilgrimage, etc. are indeed products of the land grant economy. Though the brahmanas were the biggest beneficiaries of the mechanism and may have also worked consciously in league with contemporary rulers to prepare its philosophic background, it would again be difficult to rationalise these developments only in terms of dominating brahmana ideology. Surely, it is impossible to eliminate the symbiotic relationship between the brahmanas on the one hand and the tribals on the other? The traffic of ideas was certainly a two-way one. And what about the Buddhists and the Jainas? They were also affected by the nuances of the land grant, economy. Though the sphere of the influence of the Buddhists was shrinking, this was not the case with the Jainas. In Karnataka, Gujarat and Rajasthan specially, they had carved out a niche for themselves in the mind of people. But ideas such as *bhakti,* tantric practices and pilgrimage were essential components of their creed too. The transparent weakness of the so-called 'Brahman-Peasant Alliance' in post-Gupta southern India has already been convincingly demonstrated.[230] But even the hypothesis of the rural base of the temple movement under the patronage of brahmana-king collaboration leaves many gaps if the role of *bhakti* as an ideology is to be fully appreciated. To illustrate, the Tamilakam where this rural base model has been applied, [231] also witnessed an extensive internal trade network[232] as well as an ambitious programme of maritime trade activity. What was the role of traders and merchants in the growth of the temple movement? Perhaps because of the violent attitude of the Alvars and the Nayanars, at least in the initial few centuries, non-brahmanical religions which used to get the support of these communities, had almost vanished from Tamilakam. Did traders and merchants switch their allegiance to the new temple movement? Or they did not need any ideological prop? Evidence is mounting to show that even merchants and their assemblies *(nagarams)* exercised control over land and had interest in its agricultural output. Further, did not temples also tend to erect barriers of both language and rituals between peasant laity and the priesthood? If then ideology is to be understood in terms of a mechanism of class interests in general and ruling class interests in particular, how does one explain the role of *bhakti?* This dilemma would apply to other major post-Gupta religious manifestations as well.

Apropos of Gramsci, reference was made to four levels of ideology: philosophy, religion, commonsense (called 'the folklore of philosophy') and folklore. One may not accept the gradation of these levels—particularly the despising tone in which the last level is considered, yet as a conception it has elements which make it very broad-based. The role of religion in society, particularly as an ideology ought to be seen in its potentialities to sway masses and we may conclude with a recent assessment and also perhaps a warning about ideology as a cultural system, considering ideology as a justificatory and apologetic dimension of culture, Geertz accepts that it refers 'to that part of culture which is activity concerned with the establishment and defense of patterns of beliefs and value...the patterns of belief and value defended may be, of course, those of a socially subordinate group, as well as those of a socially dominant one, and the 'apology' therefore for reform or revolution.'[233]

I thank Professors R.S. Sharma, Romila Thapar, R.L. Shukla and D.N. Jha for their comments and suggestions on the first draft of this address.

Notes and References

1. The term 'science of religions' had been used by Abbe Prosper Leblanc and Stiefelhagen in 1852 and 1858 respectively but not in the strict sense given to it by Max Muller—the sense in which it is being currently used. Cf. Mircea Eliade, *The Sacred and the Profane,* 1961, p. 216.
2. I take this opportunity to thank my numerous students who have, over the years, helped me through their intelligent and lively discussions in developing the perspective being presented here. Mrityunjay Kumar and Dr. Bhairabi Prasad Sahu deserve very special attention in this connection.
3. For the problems of defining religion and its varied dimensions, Cf. J.E. Barnhart, *The Study of Religion and its Meaning—New Explorations in Light of Karl Popper and Emile Durkheim,* The Hague. See also Ninian Smart, *The Religious Experience of Mankind,* Fontana paperback, London 1969, pp. 11-41; Donald Wiebe, *Religion and Truth: Towards an Alternative Paradigm for the Study of Religion,* The Hague, 1981. Haridas Bhattacharyya, *The Fundamentals of Living Faiths,* Stephanos Nirmalendu Ghosh Lectures of 1933, University of Calcutta, 1938, *passim* and Nalinikanta Brahma, *The Fundamentals of Religion* being the Stephanos Nirmalendu Ghosh Lectures of 1951, University of Calcutta, 1960, chs. 1, 2 and 8.
4. While it has been argued by some that at the most primitive levels of culture, 'to live as a human being is itself a religious Act' (Cf. Mircea Eliade's foreword to Douglas Allen, *Structure and Creativity in Religion,* The Hague, 1977, p. (viii), others forcefully reject the role of religion within the major cultural traditions of mankind—in the ancient worlds of India, China, Greece, Rome and Israel (Cf. James Thrower, *The Alternative Tradition,* The Hague, 1980, *passim).*
5. Joachim Wach, *Sociology of Religion,* Chicago, 1944, pp. 1-2; C. Jouco Bleeker, The Contribution of the Phenomenology of

Religion to the Study of the History of Religions', in Bianchi, Bleeker and Bausani, (eds.) *Problems and Methods of the History of Religions,* Leiden, 1972, pp. 35-45; Idem, *The History of Religions* 1950-1975, Leiden, 1975 and numerous articles on *Religionswissenschaft* by Jacques Waardenburg, published in the 1970s. Cf. also Waardenburg, *Reflections on the Study of Religion,* The Hague, 1978.

6. *Priests, Warriors, and Cattle,* California, 1981. Though linguistic analysis constitutes an important tool of this comparative study of the religion of the East African Pastorals (Nuers, Dinkas and the Masais) and the Indo-Iranians, its focal point centres round its subtitle, viz., *A Study in the Ecology of Religions.*
7. *The Religions of India,* Trubner's Oriental Series, 1881.
8. Cf. works of W.D.O'Flaherty {*Asceticism and Eroticism in the Mythology of Shiva,* Oxford, 1973 and *Dreams, Illusions, and other Realities,* Chicago, 1984, Delhi, 1987, etc.) and David Dean Shulman (*Tamil Temple Myths,* Princeton, 1980).
9. Indian reprint, Calcutta, 1958, p. 5.
10. Though Morgan spoke of unintelligibility of only 'primitive religions', we may suggest that even if the word 'primitive' is deleted, it would still reflect the situation obtainable in the field of *Religionswissenschaft* in the mid-nineteenth century.
11. Cf. Julius Gould, 'Auguste Comte' in Timothy Raison, (ed.) *The Founding Fathers of Social Sciences,* Harmondsworth, 1969, pp. 35-42. In his later writings, Comte introduced his new 'Religion of Humanity', but it was his positivism which most influenced nineteenth century historians of religion.
12. James Thrower convincingly argues against the widely held belief that the rejection of religious understanding of the world is something which begins no earlier than the period of European eighteenth century *Aufklarung.* Cf. James Thrower, op. cit; see also *supra,* n. 4. Even in the European thought ferment, a few historians of religions place greater emphasis upon the contribution of Romanticism; their fundamental objective is not the dissolution of religion but its 'transcendental' justification and foundation. In contrast to *religio naturalis* of the Enlightenment thinkers, phenomenologists of religion such as Rudolf Otto and Mircea Eliade insist upon the complexity and the *sui generis* character of the religions. Surely, this may be taken as their reaction against a 'rationalistic bias' inherited from the enlightenment. For the relevant works on this debate see Ernest Caasirar, *The Philosophy of the Enlightenment,*

Boston, 1961, p. 134f; Jan de Vries, *The Study of Religion: A Historical Approach,* New York, 1967, pp. 39-58; G. van der Leeuw, *Religion in Essence and Manifestation,* Vol. 2, New York, 1963, pp. 691-94.

13. These last two decades have witnessed the appearance of two brilliant series bearing on analysis of major approaches to study the religious phenomenon. Thirty two volumes have already been published under the series *Religion and Reason* (Mouton, The Hague) with Jacques Waardenburg as the General Editor. He has also been working with Leo Laeyendecker to produce the second series entitled *Religion and Society* (Mouton, The Hague), wherein 25 titles have already come out. Jacques Waardenburg's two volumes (nos. 3 and 4 of *Religion and Reason*) entitled *Classical Approach to the Study of Religion* (1973) and Frank Whaling, ed. *Contemporary Approaches to the Study of Religion* (2 vols.) published in the 1980s deal extensively with this problem. Between the two contributions of Waardenburg and Whaling, another substantial work entitled *Science of Religion: Studies in Methodology,* edited by Lauri Honko was published in 1979. Other useful works of the series *(Religion and Reason)* and having a bearing on the problem at hand include no. 8: Th. P. van Baaren and H.J. Drijvers, (ed.), *Religion, Culture and Methodology,* (1973); no. 15: Jacques Waardenburg, *Reflections on the Study of Religion* (978); no. 20: Donald A. Crosby, Interpretative Theories of Religion and no. 25 James Thrower, *Marxist-Leninist 'Scientific Atheism' and the Study of Religion and Atheism in the U.S.S.R.*

14. For an unusual thematic survey of *myths* see Alexander Eliot, Myths, New York, 1976, with useful introductory notes from Mircea Eliade and Joseph Campbell. Indian mythology occupies a conspicuous place in most discussions of the myths; this is seldom done even in world-perspective based works produced in the West. Other useful sources for comparing various interpretations of myth are; Joseph Campbell's four-volumed *The Masks of God: Primitive Mythology* (1959); *Oriental Mythology* (1962); *Occidental Mythology* (1964) and *Creative Mythology* (1968); Thomas J.J. Altizer, William, A. Beardslee and J. Harvey Young, (eds.): *Truth, Myth and Symbol,* Prentice-Hall, 1962; Thomas A Sebeok, (ed.) *Myth: A Symposium,* London, 1958; Mircea Eliade, *Myth and Reality,* New York, 1963, Henry A. Murray, (ed.), *Myth and Myth Making,* Boston, 1968; Perry C Cohen, 'Theories of Myth', *Man* (N.S.), no. 4 (1969), pp. 337-53; G.S. Kirk, *Myth: Its Meaning and Functions*

in Ancient and Other Cultures, Cambridge, 1970 and Jean Pierre Vernant, "The Reason of Myth' in *Myth and Society in Ancient Greece,* 1980, pp. 186-242.

15. For the evolution of Max Muller's thought process see Nirad C. Chaudhuri *Scholar Extraordinary,* Oxford, 1974, particularly chapters 1 and 3, part 2 and chapter 5 of part 3. His concern for origins and primordial forms was not accompanied by the common nineteenth century formulation of a unilinear, 'progressive' evolutionary account of the development of religion. Cf. *Chips from a German Workshop,* Vol. 1, p. 48.
16. Other comparative philologists such as Kuhn, Schwartz and Preller placed greater emphasis on storm-clouds, wind and the sky respectively. See also Richard M. Dorson, 'The Eclipse of Solar Mythology' in Thomas A. Sebeok, op.cit., pp. 15-38 and E.E. Evans-Pritchard, *Theories of Primitive Religion* (Sir D. Owen Evans Lectures of 1962), Oxford, 1965, p. 22. The latter refers to absurdities of nature mythologists.
17. For a recent writing on 'disease of language' contributing to the birth of religion, see William A. Lessa and Evan Z. Vogi, (eds.), *Reader in Comparative Religion,* New York, 1958. Further, the 'inherently metaphorical' nature and 'inherent ambiguity' of language in the scheme of Max Muller finds a prominent place in Ernst Cassirer's works, viz., *An Essay on Man,* New Haven, 1944 pp. 109-10 and *Language and Myth,* New York, 1946, pp. 3-4, 85-86. For a critical analysis of Max Muller's method and his writings providing a backdrop of the psychological theories on religion see E.E. Evans-Pritchard, op.cit., pp. 20-47.
18. E.B. Tylor, *Primitive Culture,* 1871.
19. R.H. Codrington first talked about this impersonal, dynamic and universal supernatural power. Cf. *The Melanesians,* pp. 118-20. Soon, the anthropologists began to find concepts comparable to Melanesian *mana.* Thus, we have Polynesian *mana,* the Sioux *wakanda,* the Algonquin *manitou,* the Iroquois *arenda,* the Crow *maxpe,* the *hasina* of Madgascar, the *ramat* of the Ainus, the *baraka* of Morocco and many others. See particularly E. Gellner's analysis of *baraka* in 'Concepts and Society' in D. Emmet and A. Maclntyre, (eds.) *Sociological Theory and Philosophical Analysis,* London, 1970, p. 142 and Talal Asad, 'Anthropology and the Analysis of Ideology' (Malinowski Lecture for 1979), *Man,* Vol. XIV, 1979, pp. 622-23. For other decisive criticisms of the preammistic theory of mana, *see* Mircea Eliade, *Myths, Dreams and Mysteries,*

New York, 1960, pp. 126-31 and *Pattern in Comparative Religion,* London, 1958, pp. 19-23.

20. R.R. Marett submitted 'the taboo-mana formula' as the 'minimum definition of religion'. Significant writings on taboo are those of A. Gennep, Frazer, French, E.S. Handy, R. Lehmann, Radcliffe-Brown, H. Webster and F. Steiner. See also Meyer Fortes, Totem and Taboo', *Proceedings of the Royal Anthropological Institute,* 1966, pp. 5-22.
21. W. Mannhardt had in his *Wald und Feldkulte (Cults of Forest and Field, 1875-7)* formulated his hypothesis of 'demons of vegetation', a concept of 'corn-spirits' and claimed that the lower mythology still surviving in the culture of various peasants disclosed an earlier stage than even Muller's naturalistic mythologies. James Frazer's *The Golden Bough* was deeply influenced by Mannhardt and is notable for fascinating empirical data. However, his theories have been strongly criticized in R.H; Lowie's *Primitive Religion,* New York, 1924, pp. 137-47.
22. High God (the belief in a primal being, a Maker, undying, usually moral, 'All-Father') was worked out by Andrew Lang who had argued vehemently against Max Muller and Tylor. Cf. *Custom and Myth: Myth, Ritual and Religion* and *The Making of Religion.* See also Edwin Smith, (ed.) *African Ideas of God,* Edinburgh, 1950.
23. We feel that the climax of ethnologists' writings of the first phase is reached in the works of Lucien Levy-Bruhl of France (1857-1939). His *Ethics and Moral Science* (1903) and six volumes of *Primitive Mentality* (1922) typify the caricature worked out by ethnologists, who would not attribute much rationality to the so-called primitives. Surprisingly, even sophisticated thought of China and India was also included in it by Bruhl. For a critique of Levy-Bruhl see Herbert Read. *Art and Society,* Faber (ed.), 1967, pp. 28-30; E.E. Evans-Pritchard, *Theories of Primitive Religion,* chapters 1 and 4. It may however, be mentioned that Levy-Bruhl seems to have abandoned his hypothesis of pre-logical primitive mentality, Cf. his Las *Cornets,* published posthumously by Maurice Leenhardt in 1949.
24. James Hastings, (ed.), *Encyclopaedia of Religion and Ethics* (13 vols., 1908-21) typifies this. But contrast this with two recent encyclopaedias: Richard Cavendish, (Editor in Chief), *Man, Myth and Magic: The Illustrated Encyclopaedia of Mythology, Religion and the Unknown,* 12 Vols. 1983 and

Mircea Eliade, (Editor in Chief), *The Encyclopaedia of Religion,* 16 vols, 1986, Macmillan and Free Press.

25. E. Durkheim, 'De la definition des phenomenes religieux', *L'Annee Sociologique,* Vol. II, pp. 1-28. It may, however, be pointed out that since Durkheim was basically concerned with so-called primitive, pre-class societies, phenomenon such as Hinduism may not have interested him. Obviously, the second element in his classic definition of religion, viz., its inseparability from the Church and collectivity of things would leave out such a phenomenon from the domain of religion. There is, of course, a great debate on the extent to which Hinduism can be regarded as an 'ism' at all.
26. Cf. *The Elementary Forms* ... pp. 418-9 and *passim.*
27. Though Durkheim's view of the function of religion evoked keen interest amongst sociologists, his theory of totemism being a primordial form of religion is not taken seriously. Cf. Mircea Eliade, *Australian Religions: An Introduction,* Ithaca and London, 1973, *passim.*
28. Cf, Charles H. Long, 'Prolegomenon to a Religious Hermeneutic', *History of Religions,* VI, no. 3 (1967), pp. 260-2. Division of 'sacred' and 'profane' is admissible but the identification of the profane with the individual and sacred with social creates problems. To say that the social factors in rites and ceremonies tend to fortify and crystallize the religious emotions is one thing, to regard them as its only or basic source is another (see also discussion on Raddiffe Brown under phase III). Kingsley Davis has suggested an improvement upon Durkheim's formulation which follows Parson's analysis—sacred objects, instead of symbolising society, symbolize the 'unseen world'. Cf. Human *Society,* New York, 1948, p. 529. Hans Mol, *Identify and the Sacred: A Sketch for a New Social-Scientific Theory of Religion,* Oxford, 1976, tries to resolve the 'conflicting but complementary relationship between the sacred and profane' by using 'sacralisation' (the process of becoming, or making sacred) rather than 'the sacred' (being sacred). *See* also John Sturrock, *Structuralism and Since,* Oxford, 1980 and W.S.F. Pickering, *Durkheim's Sociology of Religion: Themes and Theories,* London, 1984.
29. George Dumezil, founding father of what has come to be known as 'the new comparative mythology' and who had been influenced by Durkheim's writings has raised serious doubts against this proposition. With his extensive knowledge of comparative Indo-European mythology, Dumezil argues that the social as well as supernatural phenomena (the content of

myths) were but surface manifestations of a deep-seated set of 'ideal' ideological principles, which provide a 'method of analysis' and thus permit one to come to grips with the forces affecting human existence, Cf. *Mythe et epopee,* Vol. II, 1971, p. 15—relevant passage has been translated by C. Scott Littleton, 'Dumezil versus Levi-Strauss: Some Theoretical Implications of the New Comparative Mythology' in Charles Frantz, (ed.), *Ideas and Trends in World Anthropology,* New Delhi, 1981, pp. 91-99. See also C. Scott Litteleton, *The* New *Comparative Mythology: An Anthropological Assessment of the Theories of Georges Dumezil,* Berkeley, 1973, and Jean-Pierre Vernant, The Reason of Myth' in Myth *and Society in Ancient Greece,* 1980, pp. 186-242. For the idea of creation of community through myth and ritual, see Frederick J. Streng, Charles L Lloyd and Jay T. Allen, *Ways of Being Religious,* Prentice-Hall, 1973, Introduction and pt 2.

30. Maurice Bloch took up this theme in the Malinowski Memorial Lectures delivered in the London School of Economics and Political Science on 7 December 1976, cf. 'The Past and the Present in the Present', *Man* (N.S), XII, 1977, pp. 278-92. The notion that Durkheim's sociology developed in a substantial degree as a response to the 'problem of order' is taken as myth and analyzed by Anthony Giddens. 'Four Myths in the History of Social Thought', *Economy and Society,* I, no. 4, 1972, pp. 357-85. For the importance of Durkheim in understanding belief systems and the notion of belief as 'creating' society, see Michael Mann, *Sources of Social Power,* Vol. I, From the Beginning to 1760 AD, Cambridge, 1986, ch. I and John A. Hell. "The Land of the Brahmans' in *Powers and Liberties,* Basil Blackwell, 1985, pp. 58-83. There is rather undue emphasis on Burton Stein's recent writings in the aforesaid contribution of Hell, who supports the questionable Weberian view of Hinduism as an obstacle to capitalist growth. For an exhaustive critique of Purton Stein's assumptions and methodology, see D.N. Jha, 'Relevance of 'Peasant State and Society' to Pallava-Chola Times', *The Indian Historical Review,* VIII, nos. 1-2, 1981-82, pp. 74-94 and 'Validity of the 'Brahmana-Peasant Alliance' and the 'Segmentary State' in 'Early Medieval South India', *Social Science Probings,* I, no. 2, June, 1984, pp. 270-96.
31. *Sacrifice: Its Nature and Function,* London, 1964.
32. *The Mahabharata: An Ethnological Study,* London, 1915.
33. For the potentialities of Durkheim's method for an analysis of the interrelations between caste and religion, see Celestin

Bougie, *Essays on the Caste System,* Cambridge, 1971; Louis Dumont, *Homo Hierarchicus,* London, 1972 and Romila Thapar, 'Durkheim and Weber on Theories of Society and Race Relating to Pre-Colonial India', in Marion O' Callaghan (compiler), *Sociological Theories: Race and Colonialism,* UNESCO, Paris, 1980, pp. 93-116.

34. *The Religion of India* (first published, 1920-21) New York, 1958; for a scathing criticism of this translation by Hans H. Gerth and Don Marrindale, see Detlef Kantowsky, 'Max Weber on India and Indian Interpretations of Weber', *Contributions to Indian Sociology* (N.S.), Vol. 16, No. 2, 1982, pp. 141-74.
35. *The Religion of China,* translated and edited by Hans H. Gerth, New York, 1951 (first published 1915).
36. *Ancient Judaism,* translated and edited by Hans H. Gerth, New York, 1952; *Wirtschaft and Cesellschaft* (1922), translated as *The Sociology of Religion,* London, 1965 and *The Agrarian Sociology of Ancient Civilisations,* London, 1976 (first German edition in 1909).
37. First published in 1904-5. Translated by Takot Parsons with a Foreword by R.H. Tawney in 1930; reissued with an Introduction by Anthony Giddens, London, 1976. See also RJ. Anderson, J.A. Hughes and W.W. Sharrock, (eds.), *Classic Disputes in Sociology,* London, 1987 for a review of the Protestant Ethic Debate.
38. Anti-reductionist approach is one of the distinguishing characteristics of contemporary history of religions. For an analysis of 'the irreducibility of the sacred', Cf. M. Eliade, *Australian Religions: An Introduction,* Ithaca, 1973, chapter on Death and Eschatoiogy. The ideological ramifications of anti-reductionist approach are discussed in detail in Section V.
39. See also Nigel Harris, *Beliefs in Society,* Harmondsworth, 1968, pp. 81-85.
40. Charles, P. Loomis and Z.K. Loomis were the authors of this paper. Later, they also edited papers presented at this symposium and published under the same title in 1969 (New Delhi).
41. For an effective recent critique of not only Marxian notion of the AMP but some recent Indian attempts to resurrect it through the back door, see D.N. Jha, (ed.), *Feudal Social Formation in Early India,* Delhi, 1987, Editor's Introduction.
42. Cf. Romila Thapar, op.cit.

43. Cf. The writings of Rivers, Boas, Kroeber, Malinowski and Schmidt. See particularly V. Basilov, 'The Study of Religions in Soviet Ethnographic Science' in Ernest Gellner, (ed.), *Soviet and Western Anthropology,* London, 1980, pp. 231-42.
44. e.g., *Myths and Symbols in Indian Art and Civilisation,* 1946; *Philosophies of India,* 1951 and *The Art of Indian Asia,* 1955. See also Joseph Campbell, *Masks of God: Oriental Mythology,* 1962. More recently, W.D. O'Flaherty's writings on Epic Puranic mythology *(Women, Androgynes and Other Mythical Beasts,* Chicago, 1980; *Dreams, Illusion and other Realities,* Delhi, 1986) acknowledge debt to both Freud and Jung. However, for an incisive critical comment on the psycho-analytical approach to early Indian history, see R.S. Sharma, *Material Culture and Social Formations in Ancient India,* New Delhi, 1983, p. 11.
45. Among important works which outlive the diversification and specialisation of anthropological approaches to *Religionswissenschaft,* one can mention: Michael Banton, (ed.), *Anthropological Approaches to the Study of Religion,* New York, 1966; Allan W. Wister, (ed.) *Changing Perspectives in the Scientific Study of Religion,* London, 1974; W.A. Lessa and E.Z. Vogt, (eds.) : *Reader in Comparative Religion,* New York, 1958; Sol Tax, (ed.), *Horizons of Anthropology,* London, 1965; Anthony F.C. Wallace, *Religion : An Anthropological View,* New York, 1966.
46. Bronislaw Malinowski, *Magic Science and Religion, and Other Essays,* New York, 1954; A.R. Radcliffe-Brown, *Taboo,* Cambridge, 1939; *Idem, Structure and Function in Primitive Society,* London, 1952. See also Meyer Fortes, in 'Totem and Taboo', *Proceedings of the Royal Anthropological Institute,* 1966, pp. 5-22.
47. George C. Homans, *The Human Group,* London, 1951, reconciles certain differences between Brown and Malinowski. While the latter focuses attention on situations, in which rites originate and the functions they perform once they are established. Brown does not consider the situations of their origin; he shows how they function once they are established. For a review of differences amongst major Functionalists, see Carl G. Hempel. "The Logic of Functional Analysis' in Llewellyn Gross (ed.), *Symposium on Sociological Theory,* also published in May Brodbeck, (ed.), *Readings in the Philosophy of the Social Sciences,* New York, 1968, pp. 179-210, Hans H. Partner, "The Poverty of Functionalism', *History of Religions,* Vol. 11, 1971, pp. 91-97.

48. That the clear-cut gulf between the primitive and ourselves is dubious is also shown by the brilliant findings of Alexander Marshack, 'Cognitive Aspects of Upper Palaeolithic Engraving', *Current Anthropology,* Vol. 13, Nos. 3-4 (1972), pp. 445-77; M. Eliade, 'On Prehistoric Religions', *History of Religions,* Vol. 14, No. 2, 1974, p. 141. See also, Whitney Davis, "The Origins of Image Making', *Current. Anthropology,* Vol. 27, No. 3, 1986, pp. 193-216.
49. First published in 1958. His other major works are *The Savage Mind* (1962), *Totemism* (1963) and *The Raw and the Cooked* (1964).
50. For recent writings on Levi-Strauss, his method and significance, see Malcolm Crick, *Explorations in Language and Meaning,* London, 1976; John Sturrock, (ed.), *Structuralism and Since,* Oxford, 1980 and Anthony Giddens and Jonathan Turner, (eds.), *Social Theory Today,* 1987. The last named work claims to be an 'Obituary of Structuralism'. That this is far from being the case should be apparent from such contributions as: Bob Scholte, 'Critical Anthropology since its Reinvention', *Anthropology and Humanism Quarterly,* Vol. III, pp. 4-17; Joel S. Kahn and Josep R. Llobera, etc., *The Anthropology of Pre-Capitalist Societies,* London, 1981 and Mark Kline Taylor, 'Symbolic Dimensions in Cultural Anthropology', *Current Anthropology,* Vol. 26, No. 2, April 1985, pp. 167-85.
51. Charles J. Adams, *The History of Religions: Essays on the Problem of Understanding,* p. 178.
52. Cf. C.J. Bleeker, 'The Contribution of the Phenomenology of Religion to the Study of the History of Religions,' in U. Bianchi, C.J. Bleeker and A. Bausani, (eds.), *Problems and Methods of the History of Religions,* Leiden, 1972, p. 39.
53. *The Idea of the Holy* (first published in 1917), translated by J.W. Harvey, 1923.
54. First published in 1933 and translated by J.E. Turner in 1938.
55. *Meaning of Religion: Lectures in the Phenomenology of Religion,* The Hague, 1960.
56. Cf. Douglas Allen, *Structure and Creativity in Religion: Hermeneutics in Mircea Eliade's Phenomenology and New Directions,* The Hague, 1977.
57. *Ibid.,* p. 83.
58. PJ. Chinmulgund and V.V. Mirashi, (eds.). *Review of Indological Research in last 75 Years,* Pune, 1967, pp. 561-773.

59. N.N. Bhattacharyya, *History of Researches on Indian Buddhism,* New Delhi, 1981.
60. H.D. Sankalia, *Prehistory and Protohistory of India and Pakistan,* 2nd ed., Pune, 1974; Idem, *Prehistory of India,* New Delhi, 1977; Idem, *Prehistoric Art in India,* New Delhi, 1978; Vidula Jayaswal, *Palaeohistory of India,* Delhi, 1978; Idem, *Chopper-Chopping Component of Palaeolithic India,* Delhi, 1982; Yashodhar Mathpal, *Prehistoric Rock Paintings of Bhimbetka,* New Delhi, 1984; K.K. Chakravarty, (ed.), *Rock Art of India,* New Delhi, 1984; D.P. Agrawal and B.M. Pande, (eds.), *Ecology and Archaeology of Western India,* Delhi, 1977. See also *Man and Environment* and *Puratattva,* journals of the Indian Society for Prehistoric and Quaternary Studies and Indian Archaeological Society respectively. Former issued its Vol. XII and the latter its No. 17 early this year.
61. K.V. Soundararajan, 'Eco-Functional Frame of Early Man—Some Factors' *Puratattva,* No. 12, 1980-81, pp. 9-15.
62. G. Willey and P. Phillips, *Method and Theory in Archaeology,* Chicago, 1958; L.R. Binford and S.R. Binford, *New Perspectives in Archaeology,* Chicago, 1968.
63. D.L. Clark, *Analytical Archaeology,* London, 1970 and 1979; Idem, *Models in Archaeology,* London, 1972 and *Spatial Archaeology,* London. 1977. Also, Harold Hietala, (ed.), *Intrasite Spatial Analysis in Archaeology,* Cambridge, 1984.
64. This is despite the expanding interests of American archaeologists in India, for whom 'archaeology is anthropology or it is nothing.' Cf. Willey and Phillips, op.cit, p.2; Cf. also Gregory L. Possehi, 'Culture and Process', *Puratattva,* No. 9, 1977-78, pp. 43-46.
65. Being edited by Richard Bradley, Tim Earle, *et.al.* The earliest volume in the series is dated 1979. The relevant volumes from our point of view are : Daniel Miller and Christopher Tilley, (eds.), *Ideology, Power and Prehistory,* 1984; and Dorothy K. Washburn, (ed.), *Marxist Perspectives in Archaeology,* 1984; and Dorpthy K. Washbum, (ed.), *Structure and Cognition in Art,* 1983. Apart from this series, some other writings on prehistoric religion are provocative and challenging, e.g., Whitney Davis, 'The Origins of Image Making', *Current Anthropology,* Vol. 27, No. 3, June 1986, pp. 193-215.
66. D.D. Kosambi, 'At the Crossroads: A Study of Mother Goddess Cult Sites' and 'Pilgrims's Progress: A Contribution to the Prehistory of the Western Deccan Plateau', both included in author's *Myth and Reality,* Bombay, 1962, pp. 82-151;

N.N. Bhattacharyya, *The Indian Mother Goddess,* 2nd rev ed., Delhi, 1977. See also Debiprasad Chattopadhyaya, *Lokayata,* Delhi. 1959.

67. Numerous writings of E.O. James, *Prehistoric Religions,* London, 1957; *The Cult of Mother Goddess,* London, 1959; *Seasonal Feasts and Festivals,* London, 1961; R. Briffault, *The Mothers* (3 vols.), London, 1952; J. Marringer, *Gods of Prehistoric Man,* London, 1960; E. Norbeak, *Religion in Primitive Society,* New York, 1961. See also O.R. Ehrenfels, *Mother Right in India,* Hyderbad, 1941.
68. Regions discussed are Mesopotamia, Egypt, the Indus Valley, the North China Plain, Mesoamerica, the Central Andes and the Yoruba territories of S. W. Nigeria.
69. 'Whenever in any of the seven regions of primary urban generation, we trace back the characteristic urban form to its beginnings we arrive not at a settlement that is dominated by commercial relations, a primordial market, or at one that is focussed on a citadel, and archetypal fortress, but rather at a *ceremonial complex...religion* permeated all activities, all institutional change, and afforded a consensual focus *for social life'* (emphases added), Paul Wheatley, *Pivot of the Four Quarters,* Chicago, 1971, pp. 280-320; see also David N. Keightly, "Religion and the Rise of Urbanism", being a review of Wheatley's work, in *Journal of American Oriental Society,* Vol. 93, No. 4, 1973, pp. 527-33.
70. Max Weber, *The City,* 1921 (Eng. trans., 1958) and *The Agrarian Sociology of Ancient Civilisations,* 1909 (Eng. trans., 1976); Gideon Sjoberg, *The Preindustrial City of Fast and Present,* New York, 1960; Lewis Mumford, *The City in History,* London, 1961; V. Gordon Childe, 'The Urban Revolution' (first published in 1950), reprinted in Gregory Possehl, *Ancient Cities of the Indus,* New Delhi, 1979; pp. 12-17; Robert McC Adams, *The Evolution of Urban Society,* London, 1966; Philip M Hauser and Leo F. Schnore, *The Study of Urbanisation,* New York, 1965; Karl Polanyi, C. Aresberg and H.W. Pearson, *Trade and Market in the Early Empires,* Chicago, 1957.
71. Walter A. Fairservis, Jr, 'The Harappan Civilisation: New Evidence and More Theory' in Gregory Possehi, op. cit., pp. 5lf; David N. Keightly, op. cit. The volume edited by Possehl and a subsequent collection, *Harappan Civilisation; A Contemporary Perspective,* New Delhi, 1982, also edited by Possehl, are valuable additions from the point of view of the much-needed multi-disciplinary orientation. However, they are inadequate works in the present context. The same is true of

Shashi Asthana, *Pre-Harappan Culture of India and the Borderlands,* New Delhi, 1985 and Jerome Jacobson, *Studies in the Archaeology of India and Pakistan,* New Delhi, 1986.

72. Cf. S.C. Malik, *Indian Civilisation: The Formative Period,* Simla, 1968, pp. 99-105.
73. D.D. Kosambi, *Culture and Civilisation of Ancient India in Historical Outline,* London, 1965, pp. 66-68; Idem, *Myth and Reality,* Bombay, 1962, pp. 71, 78-79. For a more recent reconstruction of religion-based Harappan set-up, see Debiprasad Chattopadhyaya, *Religion and Society* (Stephanos Nirmalendu Ghosh Lectures of 1981, Calcutta University), Bangalore, 1987.
74. Walter A. Fairservis, op.cit.
75. Cf. Posehl's reconstruction of the pattern of Harappan settlements in Gujarat, vide, 'The End of a State and Continuity of a Tradition: A Discussion of the Late Harappan', in Richard G. Fox (ed.), *Realm and Region in Traditional India,* New Delhi, 1977, pp. 234-54; Idem, *Indus Civilisation in Saurashtra,* New Delhi, 1980.
76. Walter A. Fairservis, Jr., 'The Origin, Character and Decline of an Early Civilisation', in G.L. Possehl, (ed.), *Ancient Cities of the Indus,* pp. 66-75.
77. Grant D Jones and Robert R. Kautz, (eds), *The Transition to Statehood in the New World,* Cambridge 1981, pt. 4 which discuses 'Ideological Factors in State Formation with special reference to religion in the context of Mesoamerica and Peru.
78. Geoffrey W. Conrad and Authur A Demarest, *Religion and Empire—The Dynamics of Aztec and Inca Expansionism,* Cambridge, 1984.
79. Ildiko Puskas in her short contribution ('Society and Religion in the Indus Valley Civilisation' in Bridget Allehin, (ed.), *South Asian Archaeology 1981,* Cambridge, 1984, pp. 162-65) persists with the decades-old suggestion of John Marshall about 'priests kings', though she distinguishes between 'primitive rural form of religion' (not studied by her) and 'the sophisticated religion of the urban centre.' She also makes some fanciful suggestions such as the so-called proto-Shiva being proto-Brahma and the Mother Goddess being proto-Parvati (and later even Tara of Mahayana Buddhism). However, her suggestions about tensions amongst deities of 'bull and tiger totem line' and '*ashvatlha* and mm trees' need futher probing.

80. Cf. Marcia A. Fentress, 'Regional Interaction in Indus Valley Urbanisation: The Key Factors of Resource Access and Exchange', in Sylvia Vatuk, (ed.), *American Studies in the Anthropology of India,* New Delhi, 1978, pp. 389-424.
81. Published from Pune in 1987.
82. Shubhangana Atre, 'Lady of Beasts - The Harappan Goddess', *Puratattva,* no. 16, 1985-86, pp. 7-10. For analogous reconstruction see also H.P. Sullivan, 'A Reexamination of the Religions of the Indus Civilisation', *History of Religions,* Vol. 4, 1964, pp. 15-23. Other writings on the subject include, K.L. Sastri, *New Light on the Indus Civilisation,* New Delhi, 1957, Vol. I, pp. 7-13 and D Srinivasan. 'The So-called Proto-Shiva Seal from Mohenjodaro: An Iconological Assessment', *Archives of Asian Art,* 1976-7, pp. 47-58.
83. Shubhangana Atre, 'The Harappan Riddle of Unicorn', *Bulletin of Deccan College Research Institute,* 1985, pp. 1-10.
84. Atre emphasizes that the Harappans chose a composite animal—a combination of 'ruminants' to bear the antler on its forehead clearly illuminating the awareness of the interdependence of agriculture and animal husbandry, ibid.
85. Gregory, L. Possehl, *Kulli,* Durham, USA, 1986, ch. 5. See also, Shereen Ratnagar, 'Some Problems Concerning the Urbanisation of the Indus Valley in the Third Millennium B.C.', in J.S. Grewal and Indu Banga, (eds.), *Studies in Urban History,* Amritsar, 1978-79, pp. 18-28 where the author refers to 'merchant oligarchy' as a determining influence.
86. Shereen Ratnagar, 'An Aspect of Harappan Agricultural Production', *Studies in History,* Vol. 11, no. 2, 1986, pp. 137-53; Idem, 'Pastoralists in the Prehistory of Baluchistan', *Studies in History,* Vol. III, no. 2, 1987, pp. 137-54.
87. *Asiatic Researches,* VIII, M. 369-476.
88. For a provocative scientific analysis of legend, see D.D. Kosambi, *Myth and Reality,* 1962, pp. 42-81.
89. *Mythologische Studien von Adalbert Kuhn,* published posthumously by his son in 1912, it includes such papers as 'Ditaras as phenomena of light', 'Dwarfs a souls of the dead' and 'Dwarfs as phenomena of light'.
90. Weber pointed out the implication of Videgha's legend for the eastward expansion of the Sanskrit speakers. For the treatment of this legend as representing 'eastward march of the sacrificial cult', see G.V. Devasthali, *Religion and Mythology of the Brahmanas* (with special reference to the *Shatapatha Brahmana),* Poona, 1965, p. 121.

91. Author of *Zoolical Mythology,* London, 1873.
92. Three volumes of *La religion vedique d'apres les hymnes du Rig Veda,* published from Paris, 1878-83.
93. The fifth volume of his *Original Sanskrit Text,* London, 1872 has the subtitle, 'Contribution to a Knowledge of the Cosmogony, Mythology, Religious Ideas, Life and Manners of the Indians in the Vedic Age.' Though Muir insisted that the Vedic religion should be studied primarily from the Vedic sources, he had not Renounced comparative mythology completely. His identification of Varana with Ouraribs and attempt to link him with Ahur Mazdah are indicators of this continuing influence.
94. A. Barth, *Les religions de I'lnde,* Paris, 1879, Eng. trans, by J. Wood, *The Religions of India,* London, 1881.
95. One such recent attempt is Sukumari Bhattacharji, *The Indian Theogony,* Cambridge, 1970.
96. A. Barth, op.cit. pp. 17-19.
97. For reference to 'colonial' and the 'romantic' bias of nineteenth century West European Indology, cf. G. Bongard-Levin and A. Vigasin, *The Image of India,* Moscow, 1984, p. 61.
98. *Ibid.,* ch. 2.
99. Being Vol. I of the work, *A Study of Bacchanal Cults of Indo-European Antiquity in the Context of the Role of Ecstasy in the Early Stages of Social Development.*
100. A.A. MacDonell, *The Vedic Mythology,* 1897; reprinted, Varanasi, 1963; Jan Gonda's numerous works include *Notes on Brahman,* Utrecht, 1950; *Change and Continuity in Indian Religion,* The Hague, 1965; *Notes on Names and the Name of God in Ancient India,* Amsterdam, 1970, *The Dual Divinities in the Religion of the Vedas,* Amsterdam,' 1974; *The Vedic Cod Mitra,* Leiden, 1972 and J. Gonda, (ed.), *A History of Indian Literature,* Vol. I. fasc. *(The Vedic Literature)* and fasc. *Mythological Tracts,* Delhi, 1979; *Insights into Hinduism,* Delhi, 1979 and *Exercises in Indology,* Delhi, 1981.
101. In two volumes, published as Vols. 31 and 32 of the Harvard Oriental Series in 1925; reprinted, Delhi, 1981.
102. *Ibid.,* Vol. I, preface, p. x.
103. *Supra,* paragraphs 2, 10 and 11 and n. 29.
104. A.B. Keith, op. cit., pp. 55-57.
105. *Ibid.,* Vol. II, pp. 629-34. Much ground has been covered on this issue since the days of Keith. For a recent survey of the

problem: Madhav Deshpande and Peter Edwin Hook, (eds.), *Aryan and Non-Aryan in India,* University of Michigan, Ann Arbor, 1979.

106. *The Ancient Indian Royal Consecration,* The Hague, 1957.

107. Naama Drury, *The Sacrificial Ritual in the Shatapaitha Brahmana,* Delhi, 1981. For some useful writings on comparative studies on sacrifice and allied subjects see E.O. James' works, viz., *The Nature and Function of Priesthood,* London, 1956; *Sacrifices and Sacrament, London,* 1962 and *Origins of Sacrifice,* London, 1971.

108. e.g. Jogiraj Basu, *India of the Age of the Brahmanas,* Calcutta, 1969; Ganesh Umakant Thite, *Sacrifice in the Brahmana Texts,* Poona, 1975; G.V. Devadthali, *Religion and Mythology of the Brahmanas,* Poona, 1965; Usha Choudhuri, *Indra and Varuna in Indian Mythology,* Delhi 1981 Usha Grover, *Symbolism in the Aranyakas and their Impact on the Upanishads,* New Delhi, 1987.

109. *Priests, Warriors, and Cattle,* published in 1981 under the *Hermeneutics: Studies in the History of Religions* series of the University of California under the editorship of Kees W. Bolle.

110. *Ibid.,* appendix, pp. 179-84.

111. *Ibid., passim.*

112. *Material Culture and Social Formations in Ancient India,* Delhi, 1983 and *Perspectives in Social and Economic History of Early India,* Delhi, 1933.

113. *From Lineage to State,* Bombay, 1984.

114. R.N. Dandekar, 'Asura Varuna', *Annals of the Bhandarkar Oriental Research Institute,* Vol. 21, 1940, pp. 157-91; Contra, Wash Edward Hale, *Asura in Early Vedic Religion,* New Delhi, 1986.

115. D.D. Kosambi, 'Urvashi and Pururavas', in his *Myth and Reality,* 1962, pp. 42-81.

116. Cf. J.R. Joshi, *Some Minor Divinities in Vedic Mythology and Ritual,* Pune, 1977; N.J. Shende, *The Religion and Philosophy of the Atharvaveda,* Poona, 1952; V.W. Karambelkar, *The Atharvavedic Civilisation,* Nagpur, 1959; Chhanda Chakraborty, *Common Life in the Rigveda and Atharvaveda—An Account of the Folklore in the Vedic Period,* Calcutta, 1977.

117. N.N. Bhattacharyya, *Ancient Indian Rituals and their Social Contents,* Delhi, 1975.

118. Research on Ashvamedha and Purushamedha along these lines is already in progress under the supervision of the present author.
119. Paul Deussen, *The Philosophy of the Upanishads,* first published in 1906, Dover paperback, 1966; A.B. Keith, *The Religion and Philosophy of the Veda and Upanishads,* Delhi, reprint, 1970, ch. 28; R.D. Ranade, *A Constructive Survey of Upanishadic Philosophy,* Bombay, 1916; A.K. Lad, *A Comparative Study of the Concept of Liberation in Indian Philosophy,* Burhanpur, 1967.
120. K.M. Shrimali, *History of Panchala,* Vol. I, Delhi, 1983, pp. 173-77.
121. K. Damodaran, *Man and Society in Indian Philosophy,* Delhi, 1970, p. 45.
122. Romila Thapar, General President's Address, *Proceedings of the Indian History Congress,* 44th Session, Burdwan (1984), pp. 15-17.
123. There is need to recognise grammatical aberrations involved in the use of more popular forms, viz., Vaishnavism and Shaivism. The forms being used here need to be popularised. Alternatively, we should use Vaishnava religion and Shaiva religion. Incidentally, usage is Buddhism and not Bauddhism. Of course, the form should be Jinism rather than Jainism.
124. One of the earliest works is H.H. Wilson, *A Sketch of the Religious Sects of the Hindus.* Originally appeared in two parts in Asiatic Researches, Vols. XVI (1828) and XVII (1832); published independently in 1846, later included in Vol. I of the Collected Works of the author in 1862. Though a pioneering work, it deals largely with the Vaishnava sects of the post-twelfth century period.
125. Scholars have followed clues given by A. Barth, cf. *supra,* paragraph 3.6.
126. For historiography of writings up to the 1960s see the contributions of Ajay Mitra Shastri and G.T. Deshpande on Vaishnavism, Shaivism and Shaktism in P.J. Chinmulgund and V.V. Mirashi, (eds.), *Review of Indological Research in Last 75 Years,* Pune, 1967, pp. 597-657.
127. In J.N. Banerjea's, *Religion in Art and Archaeology* (Radha Kumud Mookerji Lectures of 1961-2), Lucknow University, 1968, it forms a major theme rather than incidental allusions. See also R.P. Chanda, *Archaeology and Vaishnava*

Tradition, Memoirs of the Archaeological Survey of India, no. 5, 1920.

128. e.g. U. Dhal's monograph on *Lakshmi.*

129. First published from Utrecht in 1954 and later reprinted from Delhi m 1969 For its limitations, see Suvira Jaiswal, *The Origin and Development of Vaishnavism,* New Delhi, 1981, p. 6.

130. *Vishnuism and Shivaism,* first published in London in 1970, reprinted, Delhi, 1976.

131. Cf. *Myth and Reality,* 1962, *passim.* For a recent review of Kosambi's hypothesis on the *Bhagavadgita, see* Vivekanand Jha, 'Social Content of the *Bhagavadgita' The Indian Historical Review,* Vol. XI, nos. 1-2, 1984-85, pp. 1-44.

132. *The Indian Theogony,* Cambridge, 1970; reprinted in India.

133. First published from New Delhi in 1967. Second rev. ed., also from New Delhi, 1981.

134. See also T.J. Solomon, 'Vaishnava Bhakti and its Autochthonous Heritage', *History of Religions,* Vol. X, No. 1, August 1970, pp. 32-48; D.D. Kosambi, 'The Avatara Syncretism and Possible Sources of the *Bhagavadgita', Journal of the Bombay Branch of Royal Asiatic Society,* XXIV-XXV, pp. 121-34.

135. *Asceticism and Eroticism in the Mythology of Shiva,* Oxford, 1973, Indian edition also from Oxford, Delhi, 1975.

136. The author writes, 'I have used 'versions' of the Siva myths written by modern *Hindu* authors (R.K. Narayan, Nirad C. Chaudhuri), eighteenth century European scholars and even one contemporary Western novelist (David Staction)' (emphasis added), op. cit, p. 13. In her enthusiasm to 'understand the myths *in situ*... and extract meanings without reducing the myths' (op. cit, p. 2), she rejects text-historical method and accepts Levi-Strauss' treatment of all 'versions' of a myth, including what are usually called interpretations, as equally relevant. This methodology creates difficulties for making proper analysis of myths from the standpoint of relevance to specific material milieu. Indeed, the nature of *Religionswissenschaft* demands a proper blend of the structural and historical approaches.

137. Published from Varanasi in 1960.

138. Published from New Delhi in 1980.

139. First published from Calcutta in 1965; second edition from New Delhi, 1980.

140. For reservations on the feudal mode of production, see A Rudra, *Some Problems of Marx's Theory of History* (R.C. Dutt lectures on Political Economy, 1985) Calcutta, 1988. For a forceful and convincing rebuttal of arguments against feudal mode of production, see D.N. Jha, Validity of the "Brahmana-Peasant Alliance" and the "Segmentary State" in Early Medieval South India', *Social Science Probings,* Vol. 1, No. 2, June, 1984, pp. 2-0-96.

141. For leading contributions in the debate on Indian Feudalism dealing with the problems of origin, feudal society, economy and ideology, see D.N. Jha, (ed.), *Feuda Social Formation in Early India,* New Delhi, 1987 and for the current position of issues involved, see specially the editor's introduction therein.

142. Cf. M.G.S. Narayanan and Velutha Kesavan, 'Bhakti Movement in South India', in D.N. Jha, op. cit, pp. 348-75 for the limits of social radicalism of the movement.

143. Friedhelm Hardy, *Viraha-Bhakti: The Early History of Krishna Devotion in South India,* Oxford, 1983 For Tamil Myths as part of wider world of Sanskrit tradition, see David Dean Shulman, *Tamil Temple Myths,* Princeton, 1980.

144. Some of the recent and influential writings on the subject include, apart from the reference cited in n. 142. Kesavan Velutha. 'The Temple Base of the Bhakti' Movement in South India', *Proceedings of the Indian History Congress,* 40th Session Waltair, 1979 (1980), pp. 185-94, reprinted in Krishna Mohan Shrimali, (ed.), *Essays in Indian Art, Religion and Society* (Indian History Congress Golden Jubilee Year Publication Series, Vol. 1) New Delhi, 1987, pp. 151-59; D.N. Jha, 'Temples as Landed Magnates in Early Medieval South India (AD 700-1300)', in R.S. Sharma, (ed.), *Indian Society Historical Probings,* Delhi, 1974, pp. 202-16 and his contributions mentioned in n. 30; M.G.S. Narayanan, 'The Philosophy and Socio-Economic Context of Land Grants in Ancient India', paper presented at the 41st session of the Indian History Congress in 1980, cyclostyled copy through the courtesy of the author; Rajan Gurukkal, 'From the Royalty of Icons to the Divinity of Royalty: Aspects of Vaishnava Icons and Kingship in Medieval South India', in Ratan Parimoo, (ed.), *Vaishnavism in Indian Arts and Culture,* New Delhi, 1987, pp. 119-24 and S. Setter, 'From Vaishnavism to Shrivaishnavism: A Study of Shrivaishnava Settlements of Pre-Ramanuja Era', in Ratan Parimoo, op. cit. The overpowering influence of land grants was not confined to

theistic Shaiva and Vaishnava currents. It had permeated the non-brahmanical monastic order as well and even worked for introducing theistic traits amongst these. These developments are admirably shown in such writings as, R.N. Nandi, *Religious Institutions and Cults in the Deccan* Delhi, 1973: Idem 'Origin and Nature of Shaivite Monasticism: The case of Kalamukhas' in R.S. Sharma, (ed.) op. cit., pp. 190-201; AK. Warder, 'Feudalism and Mahayana Buddhism, in ibid., pp. 156-74 and Ram Bhushan Prasad Singh, *Jainism in Early Medieval Karnataka,* Delhi, 1975.

145. *The Many Faces of Murukan—The History and Meaning of a South Indian God,* The Hague, 1976-77.
146. *Ibid.,* p, 194. For another substantial work with a similar orientation and a much larger canvas, see M.G.S. Narayanan, "The Vedic-Puranic-Shastraic Element in Tamil Sangam Society and Culture', in Krishna Mohan Shrimali, (ed.), op. cit., pp. 127-40.
147. *Tamil Temple Myths,* Princeton, 1980.
148. *Supra, n.* 136.
149. Suvira Jaiswal, Presidential Address (Ancient India Section) at the 38th Session of the Indian History Congress held at Bhubaneswar in 1977, Cf. its *Proceedings* p. 25f. See also her article, 'Studies in Early Indian Social History', *The Indian Historical Review,* Vol. VI, nos. 1-2. 1979-80, pp. 1-63.
150. N.N. Bhattacharyya, *History of the Tantrik Religion,* New Delhi, 1982.
151. 'Material Milieu of Tantricism' in R.S. Sharma, (ed.), *Indian Society: Historical Probings,* Delhi 1974, pp. 175-89; reprinted in D.N. Jha. (ed.) *Feudal Social Formation in Early India,* Delhi, 1987, pp. 376-90. For agrarian expansion as a result of land grants, see R.S. Sharma, *Urban Decay in India,* (c 300-1000), Delhi, 1987, pp. 168-77.
152. Thomas, B. Coburn, *Devi Mahatmya: The Crystallisation of the Goddess Tradition,* Delhi, 1984, see specially the Prolegomenon. Other recent works to highlight the Goddess tradition in early medieval times are: Cheever Mackenzie Brown, *God as* Mother: An Historical and Theological Study of the Brahamavaivarta Purana, Hartford (USA) 1974. John Stratton Hawley and Donna Marie Wulff, (eds.), *The Divine Consort,* first published from California in 1982. Delhi reprint, 1984. For a phenomenological study of the Shakti Cult, see Wendell C. Beane, *Myth, Cult and Symbols in Shakta Hinduism,* Leiden, 1977.

153. O.P. Misra, *Mother Goddess in Central India,* Delhi, 1985. See also Maheswar Neog, *Religions of the North East,* Delhi, 1984, chs. 5, 10, 11 and 12.
154. That even puritanical non-brahmanical religions were also forced to incorporate mother goddesses and tantric practices as a result of land grants is shown by studies, on trans-Vrindhyan regions. Cf. R.N. Nandi, *Religious Institutions and Cults in the Deccan,* Delhi, 1973, pp. 114-67 and Ram Bhushan Prasad Singh, *Jainism in Early Medieval Karnataka,* Delhi, 1975, pp. 23-60.
155. 'Material Background of the Origin of Buddhism' first published in Mohit Sen and M.B. Rao, *Das Kapital Centenary Volume: A Symposium,* Delhi, 1968, pp. 59-66, revised and updated in author's *Material Culture and Social Formations in Ancient India,* Delhi, 1983, ch. 7. Uma Chakravarti's *The Social Dimensions of Early Buddhism,* Delhi, 1987 is a useful addition. Though not very original, it enlightens us further on the role of *gahapatis* in the growth of early Buddhism, which is in essence, only an amplification of Kosambi's hypothesis. On the early medieval context, however, R.A.L.H. Gunawardana's *Robe and Plough* University of Arizona, 1979, is an incisive work, though dealing with Ceylonese Buddhism.
156. Warder, 'Feudalism and Mahayana Buddhism', in R.S. Sharma, (ed.), *Indian Society: Historical Probings,* Delhi, 1974, pp. 156-74.
157. N.R. Guseva, *Jainism,* Translated from Russian by Y.S. Redkar, Bombay, 1971.
158. *An Introduction to the Study of Indian History,* 2nd ed., Bombay, 1975 and *The Culture and Civilisation of Ancient India in Historical Outline,* London, 1965.
159. For an assessment of Kosambi's method see D.N. Jha; 'A Marxist View of Ancient Indian History' in Mohit Sen and M.B. Rao, op. cit., pp. 166-80.
160. *Lokayata.* New Delhi, 1959 and *Indian Atheism,* Calcutta, 1969.
161. Debiprasad Chatttopadhyaya, *Religion and Society,* Bangalore, 1987, pp. 90-115.
162. See also R.N. Nandi, 'Client, Ritual and Conflict in Early Brahmanical Order', *The Indian Historical Review,* Vol. VI, Nos. 1-2, 1979-80, pp. 64-118.
163. First published in Belgium in 1983; Indian reprint, New Delhi, 1984.

164. Krishna Mohan Shrimali, (ed.) Essays *in Indian Art, Religion and Society,* New Delhi 1987. Introduction, specially f5. 8.
165. Ake Hultkrantz, 'An Ecological Approach to Religion', *Ethnos,* Vol. 31, 1966, pp. 131-50; Idem, 'Ecology of Religion: Its Scope and Methodology', *Review of Ethnology,* Vol. 4, 1974, pp. 1-12.
166. Julian Haynes Steward, *Theory of Culture Change,* Illinois, 1955.
167. Hultkrantz, 'Ecology of Religion: Its Scope and Methods', in Lauri Honko, (ed.) *Science of Religion: Studies in Methodology,* The Hague, 1979, p. 222.
168. Ecological approach to religion is perhaps traceable to the Frankforts' description of ecological situation that influenced Near Eastern religions and was also implied in the doctrine of the older evolutionists that experiences of Nature provided man with gods and myths. Cf. H. and H.A. Frankfort, "The Emancipation of Thought from Myth" in H. Frankfort et al., (eds.), *The Intellectual Adventure of Ancient Man,* Chicago, 1946, pp. 363-73 and Max Muller's views (*supra,* paragraphs 2.2 and 3.6). But there had not been any attempt to systematise a theoretical framework.
169. Cf. Hultkrantz in Lauri Honko, op. cit., pp. 227-28. See also discussion of Levi-Stauss' structuralism, *supra,* paragraphs 220-21.
170. While Hultkrantz has clearly been influenced by the cultural ecology of Steward, another enthusiast of the ecological approach to religion, viz., Svein Bjerke ('Ecology of Religion, Evolutionism and Comparative Religion', in Lauri Honko, op.cit., pp. 242-46) adopts the model of a few other cultural ecologists, i.e. Sahlins and Service (Cf. M.D. Sahlins and E.R. Service, *Evolution and Culture,* University of Michigan, 1960 and E. Service, *Primitive Social Organisation,* New York, 1962). The latter model enables Bjerke to postulate 'new evolutionism' in religion. He argues: 'By grouping together societies of roughly the same technology and socio-political level of integration, one can distinguish between the familistic band level...characteristic of hunters and gatherers, the tribal level of horticulturists and pastoralists, which lacks any centralised political system, the chiefdom level which is defined on the basis of redistributive economic system, and the state level defined on the basis of the claim for monopoly in the use of force made by the political authorities.'

171. Marvin Harris, *The Rise of Anthropological Theory,* New York, p. 1968, p. 4; see also, Marvin Harris, 'The Cultural Ecology of India's Sacred Cattle', *Current Anthropology,* Vol. 7, No. 1, February 1966, pp. 51-66. For contra, see Alan Heston, 'An Approach to the Sacred Cow of India', *Current Anthropology,* Vol. 12, No. 2, April 1971, p. 191-209. The basic dispute between Harris and Heston is on the relative utility of ecologic and economic models.
172. For a critique of Hultkrantz's distinction between the ecologically explainable type of religion and the historically explainable features which are not part of the 'type 58 *Social Scientist* of religion', which is based on his adopting of the aforesaid model of Steward, see Svein Bjerke in Lauri Honko, op. cit. pp. 240-42.
173. e.g. Hultkrantz is aware that Steward dismissed the importance of historical factors in forming culture. Morris Freil tested Steward's cultural ecology on Negroes and East Indians of Trinidad and found that these groups, who differ in cultural traditions but make the same ecological adaptation, lack a 'common core' related to the mode of adaptation. Though Hultkrantz is not convinced of this argument because 'subsistence activities' of the two groups have not been taken into account, he is willing to consider another objection to this approach, viz., we have no fixed criteria by which to judge whether features should be attributed to the culture core or to invention, diffusion or cultural heritage.
174. Notwithstanding the need to undertake further sophistication of different fields of ecology and the need for differentiation and qualification when speaking about the ecology of religion (cf. G.C. Oosthuizen's comments on Hultkrantz's views in Lauri Honko, (ed.), op. cit, pp. 271-85), it may be said to the credit of Hultkrantz that he is not unaware of the possibilities of applying his approach to religions in modern cultures, e.g. different patterns of urban and rural religions, cf. also D Luth et al., 'An Ecological Approach to the Study of Religious Movements', *Bulletins of the American Anthropological Association,* 1-3 (1968), pp. 87f. The technological environment penetrating into the contents of belief is shown by fieldwork amongst Waldensians in Italy (cf. Manfred Buttner in Lauri Honko, op. cit., pp. 253-55) and patterns of pilgrimage and cult sites in nineteenth century France, cf. Alphonse Dupront, 'Religion and Religious Anthropology, in Jacques Le Goffe and Pierre Nora

(eds.), *Constructing the Past: Essays in Historical Methodology,* Cambridge, 1985, pp. 123-50.

175. Edmund Perry in Lauri Honko, op. cit, pp. 286-87.

176. Given this crucial importance of cattle to both cultures, the comparison between the Nilotes and the Indo-Iranians (or even Indo-Europeans) has been suggested fairly often in the past. V. Gordon Childe wrote as far back as 1926, 'In my opinion the state of things observed among many of the cow-keeping tribes of the Sudan and other parts of Africa approximates most closely the primitive Aryan economy', *The Aryans,* New York, p. 84. H.S. Nyberg, Widengren, Piggott, Lommel and Duchesne-Guiliemin have also suggested the comparison, but no systematic study had been made till Lincoln took up the problem.

177. e.g., Anaximander, the first known Greek map-maker, looked on the world as a manifestation of a religious principle, viz., the inviolability of the spatial order. The brahmanical and Jaina view of universe in India similarly look upon geographical and topographical features from a purely sectarian perspective.

178. For a brief survey of work done in the western world, see John D. Gay, *The Geography of Religion in England,* London, 1971.

179. Alphonse Dupront, 'Religion and Religious Anthropology', in Jacques Le Goffe and Pierre Nora, (eds.), op. cit., pp. 123-50.

180. D.D. Kosambi, *Myth and Reality,* Bombay, 1962, pp. 82-151.

181. *Supra,* paragraphs 3.3-5.

182. This contention has been reiterated by Debiprasad Chattopadhyaya, cf. *Religion and Society,* pp. 62-68, where Joseph Needham's analysis of Confucian China as depicted in his *The Great Titration: Science and Society in East and West,* London, 1979, pp. 168-69 has also been cited. In the context of the Harappans, it has been put forward earlier by Kosambi *(An Introduction to the Study of Indian History,* pp. 63-64) and S.C. Malik *(Indian Civilisation: The Formative Period,* pp. 99-105).

183. We have argued elsewhere about the limitations of the use of 'Aryan' and the changing frontier of 'Aryan' and 'non-Aryan', cf. our *History of Panchala,* Vol. I, 1983, pp. 23-29. See also A. Ghosh, *The City in Early Historical India,* Simla, 1973, p. 4 and Debiprasad Chattopadhyaya, op. cit., pp. 90-115.

184. R.N. Nandi, *Religious Institutions and Cults in the Deccan,* Delhi, 1973; from the two maps at the end it appears that the data for Madhya Pradesh, Maharashtra and Andhra Pradesh have not been harnessed fully. See also Ram Bhushan Prasad Singh, *Jainism in Early Medieval Karnataka,* Delhi, 1975, map at the end.

85. Cf. S. Settar, 'From Vaishnavism to Shrivaishnavism: A Study of Shrivaishnava Settlements of Pre-Ramanuja Era', in Ratan Parimoo, (ed.), *Vaishnavism in Indian Arts and Culture,* New Delhi, 1987.

86. Friedhelm Hardy, *Viraha-Bhakti: The Early History of Krishna Devotion in South India,* Oxford, 1983, pp. 256-61 and six maps between pp. 256 and 257.

187. *Ibid,* see particularly pp. 274-75 where the poetic dedication of temples is discussed.

188. Cf. Kesavan Veluthat, 'The Temple Base of the Bhakti Movement in South India', in Krishna Mohan Shrimali, (ed.), *Essay in Indian Art, Religion and Society,* Delhi, 1987, pp. 151-59; M.G.S. Narayanan and Veluthat Kesavan, 'Bhakti Movement in South India,' in D.N. Jha, (ed), *Feudal Social Formation in Early India,* Delhi, 1987, pp. 348-75: Y. Subbarayaluy, *Political Geography of the Chola Country,* Madras, 1973: George W. Spencer, 'The Sacred Geography of the Tamil Shaivite Hyms,' *Numen,* Vol. 17, December 1970, pp. 232-44. See also Kamil Zvelebil, *The Smile of Murugan,* Leiden, 1973, pp. 198-99 for the importance of the cult of places sacred to both Shaiva and Vaishnava saints.

189. For an excellent exposition of the cult, see S. Settar, *Inviting Death,* Dharwad. 1986; Idem, *Pursuing Death,* Dharwad, 1988.

190. Cf. S. Setter and Gunther D. Sontheimer, (eds.), *Memorial Stones: A Study of their Origin, Significance and Variety,* Dharwad and Heidelberg, 1982.

191. Cf. D.D. Kosambi, *Myth and Reality,* Bombay, 1962, pp. 3-32.

192. Romila Thapar, 'Death and the Hero, in S.C. Humphreys and Helen King', (eds.), *Mortality and Immortality—The Anthropology and Archaeology of Death,* London, 1981, pp. 294, 310-11.

193. Cf. *supra,* paragraph 3.18 dealing with the rise of tantricism. Yet another example of cultural integration is noticeable in the transformation of a herostone into a deity, viz, the cult of Vithoba at Pandharpur (Maharashtra). Cf. S.G. Tulpule, 'The Origin of Vithala: A New Interpretation', *Annals of the*

Bhandarkar Oriental Research Institute, Vols. 58-59, 1977-78, pp. 1009-1015.

194. *Supra,* paragraph 4.10.
195. Manfred Buttner in Lauri Honko, (ed.), *Science of Religion,* The Hague, 1979, p. 254.
196. Alphonse Duprbnt, 'Religion and Religious Anthropology,' in Jacques Le Goffe and Pierre Nora, (eds.), *Canstructing the Past,* pp. 123-50.
197. *Ibid.,* p. 132.
198. Some important writings on this aspect are: Makhan Jha, *Dimensions of Pilgrimage: an Anthropological Appraisal,* New Delhi, 1985: L.P. Vidyarthi, 'Thinking About Sacred City,' *Eastern Anthropologist,* Vol. XIII, No. 4; L.P. Vidyarthi and Makhan Jha, *Symposium on the Sacred Complexes of India,* Ranchi, 1974; S.M. Bhardwaj, *Hindu Places of Pilgrimage in India: A Study in Cultural Geography,* Berkeley, 1973; E. Alan Morris Pilgrimage in the Hindu Tradition: A Case Study of West Bengal, Delhi 1984; B.B. Goswami and S.G. Morab, 'Comparative Study of Sacred Complexes India, A Working Paper', *Journal of Social Research,* Vol. XIII, No. 2, '1970, pp. 95f: L.P. Vidyarthi, *The Sacred Complex in Hindu Gaya,* Bombay 1961: Milton Singer, The Cultural Pattern of Indian Civilisation—A Preliminary Report of the Methodological Field study,' *The Far Eastern Quarterly,* Vol. 15, No. 1, 1955.
199. P.V. Kane, *History of Dharamashastra,* Vol. IV, Poona, 1973, pp. 581-82, 730-825.
200. F.S. Sharma, *Perspectives in Social and Economic History of Early India,* New Delhi, 1983, pp. 236-37.
201. eg. V.N. Hari Rao, *The Srirangam Temple,* Tirupati, 1967; J.M. Somasundaram Pillai, *The Great Temple at Tanjore,* Tanjore, 2nd rev. ed., 1958; Douglas Barrett and Moreshwar G. Dikshit, *Mukhalingem, Sirpur and Rajim Temples,* Bombay, 1960; K.K. Pillay, *The Suchindrale Temple,* Madras, 1953, T.V. Mahalingam, *The South Indian Temple Complex,* Dharwar, 1970.
202. Debjani Paul, 'Antiquity of the Vishnupada at Gaya: Tradition and Archaeology', *East and West* (N.S.) Vol. 35 Nos. 1-3, September 1985, pp. 103-41. I owe this reference to my colleague Dr. Dilip K. Chakrabarti.
203. It is regretted that even such an intensive study as Savitri V. Kumar, *The Puranic Lore of Holy Water-Places,* New Delhi, 1983 does not note of the milieu in which the phenomenon of tirthas seems to have developed.

204. R.N. Nandi, *Social Roots of Religion in Ancient India*, Calcutta, 1986, p. 48. 205. R.N. Nandi, 'Agrarian Growth and Social Conflicts in Early Feudal India,' *Social Science Probings*, Vol. II, No. 2, June, 1985, pp. 168-69.

206. Karl Marx and Frederick Engels, *On Religion*, Progress Publishers, Moscow, 1975. 207. *Ibid:* p. 38, extract from *Contribution to the Critique of Hegel's Philosophy of Law.*

208. *Ibid*, p. 39.

209. *Ibid.*

210. *Ibid.*, p. 38. For other statements of Marx and Engels on religion and ideology see extracts from *The German Ideology* (written in 1845-46), ch. 1; *Manifesto of the* 60 *Social Scientist Communist Party* (1847-48), ch. 2 and 3; *Capital*, Vol. I (1867); *Anti-Duhring* (1878) and *Ludwig Feuerbach and End of Classic German Philosophy* (1886). For all these extracts, see *ibid.*, pp. 65-72, pp. 78-79, 117-19, 128-29, and 214-32.

211. Jorge Larrain, *Marxism and Ideology*, London, 1983, p. 42. The work takes considerable pain to show how, with few exceptions, the most important Marxist theoreticians have developed a 'positive and neutral conception' which conceives various ideologies existing in terms of the interests of opposed classes. See particularly ch. 2 where the change in the meaning of ideology from Marx to Gransci has been delineated.

212. Cf. Max Weber, *The Sociology of Religion*, trans., by Ephraim Fischoff, 1963 and A. Gramsci, *Selections from the 'Prison Notebooks'*, London, 1971, p. 376.

213. Clifford Geertz, 'Ideology of a Cultural System', in D. Apter, (ed.), *Ideology and Discontent*, New York, 1964.

214. Some representative writings grappling with these problems include, Glifford Geertz, 'Religion as a Cultural System', in M. Banton, (ed.), *Anthropological Approaches to Religion*, London, 1966; P. Hirst and P. Woolley, *Social Relations and Human Attributes*, London, 1980, S. Lukes, 'Some Problems about Rationality', in B.R. Wilson, (ed.), *Rationality*, Oxford, 1970 and M. Douglas, *Purity and Danger*, London, 1970. All the relevant extracts from these writings have been compiled in Robert Bocock and Kenneth Thompson, (eds.), *Religion and Ideology: A Reader*, Manchester, 1985.

215. A. Gramsci, op. cit., *passim*. For Gramsci's indebtedness to Lukacs, see Jorge Larrain, op. cit., pp. 69-87. See also Perry Anderson, 'The Antinomies of Antonio Gramsci', *New Left Review*, no. 100, November 1976-January 1977.

216. *Supra,* paragraph 2.22.

217. Cf. Maurice Godelier, 'Infrastructures, Societies, and History', *Current Anthropology,* Vol. 19, No. 4, December 1978, pp. 763-71 and "The Emergence and Development of Marxism in Anthropology in France', in Ernest Gellner, (ed.), *Soviet and Western Anthropology,* London, 1980, pp. 3-18.

218. Max Adler, 'Ideology and Appearance', in T. Bottomore and P. Godde, (eds.), *Austro-Marxism,* Oxford, 1978, pp. 254-55.

219. See references under n. 217.

220. *Ibid.* Cf. also Gregor McLennan, *Marxism and the Methodologies of History,* London, 1981, ch. 3.

221. Maurice Godelier, 'Infrastructures, Societies, and History', *Current Anthropology,* Vol. 19, No. 4, December 1978, p. 765.

222. Engels himself wrote in 1886, 'Every ideology, however, once it has arisen, develops in connection with the given concept—material, and develops this material further; otherwise it would not be an ideology', in *Ludwig Feurbach and the End of Classical German Philosophy,* cited in Marx-Engels, *On Religion,* p. 229.

223. *Supra,* paragraph 3.3-5.

224. Cf. particularly S.C. Malik, op. cit. *(supra,* n. 72).

225. *Man Makes Himself,* p. 154.

226. Romila Thapar, *The Mauryas Revisited*—S.G. Deuskar Lectures on Indian History (1984), Calcutta, 1987, pp. 1-31.

227. *Supra,* section III.

228. *History of Panchal,* Vol. I, Delhi, 1983, pp. 173-77.

229. R.S. Sharma, *Aspects of Political Ideas and Institutions in Ancient India,* Delhi, 1959, pp. 103-18.

230. The idea was put forward by Barton Stein in his *Peasant State and Society in Medieval South India,* New Delhi, 1980 and exploded by D. N. Jha, 'Validity of "Brahmana-Peasant Alliance" and the "Segmentary State" in Early Medieval South India', *Social Science Probings,* Vol. I, No. 2, June 1984, pp. 270-95.

231. *Supra,* ns. 142 and 144.

232. For South Indian marketing hierarchy in the Chola age, see Kenneth R. Hall, *Trade and Stategraft in the Age of Cholas,* New Delhi, 1980, *passim.*

233. Clifford Geertz, 'Ideology as a Cultural System,' reproduced in Robert Bocock and Kenneth Thompson, *Religion and Ideology: A Reader,* Manchester, 985, p. 83. Cf. this with

Antonio Gramsci's recognition 'mass adhesion or non-adhesion to an ideology is the real critical test of the rationality and historicity of modes of thinking', *Prison Notebooks,* London. 1971, p. 341. See also Georges Duby, 'The Diffusion of Cultural Patterns in Feudal Society,' *Past and Present,* April, 1968.

6

Critique of Hinduism
Approaches to Hinduism

Laxman Shastri Joshi

There is a view current even today which regards Hinduism as a body of laws conducive to the preservation or maintenance of the order and stability of society. This view has been held by some ever since the days of the Mahabharata. It is argued that since Hinduism has as its objective the establishment of such an order, it attaches primary significance to doctrines such as that of the four Varnas; the norms governing the behaviour of families or castes; the moral principles like truth, non-violence etc; various norms of social behaviour and so on. The worship of the supernatural, the divine or the spiritual occupies in Hinduism a subordinate position. Some of these thinkers carry the argument still further and point out that the conceptions of god, the other world, reincarnation, deity, apostle etc. are simply symbolic and have been devised in order that the common man may obey the laws. The fear or temptation of the other world induces him to do so.

There are others who argue that Hinduism shows the way of attaining the good in this as well as in the other world. The SHRUTIS, SMRITIES and the PURANAS preach its doctrines so that man may live comfortably in this life and attain well-being after death. It is with this object that the doctrines of the four-fold PURUSHARTHAS or three-fold VARANS have been preached in the Mahabharata and the SMRITIES. The religion in the SMRITIES has as its object the enabling of man to attain well-being and salvation i.e. God in this and the other world. It says for example that proper observation of the rules of "Grihasthashrama" enables one to lead a happy family life as well as through purification of the mind, facilitates the attainment of salvation.

Besides the above two, there is a third view also, which regards Hinduism as a pure religion of the spirit. Its principle purpose is to show the way to Nirvana, salvation or the other worldly well-being. Wealth, desire, preservation of the individual or society is all its subordinate objects. They are meant for the simple, undeveloped, child-like beings. As a matter of fact, the being is on a pilgrimage to salvation. This life or material existence is simply a halting place or a SERAI on the way. The real task of Hinduism is to show the way to spiritual well-being or salvation. The VEDANTINS, SHAIVES or VAISHNAVAS as well as the modern spiritualists, all hold this view and defend it.

Of these three, the first view is simply untenable. It is only the latter two that describe Hinduism more or less realistically in the form in which it exist today. The sense in which the first view regards Hinduism as conducive to social stability and order is wrong. In the thought and life of the Hindus from ancient times to date, there never existed religion in that sense. Barring a few exceptions the founders, perceptors or scriptures of Hinduism have always preached doctrines thoroughly inconsistent or even opposed to that view. The Vedic Yajans or rituals are all worship of god.

The Upanishads also speak of Brahma, soul, salvation, immortality and numerous other spiritual concepts. The Smrities too, in the light of the spiritualism of the Vedas, speak of the varnas, Ashrams or other social behaviour;

and in the same manner do the puranas regarding rites, pilgrimages and prayers. It is true that underneath this shell of spiritual sentiments or emotions are concealed the nature and norms of material existence. But the spiritual conceptions are not merely symbolic; on the other hand, according to those who propound them, they are the reality.

Some of the champions of the first view contend that the Vedic religion i.e. religion from the Rigveda is concerned with the things of this world and the time has now come when it should be upheld. The Vedic literature is full of prayers for material object like health, long life, power, bravery, triumph, fame, knowledge, happiness, rains, animals, grain, Gold and so on. The deities in it are simply material forces; and the Vedic religion is materialistic in its content. The impulse to work for the betterment of the material lot of the Hindus can thus be had from the Vedas. They show the way to well-being in this world; while Vedanta is spiritualistic in content. In order to rise from their present defeated and decadent stage, it is necessary for the Hindu to reject mystic, spiritualistic or devotional doctrines from the Puranas or the preachings of the saints and endeavour to establish the old Vedic religion. The religion of the SMRITIES or the Puranas has got to be now reformed. Every Hindu should now be guided by the slogan, "Back to the Vedas."

There are fallacies in this view. A religion which emphasises the material objects of this world definitely represents a backward primitive type of social organisation. Modern psychology has now clearly established that such religions arose in the early primitive communities. On the other hand, the religions emphasising the spiritual arise in more civilised and developed societies.

The former type of religion believes that God has a hand in the ordinary material affairs of man; that the desired can be obtained only through their favour or blessing and that all evils or dangers are a result of their wrath. It is thus based upon the faith that the operation of material forces is controlled by some whimsical supernatural element. It is a religion born out of ignorance of the causal relationship of the ordinary material events or phenomena; and thus constitutes a positive danger to those who desire the spreading of the scientific outlook or thought; it is exactly the opposite of scientific thought. After all, who were being prayed to in the Vedas for the sake of material prosperity and well-being? The various deities and Gods, these are certainty not material objects; they represent material forces deified by deluded mind and thus made into conscious and intelligent beings. The material forces neither listen to prayer nor confer blessings as a result of them. Does the tree bear fruit when prayed to? Does the engine or machine work because of prayers? The same is true of the force of nature. The various actions leading to material well-being according to the Vedas are the citing of the hymns, Yajnas and so on; and the Vedic people believed that these lead to the propitiation of the spiritual forces, whose blessing can bring material well-being. Magic, Mantras and similar other things have also been devised by man for the sake of material benefits; and faith in them is the same thing as faith in the Vedic rituals. It is indication of the primitive, simple undeveloped mind; for the idea of causation in it is based on complete ignorance of real causal relationship. As compared to this Vedic natural religion, the other-worldly or spiritualistic religion definitely suggests a higher stage of development. The latter definitely recognises the proper casual relationships in the affairs of this world. Religion is simply considered therein as purifying the mind and thus helping to attain salvation, but for objects of this world, it is essential to cultivate the arts of agriculture, sculpture, architecture, trading, and polity and to conform to the norms of moral behaviour. It was only after the decline of the Vedic religion that the various branches of learning and systems of philosophy were born in India. Towards the end of the Vedic period, arose the Upanishads, which made revolutionary changes in Vedic thought, and opened up the way for further spiritual progress.

It is only the second view, which takes into account the requirements of both this and the other world, that gives us an adequate and proper idea of Hinduism. It is said in one of the Puranas that the religious texts indicate certain means of spiritual good, certain other of material good and yet certain other of both. The farmer has been styled as Adrishtartha while the latter as Drishtartha. Drishta means seen and Artha means result or fruit. Drishtartha are therefore the means, the fruits or results of which can directly understood; as for example, agriculture, sculpture, trade, warfare or polity. The religious texts describe the way in which these are to be practiced and he who breaks them is bound to suffer, may be, imperceptibly. The Adrishtartha, on the other hand, are the means, the results or fruits of which are unseen. Here the relation between the means and the ends cannot be grasped either directly or inferentially i.e. through the use of human reason. It can be learnt only from the scriptures. It is only one with faith in the scriptures who will admit that the above deeds lead to results like rains, the birth of a son, the avoidance of disease, the destruction of the enemy, birth in a noble family or salvation. In this unseen causation are implicit the conceptions of heaven and hell, God and Satan, Salvation, Soul and rebirth. These are the proper objects of religious faith. The means pertaining to both of these types are those in the case of which the relation between the means and the ends is both seen and unseen as for example, the laws of marriage. Sex pleasure and procreation are both seen result of these while on the other hand the attainment of the ancestral heavens or discharge of obligations to the ancestors are the unseen results. The unseen relation between the means and the ends itself amounts to grace or wrath of God.

Some of the modern defenders of religion, interpreting the concepts of duty or deviations from duty prescribed by

God, argue that the behaviour of an individual, which on a long-period view, can be definitely said to lead to the benefit of that individual or of the society of which he is a part, may be considered as duty. It is possible to decide them only on a deep and careful study of the many–sided reality. A mind, not accustomed to such study, can see only the immediate good or well-being as well as the immediate harm; and hence the rules can be laid down only by thoughtful and meditative sages. The unseen means cannot be grasped by narrow, undeveloped minds. Action leading to immediate good, on a careful long-period view is often found to do more than harm that good; and hence the thinkers or seers consider them as being sinful.

Religion tells us that charity, truth and non-violence are the root of other-worldly happiness. It also advises us to abide by the order of the Ashramas and control the senses. The Mahabharata says that, he who behaves with all, with the consciousness that they are also the embodiments of the same soul, alone can attain eternal happiness. All the Smrities clearly argue that violence, appropriation of what belongs to others or illicit relationship with any women lead to the fall of man. If we carefully view life as a whole, it will be clear that the observance of the above rules is no doubt conducive to social well-being; while there transgression will lead to harmful results. People who, do not exercise self-control either die early in life or are affected by various dieases. Experience bears this out. Therefore, duty or sin can be indicated to man through experience or meditation, independently of faith. And religion has been propounded by those who could see these indications, interpret experience and meditate upon it.

This view is not quite tenable, for it is a half-truth. It is true that the norms of religion have been laid down by the wise and leading individuals in society. But the upholders of this view do not interpret the term “Adrishta” correctly. For example, it cannot be said that the concepts of duty or sin,when it is said that the one leads to higher birth or heaven after death while the other to lower birth or hell, have their connotation determined through the application of the norms of logic by human reason. Reason cannot establish the good results obtained in this or the other world through Mantras, Yajna, Japa, or worship. It is only on the assumption of the existence of the supernatural forces like Gods, stars, demons or the power of the shastras that the various religious rites and rituals have been prescribed. If this is not admitted, most of them will appear as vain and meaningless. As a matter of fact, it is only people with blind faith in them, who have laid down the various religious prescriptions; and frank admissions of this alone can be helpful to the future progress of the social order.

A good part of religious texts of the Hindus has been written by people with blind faith in the supernatural. Not only that but conscious defenders of the dominating class interest can also be said to have a hand in it. There are texts written by people desirous of keeping the Sudras as the slaves of the three Varnas. To keep the Sudras in slavery, to retain the domination of the three Varnas and to have for the priestly class a predominating voice appeared to be the three-fold principles underlying the social order described in them.

The third view which considers Hinduism as a purely spiritual religion is a result of the developments in Hinduism itself. It does not therefore present a complete picture of the real nature of Hinduism. It is that it deals with an important aspect of it and in modern times it is this view which appears to exercise a considerable hold over the minds of a majority of Hindus, including the educated ones.

It is one of the outstanding social duties of our times to combat this view; for, without that, the main difficulty in the way of a critical understanding of material as well as spiritual life of the Hindus in our own times will not disappear. The criticism of heaven is the beginning of the criticism of the Earth; that of religion is the beginning of the criticism of justice, right or authority. Underneath this spirituals-other-worldly garb is concealed the reality of this world; and the illusion produced by the former has led to self-deception as well as the deception of the others. With the help of these illusions, the free and subtle imagination often paints attractive pictures of the powers of the supernatural forces, pictures which conceal the hideous reality of this world. Against the background of a serious but empty philosophy devoid of all truth, is built up the edifice of these illusions. Unless they are all shattered, the thought that teaches us to combat the hideousness in life cannot grow, nor can actions aimed at combatting it, fructify.This otherworldliness or spiritualism is a dark curtain that covers successfully the sorrows and tears of millions of suffering Indian humanity. It is for them indeed a poor consolation, moonshine, a mirage. Unless this quest of an illusory world is stopped, it will not be possible to grasp the real significance of freedom and well-being. The way to a happy, healthy and harmonious social life will not be opened up unless the utter futility and falsehood of heaven is clearly exposed.

Let us now turn to a definition of Hinduism. A number of modern learned Hindu scholars find it difficult to point out what exactly is the peculiar feature of Hinduism that differentiates it from other religions. For Hinduism is a curious mixture of numerous religious forms and conflicting and contradictory tendencies. It has two important aspects. Peculiar social customs or laws of social life are its main aspect or feature; and various inconsistent or even conflicting spiritual sects are its other aspect. The definition of other religions in the world like Christianity or Islam can be deduced from their spiritual or other worldly side; and it is needless to look to their social character while deducing it. Under the external cover of every religion are to be found a peculiar social structure and social laws; but in the case of definition of Hinduism, it is this aspect which easily comes into prominence. The four-fold Varnas, the caste system, the marital rituals, the norms of family or caste life, the laws of succession or the joint family system all represent the social side of Hinduism. Hinduism thus means the laws or rules of a particular social structure. This peculiar social structure is founded on the Varnas and the caste. During the last two thousand years and more, Hinduism has always meant the religion founded on the caste system. A Hindu is a pure and proper Hindu when he abides by the laws governing his caste. Of course, behind all these social customs of the Hindus, there do exist spiritual or other worldly notions. All religious texts, for example, have amply used the concept of re-birth and the doctrine of Karma to defend all the laws of this social structure. On the other hand, the spiritual or other worldly sects among the Hindus are founded on various conflicting notions and it is futile, no matter how much one tries to do so, to think of introducing any consistency in them.

The late Lokamanya B.G.Tilak has defined Hinduism as "faith in the Vedas, variety in the means and indefiniteness of the objects of worship." This is indeed a highly significant definition for it clearly shows the utter absence of any definite, orderly, consistent, positive other-worldly basis for Hinduism. The term "Faith in the Vedas" indicates that all the Hindus accept the authority of the Vedas. But in the Hindu society, at least 70 per cent of the people have no right to study and know that authority or have their social customs and laws ordained according to it. How can they then have faith in the Vedas? They have no right even to listen to the Vedas; not only that but such listening on their part has been considered as sinful for which they are doomed to hell. It is therefore quite meaningless to say that they have faith in the Vedas. "The variety of means" or "in-definiteness of the objects of worship" cannot be components of a definition at all.

Every particular sect of Hindus such as the Shaivas, the Vaishnavas and so on, have their peculiar means and peculiar objects of worship; and there is no uniformity regarding these so far as all the Hindus are concerned. But this negative feature cannot furnish us with a definition. In an endeavour to define something, we have to state its positive feature which pervades it completely and is all its own and cannot therefore be found anywhere else outside it. The "variety of means" or "the indefiniteness of the objects of worship" simply proves that there is nothing like a particular religion of all Hindus, know as Hinduism. There are several religions of the Hindus and there is no consistency amongst them.

The caste system is an important positive feature of the Hindu social order. The vast majority of Hindus barring a few exceptions order their behaviour according to it. Even these exceptions like Prarthana Samaja or Arya Samaja have in their fold people who recognise the caste system and abide by it. While Jainism does not recognise castes, the Jains recognise them. Even amongst the Christians and the Muslim in India, there are many who accept the caste divisions. Even they have been influenced and affected by this outstanding principle of Hindu social life.

It is extremely difficult to describe comprehensively the nature of Hinduism by trying to find out its common feature; for it is not a phenomenon which can definitely and consistently be described. It is far too complicated and many-sided for such a description. In order to understand it fully, therefore, it is necessary to go into its various peculiar forms under different circumstances. It is not logically quite sound to search for a common feature of such a disorderly object and it will be better if we therefore try to examine its various forms found at different stages of its development.

Hinduism is not a thing based on certain particular spiritual or other–worldly thought. It is, on other hand, a collection of different social laws, customs and there is, further added on to these, various mutually inconsistent and contradictory spiritual notions. Hinduism does not consider the social customs or laws as merely “things that are Caesar’s” but ascribes to them a spiritual value and sanctions. The customs pertaining to marriage, those of various castes, and sub-castes, the behaviour of the sexes, the laws of succession, the life of the widows or the taboos regarding food and drink all have a religious significance. The caste system no doubt is its outstanding feature but even there it is difficult to describe it properly. For example, though a number of castes recognise the supremacy of the priests and accept the Brahmins as priests, there are some which have priests from amongst themselves or the non-Brahmins. Though Islam or Christianity is different from Hinduism, there are Hindus who worship the Christian deities or the Muslim Pirs. All these things simply indicate that Hinduism often attaches a far greater significance to social customs rather than to the idea or behaviour in worship. It is necessary therefore, to examine historically this religion which is so full of various conflicting spiritual ideas. In analysing and examining it in this manner, we shall discover in it various primitive or developed layers.

Nature of Hinduism

The historical method does not attach the same significance to the different religious conceptions in the course of social evolution. Just as society passes through the various primitive or civilised forms of social development, it gives rise to various primitive or civilised religious notions. The worship of objects like the trees or the stones or that of ghosts, magic or sacrifice of man or animal in Yajna are all features of primitive religion. In a more developed society, we have monotheism. In Hinduism are to be found these various forms, even the other monotheistic religions like Christianity, Zoroastrianism or Islam have in them the relics of religious notions of a backward undeveloped society. But monotheism have successfully eclipsed or concealed these earlier and more primitive forms. These monotheistic religions arouse to shatter and destroy the primitive religious notions and forms. But they could not succeed in this beyond a limited extent. The greatest measure of success has been attanined by Islam. Hinduism, on other hand, was not very successful in that respect; rather it failed; and the proof of that failure is its present form. The most primitive or barbaric forms are to be found prevalent in it; on occasions they are even highly revered and respected; and are sought to be defended with subtle and sophisticated arguments. Orthodox scholars have showed this tendency to seriously defend these primitive features, which have been still sticking on to Hinduism and have thus practiced self-deception.

Religious notions at three different stages in the development of religion are to be found in Hinduism. Of course, besides these, there are various others belonging to various levels in each of these stages. But for the convenience of our discussion, we can safely take this three-fold division; (I) magic; animism, ancestor-worship or worship of ghosts and demons; (II) worship of deities imagined in the image of man and worship of power; (III) monotheism, the doctrine of Brahma, pantheism and philosophical religion.

Magic, the earliest form of religion, is found in almost all the primitive communities of the world. Even in the modern civilised societies, it is seen in existence in the backward strata of the community. It is a very primitive form of religion; and has at its root a complete ignorance of the causal relationship of phenomena. Magic generally is of two kinds; one that precedes theism and the other succeeding the theistic religion. Both of these are found in Hinduism. Magic has a place in the religion of the Atharvaveda and the Grihya Sutras. It also finds a place in the rites prescribed in the other Vedas. Some of the Yajnas are like magical acts or have relics of these in them. They are to be performed for getting rains, destruction of the enemies, avoidance of disease etc. There are certain magical rituals or Yajnas named Abhichar as prescribed in the Vedas. The rites accompanying the attainment of maturity or conception also fall in the same category. Magic is Sadhana. By Sadhana is meant the use under particular conditions, of particular rites, objects or Mantras, believing them to be possessed of supernatural power, for the purpose of attaining the desired or avoiding the evil. Even the medical remedies of the earlier times, based as they were on ignorance of the properties of the various objects, had an element of magic in them. Some of the remedies in Atharvaveda and the Grihyasutras are of this kind; and magical herbs and mantras have been stated in them.

The other relic of primitive religion in Hinduism is nature worship. The worship of the various natural objects like stones, mountains, rivers, trees, animals etc. comes in here, on the basis of a faith that these objects possess some supernatural power. In Hinduism, for example, we have the worship of stones and pebbles, of mountains, of rivers like the Ganges, of trees like the Banyan or 'Pimpala', of animals like the cow or the monkey, of heavenly bodies like the Sun and the Moon; of natural elements like fire, wind or the rains. And this still persists; even in the monotheistic devotional religions which prescribe the worship of these objects as symbols. Originally, however, they were not considered as of symbolic significance but were sacred in themselves. The trees like the Pimpala or the Banyan still continue to be worshipped in the original sense; and the Puranas have linked them up with various deities in the developed form of religion. But their existence as worshipful objects is an independent existence. The cobra and the cow still remain as independent objects of worship. Though the fish, the tortoise, the lion, the tiger or the eagle are no longer themselves worshipped, the worship of their images still continues. The Sun and the Moon still enjoy an important worshipful position. Even outstanding leaders of the Hindus like Pandit Madana Mohana Malaviya still preach the worship of cow or the Tulsi plant as an important feature of Hinduism. This natureworship arises in the form of primitive totemism. It is born out of faith that particular natural objects or animals are possessed of powers for good or evil; a faith based on complete ignorance. There is, for example, an idea in the Rigveda and the Atharvaveda that the sight of crow or a pigeon is indicative of death. In the smrities also, there is a belief that the sight or touch of particular objects or even persons belonging to particular castes is either purifying or polluting. Thus, the concepts or Mana or Taboo, found in the primitive communities, are still seen lingering in Hinduism. There is ample evidence of this in the Shruti literature. The taboos concerning food as well as touch in the smrities are all indicative of this.

In Hinduism, certain natural objects or their images have been considered as worshipful, while the worship of certain others is a result of the influence of the later, more developed forms of religion. For example, the eagle, bull or the apes are cases in point. The eagle or bull worship comes in because of their being the vehicles of Vishnu and Shiva respectively, while the ape is worshipped as the messenger of Rama. As a matter of fact they were considered worshipful in the beginning quite independently of these factors. The bull is still independently worshipped by some Hindus. The same holds good in the case of the monkey, who is worshipped as Hanumana. The worship of tree, the Sun, mountain, river and the stars still continues almost in the same form in which it existed in the earliest times.

It has been already pointed out that this worship originates in the most primitive times. It arises out of a belief in man that the beasts or the birds around him are more powerful than himself. When man realises his position in nature as superior to the other animals, the worship of animals, deities possessed of power, symbolised through the possession of limbs or organs, begins to decline. Man has created these various deities possessing the limbs of the ape, the lion, the elephant etc, before releasing his own importance. On the other hand, nations or society which had attained a certain amount of stability, created gods in man's own image and endowed them with various human qualities. Thus, god was created by man with his reason in his own image, when he realised his superiority over the animal kingdom. Human society had to pass through centuries of development, before human triumphs came to be attributed in an exaggerated form to Gods. Man then began to imagine the deities of various animals, birds, rivers etc. as being possessed of human qualities, while retaining their externals.

The worship of natural elements like fire, wind or rain arose similarly out of an ignorance of causation. These deities were created out of a failure to causally interpret natural events like wild fire, the blazing sun, stones, draughts and floods, high or low tides, sunrise and sunset etc. A proper and correct interpretation of these events was impossible in the absence of science; and therefore man had to carry on with his numerous deities or one God. The only way open to him under those conditions was to pray, to worship, to perform Yajna; and that became his religion.

Ancestor worship or worship of the dead is also to be found in Hinduism. The existence of the youngster in the family depend upon the elders; the latter alone provide him with the equipment for life. They therefore naturally dominate and influence him. The death of the elderly person is therefore a big calamity naturally felt by everyone in the clan or the family. The feeling prevents them from accepting the idea of the complete end. The existence of the elders is felt to be there either in dreams or in solitude. When the group is overtaken by a calamity, it is regarded as the result of some unfulfilled desire of the dead. The survivors thus entertain the desire to fulfill the wishes or desires of the dead. Out of this arises animism. The worship of the dead is born out of the belief that in the body there exist some entity like it, but independent of it and it survives the body after death. It is this very idea that underlies the faith in ghosts of various kinds believed to exist according to some of the Hindus. The concepts of deity or rebirth also arose out of it. The belief that mountain, river or tree, for example, has some such entity in them is also born out of this faith.

Hinduism attaches great significance to the mortuary rituals and the 'Shraddhas' of numerous kinds. There are Yajnas which are also based on there rituals. These 'Shraddhas' are also performed by the Hindus when they visit places of pilgrimage like Benares, Gaya or Prayaga (Allahabad). The custom of worshipping the dead kings, noble men or priests was also widely prevalent in ancient Egypt. In Hinduism also, hero-worship of Rama, Krishna, Jina or Buddha is simply a higher form of this worship of the dead.

The law of succession in Hinduism is closely connected with 'Shraddha'. One of the principle objects of the successory right according to the Smrities is the performance of the 'Shraddha'; and the purity of the family is also to be preserved for the same purpose. According to some of the Hindu religious texts, the property of the family is mainly meant for the performance of 'Shraddha' ; and one who does not perform it should not be allowed to inherit it, say the Smrities. This ritual has contributed a great deal to preservation of the caste system, because it is closely connected with the purity of the family.

The ancestor-worship prevalent among the Hindus has also influenced the idea of God. A number of religions in the world regard God as the mother, the father or the king. In ancient times, the chief of the gens or the clan used to be considered as the king or the father. Similarly the worship of mother earth is also prevalent among the Hindus since the earliest times. The worship of a

Goddess is fairly old and the Goddess is generally regarded as Mother.

We have discussed so far the earliest and the most primitive forms of religion in Hinduism. Along with them exists the relatively more developed forms also. One of them is the faith numerous deities, created in the image of man. There is an important place in Hinduism to the thought that beyond the visible objects of the world, are certain invisible superior powers ; that these are like human beings, possessed of human qualities and they control all the various material objects ; and that behaviour in conformity with their desire leads to well-being in this and the other world.

The various Gods in Rigveda like Indra, the Sun, and the Vauna are not merely the powerful elemental forces of nature, but the Rishis have also attributed human qualities to them all. Indra is a brave and powerful king. The Sun or the Varuna are the law givers and the dispensers of justice. The various human qualities such as art, knowledge, mercy, charity, piety, joy, bravery, love, hatred, anger and so on are to be found in them in perfection and they can be won over through devotion. The various Gods in present day Hinduism like Rama, Krishna, Hanumana, Shiva or Ganesha are also of a similar type. They have all the virtues and even the vices of man. They are proud, jealous, whimsical, full of hatred and amenable to flattery. The Yajnas in the Vedas, the various sacrificial or holy fires in the Smritis or the rites and the rituals in the Puranas have all been devised to please them and when pleased, they can be made to perform any miracle. The Vedic Gods are pleased by the sacrifice of goat, horse or the cow; or the offerings of bread, ghee or rice. The Gods from the Puranas are pleased through the offerings of Tulsi, grass or water, for they are the Gods of the poor. They are extremely happy when offered sweets, a palace, a bed, flowers, etc and confer boons. The devotee can then have any miracle performed by them.

In Hinduism, there are found still more developed concepts of Gods. These are the emotional contents of the objects and they too are worshipped. The life or consciousness, for example, is imagined as a God in the Vedas. Indra is the god of power, Varuna of Empire, Savita or the Sun of command; Saraswati the goddess of plenty or learning, Shree, the goddess of all the virtues in their perfection. (Shatapatha Brahmana ii).Prajapati is the lord of Procreation, Brahma of creation, Vishnu of preservation or protection, Rudra of destruction. Here God takes up a more subtle character.

Hinduism, attributing human qualities to Gods, has been described in the Shruties, Smrities and the Puranas. A religion, suggesting devotion to them all, establishing harmony between them or making one of them supreme and worshipping it, is found in a developed form in the Rigveda. Various religious sects, worshipping different deities arose in Hinduism and they have their peculiar marks, dress, rules of behaviour among themselves, and notions of purity or pollution.

In Hinduism is to be found further a more developed form of religion which consists of the spiritualist doctrine of the Brahma, monotheism and a philosophic religion. The doctrine of Brahma implies that all the deities are contained in a single all-pervading principle, and are parts of it. Everything arises out of that single principle and ultimately vanishes in it. It is a principle pervading the entire Universe. This is known as doctrine of Brahma. This arose in the roth Mandala (chapter) of Rigveda and attained its full development in the Upanishads. This Brahma is more subtle than the human soul of the omniscient and omnipotent God. The man who has known it can be said to have attained the highest. Self-control, peace of mind or generosity is more essential for its knowledge than the rituals. It is not a person but a principle, and hence more subtle than God, which is responsible for the Heavens, the salvation, the good or the evil results of one's actions.

Monotheism, which is a higher form of religion, is also found in Hindusim. The view that there is only one God who controls the Universe and all else is a result of his dispensation is Monotheism, the Shaiva and the Vaishnava sects believe in this. To devote oneself completely to him or to fully surrender to his desire is the only way to salvation. Truth, non-violence, mercy or self-control facilitate such devotion and are therefore the essence of religion. In the Upanishads also is to be found on occasions the idea that the favour of God leads to happiness and salvation while His wrath is responsible for sorrows, sufferings and degeneration (Chandogyopanishad and Shwetashwataropanishad). The monotheistic sects are non-Vedic in their origin. There existed such sects, inconsistent with the Vedic rituals as well as path of knowledge preached in the Upanishads in ancient India. The various Monotheistic sects like Vaishnavism, Shaivism, or the Shaktas arose out of these. Even the Bhagavad Gita was written after the Vasudeva sect was reconciled with the Vedic teachings.

The other developed form of religion in Hinduism is philosophic in character. Its earliest form is the Kapila and the Sankhya schools. These do not accept the existence of God. According to them, the soul of man attains salvation by recognising the principle underlying the Universe. This can be done only through a purification of the mind; and the mind can be purified through a pure and controlled behaviour, in conformity with moral norms like truth, non-violence and so on. The Jains or the Buddhists are also sects of similar nature; and they too do not accept the existence of God.

All these sects relegate the various rituals, forms of worship, pilgrimages, temples or the order of Varnas or Ashramas, to a subordinate position. But of all these, the Monotheistic or the pantheistic devotional religion is really the developed form of religion. The essence of all religions is the surrender to God. Monotheism or pantheism is the highest form of the development of human faith or devotion. With the philosophical forms or the doctrine of Brahma begins the critical examination and intellectual research of the foundation of faith. When these commence with a well developed logical rigidity, the foundations of religion begin to shake. The supernatural causes or interpretations disappear making room for logical reasoning.

Some of the modern scholars are seen often defending this eclecticism in Hinduism. Dr. S. Radhakrishnan is, for example, a leading case in point. He writes, "Hinduism is not based on any racial factor. It is an inheritance of thought and aspiration to which every race in India has made its distinctive contribution...Many features of modern Hinduism are derived from very primitive sources...While the vedas represent the religion of the classes, the masses continued to worship their traditional deities, Yaksas and Nagas. Behind the facade of Vedic orthodoxy and its tendency to abstract symbolism, an extensive and deep-rooted system of popular beliefs and cults and a decided tendency to anthropomorphic presentation prevailed. The Vedic religion, however, absorbed, embodied and preserved the types and rituals of older cults. Instead of destroying them, it adapted them to its own requirements. It took so much from the social life of the Dravidians and other native inhabitants of India that it is very difficult to disentangle the original Aryan elements from others. The interpenetration has been complex, subtle and continuous with the result that there has grown up a distinct Hindu civilisation which is neither Aryan nor Dravidians nor Aboriginal. Ever since the dawn of reflection the dream of unity has hovered over the scene and haunted the imagination of the leaders... Though the religions of Islam and Christianity by their militant attitude occasionally provoked similar developments in Hinduism, its prevailing note continues to be one of understanding and acceptance of the *bona fides* of other faiths...As a result of this tolerant attitude, Hinduism itself has become a mosaic of almost all types and stages of religious aspiration and endeavours."*

A number of scholars in the last century also advanced a similar defence. But this is fallacious. Preservation or acceptance of primitive notions is not a mark of tolerance and generosity; it is rather a sign of weakness. Since the primitive notions lead to a general decay and demoralisation, they come to be replaced by the more developed ones. It is, therefore, an illusion to go on believing that they too contain an element of truth. It becomes on the contrary, in the course of evolution, a duty to destroy them. It may be argued that the ignorant mass cannot assimilate the more developed notions; but this is not true. All those backward social groups which were barred by Hinduism from inheriting the religion of the classes were actually converted by the religions of Islam and Christianity and were made the basis of more developed religious institutions. That the destruction of primitive religious ideas or institutions and the creation of new and more developed ones in their place do prove that at a certain stage of social development, conducive to progress, has been clearly demonstrated by both Islam and Christianity. When Buddhism, Islam, or Christianity rushed forth to destroy the earlier primitive religions, they shattered a number of such illusions; and cleared the human mind of them, Hinduism on the other hand tried to preserve them. It was neither noble nor heroic, but it was weak and unable to do what it ought to have done.

Hinduism is not a religion; it is rather a mosaic of various primitive and developed religious forms. It is wrong to argue that it has no dogma; in fact, it has a number of dogmas. If it is to be considered as tolerant because it does not demand faith in any particular prophet, dogma or sect, it will be equally legimitate to consider the entire humanity as tolerant, for it too allows various religions and does not demand faith in any one of them. There is not a single thing in Hindu life which is not controlled by dogma or custom. The authority of a dogma or prophet or customs or traditions is applicable to every one of them. There are numerous dogmas and numerous prophets which have made Hinduism almost a museum. That Hindus worship the prophets of Islam or Christianity is not due to generosity or freedom of thought and opinion. It is rather a result of weakness, of imbecility. The tendency to surrender to any deity or prophet shows that weakness. When faith blinds vision, illusions throttle reasons, emotions are entangled with delusive ideals of other worldly blessings, and the mind naturally becomes weak and prone to surrender to anyone.

It is historically wrong to interpret this feature of Hinduism as motivated by a desire to enable the various groups and sects and live amicably together. Hinduism did not preserve or assimilate them with that purpose. The different communities that had come together in India also had their religious or social life and institutions. They intermingled with each other. It is not that the preservation of their religious or social thought and institutions led to their assimilations into the Hindu fold; but rather their coming together was responsible for inter-mingling of their thought and institutions. And this mixing up was not due to any humanitarian love but had its causes in migration, wars and search for the means of subsistence. Generosity is not its cause. The caste system or the system of Varnas is full of absence of this generosity. If it were really generous, the subjection of the Shudras, untouchability or the gradation of the caste system based on birth, which have been prevalent in it for centuries together, would never have become its important features; nor would the Smrities have propounded laws prescribing capital punishment to Shudras, transgressing the laws of the Vedic religion. The numerous primitive forms could survive in Hinduism, because an adequate organised force was never created in support of its more developed ones. There did not arise many prophets in it, moved by the inspiration of nobler ideas, and determined to show humanity, at various stages of development, the path of well-being, thus freeing it from the grip of primitive notions and illusions; and those who did arise could not succeed because of the peculiar social environment. Islam wielded together hundreds of nomadic tribes of the Turks, Arabs and the Central Asian people, fighting for centuries together amongst themselves, into a forceful and vigorous society. If the earlier history of these tribes is closely seen, it will be clear that they were in no way superior to those lower strata of the Hindu society. The same can be said about Buddhism or Christianity. To allow a various low and primitive illusions to remain under the garb of tolerance is a sign of intellectual and mental degeneration.

The monotheistic, pantheistic or philosophic religions contain broad principles conducive to a descent existence and leading the primitive communities onwards along the path of progress, when those principles themselves come to occupy a predominant position, the religious institutions founded on them start spreading. The primitive religious forms disappear, and scope is provided to the development of art as well as various natural and social sciences based on reasons. These higher forms of religion cannot develop and expand unless they have relegated the particular primitive rites, the peculiar narrow social customs and rituals to a definite subordinate position. The ability to transgress the limits of a particular community, race or nation and to take up a universal form can arise only out of such subordination. Where on other hand, rites, rituals and customs dominate religions can never become effective and powerful, no matter how broad principles, on which it is based, are. The traditions and customs of any particular community cannot be adopted by other communities to any significant extent. It is only religions which provide an important place to broad principles or which accept simply one particular prophet and dogma, that have the capacity of quickly spreading out.

Hinduism does not belong to any of these categories, the rituals of different communities, religious forms in family, caste of regions as well as various mutually inconsistent traditions and customs acquired permanence in it. Numerous tiny communities, their customs, traditions and rites acquired sanctity, purity and respectability. Political or social forces, making a clean sweep of the narrow limitations and restrictions as impediments in the way of progress and organising the social life on broad premises with a powerful authority at the centre, did not hold their sway for a long time in India. They waned, before fully developing, with the result that the narrow restrictive laws of the Shruties and Smrities themselves continued to dominate till the end. Broad religious principles remained in suspense and had never the power to destroy the old primitive religious forms or build up a new social organisation.

The task of keeping this mosaic of Hinduism alive was performed by the priestly class. The realistic thought pertaining to things of this world could not therefore develop nor could a social organisation sustaining it. The priestly class, sustained by the primitive religion, is itself alone responsible for this confusion, caste system and social backwardness. A class maintaining itself on the basis of faith in the stars, the dead, the ghosts and various other similar illusions, sought to preserve and foster that faith out of simple selfish considerations. It could perpetuate its domination over the community only in that peculiar manner. The religion of the Puranas can bear clear testimony to that.

New thought tends to become effective in societies where other productive classes succeed in overthrowing the domination of the priestly class. With the relegation of the priests to the background, arise science and philosophy. The universal religion of Christianity dominated Europe owing to the stability of the Roman Empire for a long time. The rise of the trading and the warrior classes in Arabia led to the rise of Islam. It was classes other than the Brahmins that established in India Universal religions like Buddhism. Modern western civilisation also arose after the decline of the power of the priests. It is only when human society emerged out of its primitive barbaric stage, this class played a progressive role; but thereafter it has been a continual impediment in the way of progress. The history of India clearly show this fact and the confused form of Hinduism is also result of this.

Hindu Philosophy of History

Let us now turn to the statement of the philosophy of history that we find in Hinduism; its view of social events, their dynamics, growth and decay. The divine as well as the material or human interpretations are both found in it. The doctrines of reincarnation as well as that of the Yugas belong to the former category. That God takes birth as a human being from time to time and saves man from various calamities is the statement found in the Mahabharata, Gita and the Puranas, which is a statement of the theory of reincarnation. Various Puranas point out that human or social life degenerates when Rakshasas or Asuras are born in society, while it progresses and prospers with the birth of the Gods. There is also the theory of the cyclical movement of the four Yugas. Life decays in the Kali Yuga while it prospers in the Krita Yuga. Thus, its decay or prosperity is a result of the times. There is a tone of inevitability about these movements. All this implies that prosperity or decline is an outcome of the divine, supernatural beings or forces and that man entirely depend upon these and is helpless. He is poor victim of fate or the Gods.

The worldly or material interpretation of history on the other hand, has been narrated by Bhishma in the Shanti Parva of the Mahabharata. With a good king, comes in prosperity while degeneration is a result of a wicked person coming to the throne. Social prosperity or decline is thus a result of the institution of kingship. The king can make a particular Yuga Krita or Kali. He is the cause of the times.

There is another theory also to be found in the Mahabharata. It says that the people themselves are the cause of social prosperity or social decline. It is they who make and unmake the king. They used to manage their own affairs on the basis of norms decided by them among themselves in a peaceful and harmonious manner. In course of time anarchy prevailed and the law of the jungle came to dominate. Hence they made Manu their king. It will thus be seen that even in the early times, Indian thought had advanced to the stage of furnishing a secular explanation of historical development in place of one in terms of the supernatural or divine causes. Social life unfortunately was not developed to an adequate extent so that this bold thought may thrive with the result that it was defeated in the end. There is another interpretation also to be found in the Shruties and the Smrities. It says that the conditions of social existence are dependent upon the priest and the king. If they are conscious and dutiful, society prospers or else it declines.

The various other religions such as Judaism, Zoroastrianism, Christianity or Islam simply furnish the divine interpretation. According to Zoroastrianism for example, the domination of falsehood means the beginning of the dark ages in human history. Those dark ages still continue and will in course of time gradually disappear when the dawn of enlightenment and truth will appear. The kingdom of God will then be established on the earth. Christianity or Islam considers Satan as the source of evil, and responsible for decline and decay. A concept similar to that of the above one in Zoroastrianism is also found in them. From time to time the holy prophets of God come in order to show man the path of the right. Jesus according to Christianity, and Mohammad, according to Islam, was the last and the greatest of such prophets. All the religions subscribe to the view that the satanic forces make life vicious while on the other hand, the divine forces are responsible for the establishment of a happy and prosperous kingdom of God.

With the rise of the various systems of philosophy in Hinduism there came up along with the idea of social prosperity or decline, that of individual salvation or Moksha also.

Hinduism - An Historical View

Hinduism has come to its present form through a long process which is marked by various stages. Some of them can clearly be defined such as tribal religion; the pre-Vedic polytheistic religion; the religion of the Shruties and the Smrities professed by the Vedic Aryans; the various universal religions like Shaivism, Vaishnavism, Jainism, Buddhism and the Hinduism of the Shruties, Smrities and the Puranas.

The existence of a number of tribal religions was a mark of humanity in its most primitive stages. Religion exists in this form in the nomadic stage of existence before the rise of a stable social order based upon elementary division of labour and marked by the beginnings of agriculture and other arts. The Sun, the Moon, the Fire, the cobra etc where all early tribal Gods, the festival of 'Naga Panchami' is a relic of the customs of the tribe of Nagas which existed in earlier times in India. The Ramayana indicates the existence of the tribe of Vanaras with Hanumana as their tribal God. Some of the Vedic scholars contend that the different Aryan tribes had their different tribal Gods. Every tribe had its own God and often they both had the same name. When a variety of social factors brought these tribes together, there took place a mixing up of their customs and their objects and modes of worship, many of which are still seen in Hinduism. Tribal magic is one such primitive form of religion. The primitive tribes similarly used to celebrate some common festival on which occasion all the members of the tribe would assemble together for the celebration in order that the tribe may thrive or there may be general prosperity. Some religious rites as well as communal dances used to be important constituents of these festivals. The festival of Holi is a significant ritual of tribal magic. There are also village gods, and regional gods, which were earlier merely tribal Gods. The Goddesses of Manasa and Kali are worshipped. in Bengal; that of Shitala in U.P.; the Gods of Goriya and Dilligoriya in Bihar, Kartikswami in Tamil Nadu or Biroba and Khandoba in Maharashtra. These regional and similar other village Gods also arose from the primitive tribal Gods.

The worship of various trees and animals is also a form of primitive religion. Some sociologists argue that this might have been the religion of the earliest inhabitants of India namely, the Negritos. It may also be a possible Vedic tradition. In Atharvaveda, for example, herbs are worshipped as Gods. In the Yajurveda, certain trees, used on the occasion of the Yajanas, are considered sacred and are worshipped. These may be therefore the relics of the very ancient primitive life of the Vedic Aryans. Umbara, Pimpla, Banyan are all sacrificial trees while the cow or the bull are sacrificial animals. In many other religions also, is found this custom of attributing sacredness or sanctity to the sacrificial animals. The custom of offering human sacrifies is found in the earlier stages in almost all the communities of the world. The British law in India has prohibited human sacrifice; but the custom is still found, though very rarely, in certain parts of the country. Human sacrifice is also prescribed in Vedas. The custom might then have disappeared. But there is evidence to show that it must has existed among the Vedic Aryans at some stage of their development. That the soul in the human body should be sacrificed for attaining general prosperity was a widely prevalent belief which must have been responsible for this custom though it has fallen into disuse for a long time in Hinduism.

The pre-Vedic religion in India has a striking similarity with the religion of the ancient communities in Egypt, Persia and so on. The oldest Indian culture bears this resemblance with the culture in the Mediterranean regions or in central and western Asia; according to Dr Guha and Keith, the unearthed relics of ancient Indian civilisation at Mohenjodaro and Harappa indicate a racial similarity between the earlier Indian inhabitants and the inhabitants of these regions. The pre-Vedic religions existed five thousand years ago along the banks of the river Indus. The human race that established this civilisation is known as the Mediterranean or the Armenoid race. The historians, owing to this similarity, can now disclose one of the earliest and unknown chapters and Indian history. In the earlier civilisations of Egypt, Crete and Mesopotamia are also found the Gods of Shiva, Vishnu, the Goddess of Kali, worship of the Naga (cobra), Linga (genital organs), the Moon, the Graha (the planets), and the ancestors. The terms Linga and Puja or not be found in the Vedas at all; they are non-Vedic terms. The worship of the Linga, the nine Grahas or the Goddesses is nowhere mentioned in the main Vedic literature. The custom of Devadasis (religious prostitutes), idol worship, astrology, seven days, the art of writing, the hereditary priest in temples etc. are all features of the Mediterranean civilisation. Hinduism thus inherits a number of things peculiar to the civilisations which arose along the banks of Nile, the Tigris and Euphratis and the Indus. This indeed is the pre-Vedic Indian civilisation; and the religion of it is an important constituent of Hinduism. It is on this foundation that the religion of the Hindus has grown for centuries together.

The Shrouta-Smarta religion is the religion of the Aryans. They came and conquered the pre-Vedic inhabitants of India; but could not establish their domination all over the country. Their domination began with the western and north-western India and gradually spread directly or indirectly all over in two ways-through direct conquests by the kings or indirect spread of the influence persists. They were originally nomadic, hunting tribes, with ambitions to conquer and used to rear up herds of cattle. It is believed that they might have conquered the earlier inhabitants through the use of the horse in warfare. Being nomadic they had a number of qualities useful for warring tribes and could become therefore easily victorious over the stable agricultural communities. The sacrifice of cow, goat, or horse was feature of their religious institutions. The priests in their Yajnas used to be offered cows, horse, goats and other animals or precious metals like gold and silver, which simply goes to show that they were mainly cattle-rearing tribes. It is only in the later stages that we find the offer of land. There is no mention of it in the Rigveda; most of which was written considerably after their conquests. The main feature of their religion in those days also was the worship of natural elements of forces, believed consciously to be possessed of power. This worship is the Yajna. The main object of that worship or the Yajnas was to attain with the help of these forces the requisites of a proper material existence. Magic also had a place in their religion; and is mainly stated in the Atharvaveda. The earlier form of Yajna was also magical as it appears from the Kamyeshti Yajna.

The Sun worshipped under various names by the Vedic people. Similarly there other Gods like Varuna, the Earth, Vishwakarman, Aditi, Ashwi, Indra, Marut, Rudra and so on, mentioned in the Vedas. The composer of the hymns in Rigveda often mentions each one of them as an omniscient and an omnipotent being. The original differentiaion in their powers thus appear to vanish in the times of the Rigveda; and each one of them is elevated to the position of God. Though, the Yajurveda in its present form dates after the samhitas or hymns of Rigveda, its description of rituals of Yajana can be said to be older since it mentions separate identity of this deities. These deities are also mentioned in the Atharvaveda, though there, they seem to have been used for magical purposes.

The magic in Atharvaveda also belongs to the Vedic Aryans. Several Rishis from Rigveda, Vashistha for instance, knew magic. Bhrigu, Angiras and Atharvan were also conversant with it. Ayurveda or the medicine of those days was also magic. The quality of being a deity has been attributed to the natural objects or elements. When man, for example, was incapable of understanding the material nature of objects like the sun or the fire, it was quite natural for him to imagine these to be possessed of supernatural powers. Mitra and Varuna are the day and the night thus imagined to be Gods. Savitr is the autumnal sun, for in autumn the seeds germinate and begin to grow. Pushan is the sun that feeds and strengthens the crops and the herbs. It is difficult to state exactly the nature of Indra and Bhaga, though it is quite possible to imagine it. Indra is a warrior, who attacks the enemy, is fond of Somarasa and who can easily devour a whole roasted bull or some other animal. He is the lord of the thundering skies. Marut *i.e.* the killer is his helpmate. The sprit, energy and zeal of the Aryan, hunting the wild animals, and defending his cattle from them and getting fully intoxicated and violent with a good drink of somarasa, is thus Indra. Sometime this Indra used to haunt the seers and the sages. There are hymns composed by Indra, found in the Rigveda. When the Rishi began to compose the hymn, he and the people around him imagined that Indra had hunted him and was composing it. Rudra is a deity of storms, while Aditi of the endless or infinite skies.

It may not be possible to indicate the material basis of all the deities in the above manner; but it is no longer a matter of controversy among the scholars that many of them have such a basis; and that they were prayed and worshipped in order to obtain the requisites of material existence. Thus, religion and its ancillary notions arose in the beginning to satisfy the material needs of mankind. Many of these, for instance, are dependent for their satisfaction upon the sun and the fire, which were continually worshipped by the Vedic householder, the worship being known as Agnihotra. It was the main mode of worship of the Aryans who were preoccupied with the rearing of cattle and who regarded agriculture as subordinate to it. Another important ritual was the *Darshapurnamaseshti*, which had the preservation of the cow as its important feature. The attainment of salvation as its result has been mentioned only in the later Vedic literature or the Brahmanas. In the Vedic mantras and prayers, it is only the material needs that are continually talked about. There is a continual demand for grains, animals, wealth, physical strength, woman, salve, a brave son, destruction of the enemy, averting of disease and similar other material needs. The heavens appear much later in the Vedic literature in the Brahmanas. There is reference to the other-worldly life in the Vedic rituals but there is nowhere a comprehensive or elaborate statement of it. Many of the otherworldly ideas are similarly found in the Vedas but their elaboration or discussion is found only in the later Vedic literature and the Upanishads.

The various rites as well as the doctrine of the Ashramas or stages of life are found in the Vedas. But in the period of the Rigveda it is only two stages of life, the student and the householder, that seem to be recognised. It is only in the Upanishads that we have a mention of the four stages. That there is even a statement in the Vedas that they accept only one stage that of the house-holder; and that the other stages are rejected by them is the opinion of one stage mentioned in the Gautama Dharma Sutras. There are one or two statements in the Rigveda which indicate that the first Ashrama, namely the Brahmacharin, was mainly meant for the attainment of knowledge. An elaborate statement regarding this stage is found in the Brahmanas as well as in the Atharvaveda; while all in the four stages have been mentioned in the *Chandogyo-panishad.*

The Vedic Aryans seem to have taken the other two stages viz. the hermit retiring to the jungle and the

Sanyasin from the culture of the non-Vedic people; but it took a long time for them to assimilate these forms. Long before the Vedic Aryans were civilised, the non-Vedic people had developed civilisation to a very high degree in Egypt, Iraq and India; and it is these non-Vedic civilisations that left their imprint upon the Vedic civilisation which borrowed a number of social customs and traditions as well as a vast store of knowledge from them. But this was done under social conditions in which there arose the need for Sanyasa or renunciation.

The concept of the sixteen rites is found only in the later SMRITI literature. The Gautama Dharma Sutra, which is an earlier work then all the SMRITIES, includes even the YAJNA as a rite; and has mentioned forty types of them. The sixteen rites are mainly connected with the ATHARAVAVEDA. In the KAUSHIK and GRIHYA Sutras of the ATHARVAVEDA these are elaborately mentioned but there is no mention of sixteen types or any other classification in the older GRIHYA Sutras. Besides these sixteen types of rites, there are also mentioned SULA-GAVA, indicative of a primitive life. The caste rites, the naming (NAMAKARANA) thread ceremony, (UPA-NAYANA), marital rites (VIVAHA), ANTYESHTI (the mortuary rites) are all found from the Anthropological studies and traveller's accounts, to be still existent among the primitive communities in Africa, Australia, America and the Pacific islands.

The beginning of the doctrine of the Varnas is to found in the Rigveda. The mention of the four Varnas in the tenth mandala of the Rigveda belongs to the later Rigveda period. The mention of Brahma and Kshatra is of a much earlier period and is found together, the terms "Arya Varna" (the masters) and the "Dasa Varna" (the salves) also occur at one place. Dasa Varna means the lower Varna or the Sudras. If the entire Vedic literature is seen carefully, it will be found that the Vedic Aryans had created a new class of the conquered slaves; and the conquering Aryans were their masters. The dominating classes of the Aryans were the Brahmins, the Kshatriyas and Vaishyas; and the entire power in society was concentrated in the hands of the former two. The social laws and restrictions were laid down in order to make the Sudras toil under the domination of Aryans. The right to perform the Vedic Yajna was kept by them to themselves. There is no historical basis for the view that because the non-Vedics were more backward or primitive, they were put in a subordinate or inferior position. The non-Vedic people were proficient in agriculture and various other arts. They had their huge kingdoms in existence in India; some of which were conquered by the Vedic Aryans. The people under these kingdom came under the Aryan domination and the institution of Varnas was created; and thus an attempt was made to monopolies the wealth, power, honour and purity in society. The vast bulk of the community (nearly 75 per cent) on the other hand, proficient in agriculture and other arts, was reduced to the position of slaves.

The institutions of religion were thus used by the Vedics to bring the non-Vedic masses under their domination; and the Vedic Yajna served them well in this connection. They fostered, for example, the idea that wealth has been created by prajapati for Yajna; and thus made it religious to deprive the Sudra of his wealth. Even milk obtained from the Sudra's milking the cow was considered impure for the purposes of the Yajana. Any Vedic Aryan possessed the right to punish the Sudra in anyway he liked or to drive him out of the community.

The Sudra was assigned a three-fold duty; agriculture, craft and service of higher Varnas. Agriculture or craft are in sense important professions. But the Sudras had to undergo a hard life, full of sufferings, for they were deprived of most of the fruits of their toil. With the help of tyranical laws, the Vedic Aryans appropriated a large bulk of their produce. There were incomparably higher rates interest and rent for the Sudras than for others. The burden of these was reduced by law so far as the higher three Varnas were concerned; while it was the heaviest on the productive class of Sudras, who produced most of the wealth of the community and thus constituted the foundation of its social existence. Rate of interest or rent as high as 60 per cent was allowed legally under the laws of the Smrities, to be recovered from them.

The followers of the Shrouta-Smarta religion utilised the sanctity of the Vedas for strengthening the bonds of social slavery of the non-Vedics. They refused the right to order their conduct in conformity with the Vedic injunctions, to the rest of the community. There is a rite named Vratyastoma, mentioned in the Tandya Brahmana of the Sama Veda as well as in the Katyayana Shroutasutra, the object of which seems to be the conversion of the non-Vedic into the Vedic; but it appears to have been very rarely performed. In the old Sutras and Smrities, a Sudra trying to study the Vedas has been condemned to capital punishment. It was thus only the Aryan, purified by the performance of the Vedic Yajna and observance of the Smriti religion, who was the real master of society. His birth gave him the right to follow the Vedic religion and his right brought him his superiority and mastery. The Brahmin got this superior position by virtue of this priestly function. There are some who have argued that by Brahmin was implied a self-less, self-controlled, learned, and hermit-like being. But this figurative meaning is not correct according to the shrouta-smarta law. That law prescribes a very mild punishment to a Brahmin even guilty of adultery with a woman of the other Varnas; and he is also allowed to marry her. Even important shruties and smrities permit him to have concubines from among the women of the sudras. On the other hand, Sudra marrying or commiting adultery with Brahmin women or of any other higher Varna is to be awarded a deliberately painful capital punishment.

There is no offence for which the Brahmin can get the death sentence. In fact, there ought to have been a severe punishment prescribed for a Brahmin deviating from the path of selflessness control or penance. But the law of the shruties and the Smrities says exactly the opposite. The Brahmin and the others Aryans according to that law, enjoy a large number of rights and privileges as compared with the Sudras. The facilities provided by this law to the Brahmins in connection with the enjoyments of wealth, power and honour are indeed almost unparalleled anywhere. The various virtues often associated with the Brahmins are in fact that not very important in the eyes of the laws of the Smrities. The only learning that it valued was the learning of the Vedas and the task of priesthood. The Brahmins generally were the only dispenser of justice, and failing a Brahmin, the Kshatriyas and the Vaishyas would do it. But the Smrities very categorically assert that no matter how learned, the Sudra can never dispense justice. Rates of interest and rent were to be the lowest for the Brahmin according to the Smrities. In dispensing justice, the Brahmin was to be dealt with first. The Brahmin and the other higher Varnas were allowed to pursue the occupation of the Shudras, but the Sudras were prohibited from taking up those of the other higher Varnas; even when in serious difficulties. It was considered to be a serious offence.

It may be felt that the above discussion is a digression since we have referred more to the Smrities and less to the Vedas. It is well known that the laws of the Dharma Sutra and the Smrities were those of the Vedic Aryans. The social law of the Smrities is founded upon the gradation of the various Varnas. This law is found in the Vedas themselves actually to a very little extent. The general and particular principles underlying this law are only found there. The rituals of the Yagnas and the knowledge of the Brahmans are alone found in the Vedas and the Upanishads. On the other hand, the Sutras and the

Smrities provide a collection of the laws which were gradually coming to prevail in the Vedic times. The meaning of the term 'Smriti' is itself a compilation from memory of the customs, laws and traditions prevalent among the Vedic Aryans. The Vedas on the other hand are a presentation together of the rituals, the hymns sung to the gods and the knowledge of the Brahman possessed by the Vedic Aryans. The compilation of the Smrities was done in the period after the Vedas were composed. If they had been compiled when the Mantras or the Brahmanas were written, they too would have been styled as the Vedas. It is essential because of this old tradition of the religion in the smrities that the authors of the Sutras as well as Manu could assert that the religion from the smrities is also Vedic or has originated from the Vedas. It is true that in the post–Vedic period there was a considerable addition or change made in the religious code of the Smrities. But barring some of the Smrities like Parashara, the main framework of the religious code in the Smrities and the Sutras is mostly one and the same. The form of the varnas institution or the social system founded on it, as described in the smrities of Gautama, Apastamba, Vasistha, Shankhalikhita, Manu, Yajnavalkya, Narada, Brhaspati, and so on in the almost alike; and it is this that has been described above.

The Vedic religion is not the religion of all. It is simply the religion of a group of people; and was kept by them aloof from the rest of the society; and utilised for establishing their domination over the vast masses of the people.

The domination of Brahmin and the subjection of the Sudra are the outstanding features of the social system of the Vedic Aryans. Even in the Vedic times, there arose a reaction among the Kshatriya against this domination of the Brahmins, and it took two forms. Some of the kings began to claim the privileges of the Brahmins. This was the point in the dispute of Vishwamitra and Vasistha; and the story of Vishwamitra shows that the kings could get those privileges at least to some extent. The Puranas also mention that a number of royal families attained the position of the Brahmins. The other forms of the reaction was the dispute regarding the extra rights and privileges enjoyed by the Brahmins. A number of kings fought against this Brahmanic superiority. The King Vena was against the Yajna and the offering made to the priests on that occasion. Haihaya and Vaitahavya fought against the freedom enjoyed by the Brahmins from all taxes as is clear from the facts that they tried to forcibly take away the cows of the Brahmins. Animals were used in those days as means of exchange instead of money. Parashuram again tried to establish the Brahminic privilege by the defeating and destroying the Kshatriya. The wars of the Mahabharata settled the issues in dispute. The Kshatriyas were almost destroyed. The internecine conflict in Mahabharata achieved what Parashurama had failed to achieve. The domination of the Brahmins was once again established and the Kshatriya had to take up the subordinate position.

It was only after this that the Brahmins developed the various branches of learning. The doctrine of the salvation arose. The Upanishads proved the futility of the Vedic Yagna and the deities. Out of their subtle criticism arose the doctrine of Brahma and spiritual worship. The general rituals of worship of numerous deities began to weaken and to decline. The social atmosphere, unsuitable to the Yagnas and the religious institutions founded on it, helped the process. The roots of this weakness lay in the social system of the Vedas itself. The prevalence of non-Vedic customs and rituals among the non–Aryans who were now coming into contract with the Aryans also had its influence. The stable social order established along the Vedic lines began to show signs of senility. Thinking sections of the community began to show signs of senility. Thinking sections of the community began to subject the Vedic traditions to a searching and critical analysis.

Old ideas, old deities began to melt away making room for a new thought. The various religious notions like Brahmans, renunciation, detachment, monotheism and pantheism are born during this period.

In the days of the Upanishads, the meditative thought which attached great significance to renunciation detachment or hermit like resort to the forest came into prominence because it was becoming increasingly difficult to perform the Yajnas or the duties of the householder under the existing a social conditions. In the process of social disintegration, many a household was disturbed and ruined. It began to be believed that the religion of the Sanyasin was superior came to be regarded as more important than those of the student (Brahmachari) and the householder.

The religions of Shaivism, Vaishanavism, Jainism and Buddhism were the creation of the non-Vedic classes; and the royal families not connected with priests took the lead in the matter. When the Vedic institution of Yajnas with its domination of the Brahmins began to decline owing to the operation of various internal and external factors these religions began to prosper. That was nearly twenty five centuries ago. Their superiority over the Vedic religion consisted in the fact that they showed the way of well being to all. Universal religions, proclaiming that man, irrespective of his birth or environment, can attain the highest position possible, arouse in India earlier than in any other country of the world and they led the revolt against the social system established by the Aryans. According to the Vedic religion, it was only the three Varna's that were regarded as pure in the eyes of religions, and with the help of this religious holiness of things, they made the Sudras toil for them and appropriated to themselves all the enjoyments of this world and the claims to religious superiority. This sanctity of a few and degradation of many, both determined by birth, came to be destroyed under the impact of the new Universal religions.

Vaishnavism and Shaivism have a tradition from the pre-Vedic times. They prevailed in numerous civilised groups other than the Vedics. In the western and north-western parts of India, the followers of these religions began to preach monotheism. Devotion to Vasudeva was prevalent in the times of the Vedas and has been styled as Narayaneeya religion in the Mahabharata. Devotion to Shiva was also prevalent from Kashmir to Bengal and from the Himalayas to Rameshwaram. A number of leading thinkers arose in these religions who condemned the institution of Yajna, sacrifice of animals, and the importance of the Brahmins. They were mainly responsible for the spread of the idea that God is one; and that all can reach him through devotion; that all other religious rituals have no significance as compared to devotion; that devotion and moral behaviour can lead the individual to salvation; and that this can be attained by any one, be he a Brahmin, a Kshatriya, a Vaishya or a Sudra.

Originally these sects were opposed to the Vedas, but their acceptance by the Vedic Brahmins dissolved this opposition. In the post-Buddhistic Hindu society, they occupy a very important position. Bhagavad Gita appeared when Vaishnavism became merged into the Vedic religion. The religions of the Puranas were also brought into being by those who accepted the monotheism of these sects. The low non-Vedic notions were attached with great importance by the puranas. Astrology, worship of the stars and the planets, rituals and pilgrimages and various other similar things were picked up from these religions by the Brahmins who used them to maintain themselves and to foster ignorance and fatalism in society.

In the eastern regions of northern India, there arose the other two important religions of the world, Jainism and Buddhism, among the non-Vedic civilised communities. These are also universal religions; because in them also the central thought was that anyone with the help of pure and moral behaviour can attain spiritual well-being. These were however more sceptical religions and attacked vehemently the Vedas, God and the Yajna; Shramanas belonging to the ruling Kshatriya class, created these religions, in order to attack the social system based on Brahmanic supremacy, and change it, they attacked its three-fold roots.

From the religious literature of the Jains and the Buddhists as well as of the Brahmanas, it appears that the main heresies were spread by the shramanas and the monks. Charvaka was a profound critical intellect; but the Mahabharata also regards him as a monk. The culture of the shramanas arose in the beginning among the non-Vedics; for their society was still more ancient. They therefore began to feel much earlier the evil results of the social system of the dominating Vedics. The Mahabharta mentions Takshaka, a king from the Naga tribe, as a nude shramana. The story of the sarpasatra form the Adiparva of the Mahabharata clearly shows that the Vedic Aryans were the enemies of the Nagas. On the other hand, the tales from the religious literature of the Jains indicate that Nagas were the friends of the Jain Tirthankaras (religious apostles) and had defended them against dangers on many occasions. Buddha similarly was born in a tribal society. It was among the non-Vedics that sects like Jatila, Mundi, Tapasa, Parivrajaka, Ajeevaka etc. arose in the beginning. Later on they found a place in the Vedic Aryans also.

The various non-Vedic communities lifted up their head when the need for a new order became patent as a result of the decline of the Vedic social system. They felt the necessity of the breaking the dependence of society on the priests; combatting the domination of rites and rituals that had arisen out of the selfish and pleasure-seeking attitude of the priests. Thinkers like Charvaka, for example, very vehemently attacked these rituals and there upholders, the parasitic priests.

The Brahmins use to kill various animals like, cow etc. for the sake of Yajna and their feasts. The kings were continually engaged in fratricidal wars, which prevented the peaceful pursuits of agriculture, commerce and such others things from developing. The need arose thus of some overriding sovereign power. The social parasites drawing their living from the toil of the productive classes had considerably increased. The Sudras were mainly these classes but since they belonged to the lowest of the social ladder, the political authority never cared to defend their interests. Both production and distribution of wealth were thus disorganised and the entire society faced the prospect of disintegration with its concomitant evils. It was this social environment that bred religion which emphsised renunciation, control and contentment and which taught to look at everything in this world as an illusion. The knowledge and understanding of the social order on the other hand had not developed upto a point at which the idea of remodelling the entire social structure with a view to making it conducive to harmony and progress could arise. There was therefore no alternative to rise of the spiritualistic outlook which regarded destruction or conquest of desire as eternal truth and a noble idea. The social system of the Vedic had no capacity to establish harmony or order. There was no doubt that thought of material well being in the Vedic tradition but it was not adequate to solve the great social problem. There was no scope for material development and progress beyond a limited extent in the social order of the Vedas. It is not enough to have material ideals; they must be capable of guiding social change in order to be attained and to be conducive to social development. But the Shrouta-Smarta social order had exhausted its possibilities from that point of view and had become a fetter on social progress. The soul, cramped and crumbled under the strong and rigid restriction, cried out that life is all misery, and nothing else but misery. Kapila, Buddha, and the Jain apostles all proclaimed with one voice that it was misery.

Every philosophy of life is a product of peculiar social conditions. This pessimistic philosophy, characterising life as all misery, was thus a product of the existing social order, twenty-five century ago. It was the cry of humanity seeking and struggling to emerge out of those conditions. Religion, philosophy or literature is not merely the expression of individual thoughts or feelings. They also inform us regarding the social forces and struggles. Buddha was the greatest leader of this new religious upheaval; and he had among his disciples from all classes and strata of society. Brahmins, Kshatriyas, Kings, Merchants, Sudras, and women all had joined the ranks of his followers. It was his rule that people should be taught and advised in the language of their everyday use; and he used the Prakrita language of the two kingdom- Magadha and Kosala, for his purposes; while commentaries on his message were written in the Pali, Paishachi, and Apabhransha languages.

Truth, non-violence, plain living, limited food, conquest of desire and the transitoriness of life were the main planks of his advice. It was his opinion that one should better not go into the root cause of the universe and the God. He did not support any one-sided view; nor was his whole emphasis on renunciation. He used to claim that his was the golden mean; but there was the belief that the condition of the monk is higher and nobler than the rest, and that through purification of the mind and conquest or destruction of desire, one can attain Nirvana or the highest bliss. The post-Buddhistic Hinduism has completely accepted that life is transitory and that destruction of desire can lead to salvation. The Gita, for example, clearly states that this life is full of misery and transitory and that the stage of Sthitaprajna means the end of all desire. This doctrine originated in the Upanishads, was strengthened by Buddhism, and at last was accepted in its entirety, by

Hindusim. The non-violence preached by Buddha was opposed to the violence committed at the time of the Yajnas. He did not, however, preach the renunciation of kingship.

Movements based upon human reason and rational thinking were developing in India when Buddhism arose. It was an age of social transition. The religious laws were yielding place to those of polity. Thinkers were arising, who subjected the concepts of God, the Vedas, Yajnas, society, the world, morality, religion and its authority all to a fundamental criticism. The criticism of the Vedas, God and the Yajnas began in the Upanishads themselves. God no longer remained an individual in the Upanishads; he became a broad, universal principle. Thinkers like Buddha and others came to the conclusions that he was not a proper subject for criticism nor could he be proved with reason, Kapila and others on the other hand, proved his non-existence. Vaishnavas proved that futility of yajnas for religious purposes. The monotheists and the atheists both raised morality to the status of religion. Some writers on polity regarded the otherworldly concepts as merely symbolic and tried to establish that the utility of religious institutions was simply in this world. Even the supposed eternal notions like truth, non-violence, etc. were proved inadequate in the Santi Parva of the Mahabharata. It was proved logically and in the light of experience that no exceptional occasions even untruth or violence become inevitable. Thus, loftiest heights were scaled by the intellectual thought in India from the time of Upanishads to the rise of the system of philosophy.

Professor Max Muller has characterised this period as "The age of Indian Renaissance"; and has argued that it was due to the contact with Greece which was established owing to the invasion of Alexander the Great. But the history of this Renaissance for a century and a half previous to this invasion is available today; and Buddha was the brightest star of this period of great intellectual conclusion. He arouse about a century earlier than the invasion; a number of outstanding thinkers like Charvaka, Brhas-pati, Ushana, Kapila, Kanada and so on preceded him.

Against the background of this great intellectual movement, arose the empire of the Mauryas, the biggest ancient empire of the Hindu known to history. It arose in the post-Buddhist period; but did not last for long time like Roman empire.The Roman empire, owing to its spread over most of the known parts of Europe, laid the foundation of Christianity; it destroyed most of the earlier paganistic forms of primitive religions. The Maurya Empire, on the other hand soon came to an end, as a result of the Brahmin minister, Pushyamitra, capturing the throne. This opened again the way for a revival of the Brahmanical religion and thus ruled out the possibility of any universal religion again exercising its sway in India. The Brahmins, of course, could no longer establish the old Vedic religion but resorted to some sort of an eclectic combination of the old and the new. Various sects, with their primitive or developed rites, rituals and forms of worship were pooled together for the purpose. Shaivism and Vaishnavism were also absorbed and were given a form suitable to priests.

The decline of the power of the atheists, materialists and rationalist led to the weakening of the heresy; and the Brahmins again revived the old Hinduism. The material or social law was coming to be accepted in the social and political affairs of the community but the Brahmins checked the process and once again established the law of the Smrities. The secular laws of social polity were not permitted to remain. While the western legal system still take the Roman Law as their sources and the Romans are being credited with having given humanity a legal code, in India, a similar development was nipped in the bud by this rise of Brahmanism.

With their taking up a sectarian form, the intellectual movement of the Jains and the Buddhists began to be blunted. There was again a relapse into primitive barbarism and the number of idle, parasitic vagabondish monks and sanyasins began to increase. The status of Brahmins was more stable in society than that of these. The Brahmins were related to the day-to-day existence and life of the people. Being householders, they had a hand in the daily life and behaviour of others. It was therefore easy for the Brahmins to combat and defeat these monks. (pg. 117) The Brahmins created the new religion, in a palatable and attractive form to the people, incorporating in it numerous deities, modes of worship, rites, rituals, conceptions and anecodes acceptable to all sorts of people. Mixing up the Vedic mantras and notions with it, they created the code of rituals for the higher Varnas. The old idol worship, deities and their prayers were thus given a new form. The old varnas system was transformed into the new caste system; and with its help was consolidated the social position of the Brahmins. The monotheistic sects were also absorbed in the polytheistic and pantheistic religions. With the use of the doctrine of Brahma, all the deities were raised up to a level of dignity. In fact, the doctrine of Brahma from the Upanishads would have eliminated the crowd of deities, but the Brahmasutras of Badarayana saved them all, not only that, they also saved the non-Vedic Deitied. Various primitive, pagan and tribal gods were thus revived. The worship of lingam was associated with the Rudradhyaya from the Vedas, and the Brahmins ousted the Sudras from most of the temples of the lingam from the position of the priests. They also established their domination in the temples and the places of pilgrimage of non-Vedic origin. The priests at these places in the begi-nning were the non-Vedic, non-Brahmins. But now that the higher Varnas accepted them, the Brahmins to enter everywhere, barring exceptional sects strongly and funda-mentally opposed to the Vedas, precluded the rise of an orderly uniform and well-organised religion. The various sects are given varying degrees of authority. The result was the rise of a feeble eclectic Hinduism. What is not told in the Shruties was stated by the Brahmins on the authority of the Shruties. The religion accepted by the Hindus today arose in this manner, the norms of which have been stated in the Smrities and elaborated in the Puranas.

Everything pertaining to the religion based on the caste system is found in the Smrities. The Taboos of Food, drinks and contact or touch are all found in them. Similarly the marital rituals as well as the relations of different castes with each other are also elaborately described. Thus, the traditional Hinduism is to be found in the Smrities and the Puranas. The Vedas mentions a very negligible part of it. In the Upanishads, there is the doctrine of Brahma, in the Sankhya philosophy, the ideas of Satva, Rajas, and Tamas and in the Yogasutras of Patanjali, there are the notions of the Yogic vision, an insight into the past, present, future and various other miracles. Thus, the authoritative scriptures of modern Hinduism are the Vedas, the Upanishads, the Smrities, the Mahabharata, the Brahma Sutras, Purvamimamsa, Sankhyashastras, Yogashastra and the Puranas.

Since the establishment of this religion, there never arose in the Hindu society any revolutionary intellectual movement, leading to a renaissance of Hinduism. There were no important social upheavals either. Numerous empires arose and disappeared, but the general social pattern remained the same. Thus, there began the age of a great stagnation. In this age also there was some progress in poetry, drama, commentaries and science. Towards the end of this long period, i.e. in the seventh and the eighth centuries A.D. arose, the two leading thinkers namely, Kumarila Bhatta and Shankaracharya. The former critically examined the idea of the authority of religion as developed in the Purvamimamsa and proved the various concepts of the monotheists as well as the Jains and the Buddhists to be wrong. He further proved the self-evident authority of the Vedas and thus established a particular method of judging and proving the same. This method dominated the religious thought of the later days so strongly and so well that it has been scrupulously followed by all the scholars in their religious thinking. Kumarila Bhatta wanted to combat the tendencies towards asceticism and renunciation and to establish again the supremacy of this worldly laws the religion of the householders and the Yajna. But he could not succeed in achieving that. The triumph of Shankara defeated that purpose; and Purvamimamsa was put in a subordinate position. It was only the scriptural authority proved by him that charmed all the scholars and even Shankara accepted it. Thus, while on the one hand he combated the notions of omniscience, God Yogic miracles etc, on the other hand by establishing the self-evident scriptural authority of the Vedas, he gave them a strong foundation of blind faith. All these miracles however originated from the Vedas, the Smrities and the puranas themselves. The secular outlook supported by Kumarila Bhatta was that of the shruties and smrities. It was not one founded on rationalism and materialism. It had already become weak and futile centuries ago. The institutions of Yajna and Varna had already lost their meaning. On the other hand, thinking minds were worried over the poverty and meagreness of social existence. A weak political authority, tyrannical Smriti law and the unrestrained domination of the priests, kings and the noblemen all had reduced the existence of productive classes of traders, agriculturists and artisans to a miserable position. The classes, producing wealth were themselves afflicted by poverty; while the higher classes were generally degraded. Under conditions like these, the thinking section in the community could have no other feeling excepting pessimism. It was stagnation all around. The philosophy of this stagnation was the doctorine of Maya enunciated by Shankara.

The intellectual attainments of Shankara were of the highest order. He examined closely and critically all the different philosophies and doctrine existing in his times and showed, on such examination, the shortcomings of each of them. The result of his critism was the conculsion that every interpretation of the universe or reality proved to be full of fallacies beyond a certain limit. He even established that his own doctrine of Brahma could not be proved logically. Reason, he showed, cannot determine or inform about the nature of the soul, or the doctrine of rebirth. All human thought in search of truth in life and the universe comes to a standstill at a certain stages; and hence the doctrine of Maya. The stagnant position of all thought regarding reality thus proved to be a breeding ground for the doctrine of Maya. The nature of the Universe cannot be described; you cannot say anything either positive or negative or both ways about it; hence it is illusory. But this illusory nature of the universe could not be proved by Shankara excepting on the authority of the Shruties. Since the Shruties had contended that Brahma alone is the truth, Shankara could content that the universe is an illusion or maya. Thus, the doctrine of Maya enunciated by Shankara, is a result of critical reason accepting its defeat. It is the logical culmination of the Hindu philosophy which could not break the intellectual vicious circle.

Since Shankara could clearly see that the religious institution, the doctrine of Brahma or of Maya could not be established through critical reason, he had to resort to the authority of the shruties. This simply meant a safe burial of the growing thought and philosophy since the days of the Upanishads under the crushing weight of scriptural authority. Philosophy is a critical examination of reality by human reason. This continually developing critical understanding was sought to be restrained by the observations in the four Vedas and their authority. Attributing perfection to reason that produced the Vedas, Shankara successfully blocked the way of its further development. This is not surprising an outstanding intellect like Shankara took this way in the midst of a social atmosphere that had become entirely stagnant. If the environment were ripe for the growth of scientific thinking, the destruction of the cobwebs of old thought and philosophy by Shankara would have led to the rise of new thought and a new philosophy. A critical examination of all spiritual philosophy could not have led to any other results. Either the result would have been the rise of Zeroism, Scepticism and "Maya vada", or a higher form of rationalism and materialist philosophy. The social environment was not however favourable to the development of science, hence the rise of the doctrine of Maya and the waste of all intellectual effort. When society itself was in a declining and degenerating stage, "What could philosophy come to, if not solipsism and dream"? All that remained of religion was, therefore, renunciation, surrender to God and devotion. Since the twelfth century with the break up of the Hindu empires, Hinduism has simply come to mean the doctrine of Maya, the cult of devotion and the caste system and it has remained in that form under the Muslim, Maratha and the British rules.

Recent Developments in Hinduism

An effort to defend the old customs with the help of new sciences has been made by numerous scholars under the British rule and is being made still. This revival of the old traditions and customs is the basis of Indian nationalism; and respect for those traditions is the main constituents of the mental makeup of an average nationalist. Some of these people have attempted to defend the caste system with the help of modern race theory and we may now briefly examine this defence.

It is argued that the modern classification of mankind into different races is connected with the older classification into Varna's and castes. The argument, however, is wrong. There are attempts being made at present to classify human society into various races on the basis of certain biological features such as the cephalic index, the shape of the nose, the peculiarities of the face and eyes, colour, blood, height, etc. But all these are mostly unconnected traits, for instances, it cannot be said that a person with a peculiar colour will have only a given type of facial or other peculiarities and so on. It is on the other hand being established that all these traits are an outcome of variety of external and internal factors such as heat, cold, weather, water, food, etc. The best criterion of racial differentiation is the cephalic index. But Franz Boas and other anthropologist have argued that even that undergoes a change within a couple of generations. The other biological traits also have very little to do with the division of varnas or the castes. It is impossible to fix up ones' being Brahmins or Sudra with the help of these biological traits. Nor have they anything to do with the Psychological traits of these groups described in the Shruties and the Smrities. The Aryans are generally proud of their racial superiority, but Aryan civilisation and race have little to do with each other the people with the Aryan culture are not at all of a homogenous race. On the contrary numerous racial groups are found to have that culture. On the other hand, racial similarities can be seen between, for example, the Telugu Brahmins, who have still kept the Vedic traditions alive and the Sudras, the Kalla and Illuva from Kochin. The Brahmins in the south and the cobblers in the north have the same racial traits. The Nagar Brahmins from Gujarat, The Kayastha from Bengal and the non-Brahmins from Karnataka appear to come from the same race. It would be quite easy and possible to multiply these illustrations.

Indian society, barring the primitive savage tribes still found in India, indicates racial traits of three mainly different types. The racial groups found in Europe, Central and Western Asia, in Australia and in China are all found here. But this indicates neither a higher nor lower level of culture nor any of the different character traits.

Those who feel proud of these Aryan race, should also remember that there had been in existence numerous civilised communities in the world, when the Aryans were virtually savages, many of these are still in existence and the history of China, Egypt, Crete, Palestine and others bears out the truth of the above contention. The history of Egypt and Central Asia further shows that those who call themselves Aryans even endeavoured with their savage enthusiasm and force to destroy higher forms of civilisation.

The doctrine of the four Varnas has therefore no relation with that of the races. A change in the means and modes of production helps to brings about a change in culture. A society knowing the use of iron can, for example, easily defeat another ignorant of that use, with the help of its superior weapons and thus make the vanquished its slaves. A number of Kshtriyas have become Sudras under the British rule, not because the English were better or higher type of Kshatriyas, but because they had higher and more developed types of weapons. History shows cases of communities knowing the use of the horse having defeated brave members of other communities, ignorant of its use and conquering them, making them Sudras, becoming Brahmins and Kshatriyas themselves. A change in the social environment has thus made Brahmins and Kshatriyas into Shudras. These changes are result of the changes in the social or political environment and not of any disappearance of character traits of Varnas or change of Varnas. There is nothing in history to show that the life or doings of the Brahmins or the Sudras are determined by any natural biological traits or factors. There are thousands possessed of knowledge, controls, bravery and capacity to hard and strenuous work, ability to mass wealth and so on. If it is said that learning or control are traits of the Brahmin, courage, bravery of the Kshatriyas, ability to mass wealth of the Vaishyas, or capacity to hard and strenuous work of the Sudras, there is nothing to show any inherent impossibility of two or more of these virtues being possessed by one and the same person. They are not mutually exclusive. Therefore, there is nothing to show any relation whatsoever between the doctrine of the four Varnas and that of the races.

Under the British rule, a number of movements of religion reform have arisen in Hindu society. There has been a vast change in the social life of India owing to the advent of that rule. The Englishmen arrived here with the new sciences and a new age of machine and manufacture. He established his domination over the country; a phenomenon which has fundamentally affected the social life in this country. The Indians thinkers, finding the incompatibility between their traditional ideas and thought with the new knowledge, began to reform these. Some of them founded new sects, others carried on a movement of reform. Of the new sects the more important ones are the Brahmo Samaj and the Arya Samaj. Brahmo Samaj has very little place for the various beliefs or philosophies. Its main emphasis is on devotion to one God, and observance of the norms of civil behaviour and morality. It is thus a very simple sect, but it could not hold its sway for a long time; and never spread beyond a limited number of urban, educated people. Arya Samaj on the other hand has a considerable influence in the Punjab. It made god headway in the direction of religious reform, especially in northern India. Those who simply took to religious reform, without establishing any sect can also be divided into categories. One is that of rational reformers, while the others is that of the spiritualistic religious-minded persons. The former tried to revalue the old customs and traditions in the light of the new knowledge and thus bring about some reforms in the life of the urban middle classes. Abolition of child marriage, remarriage of the widows, the condition of the age of consent, removal of taboos regarding food and the endogamous rules were some of the things mainly emphasised by them. Many of the educated persons from the second group tried to pull the leg of these reformers and attempted to defend the old customs and traditions in their hunt for cheap popularity. The tradition of these spiritualist reformers continues for the last half a century or so, Vivekananda, Ramteertha, Tilak, Gandhi, Dr. Radhakrishnan, all belong to this tradition. They have tried to brighten up through window dressing the old Hinduism and its philosophy. It is a mistake to call them rational reformers. For, they are defenders of divine revelation, yogic vision, reincarnation, and various other mystical doctrines.

The sect of Arya Samaj has arisen on the basis of an acceptance of the authority of the Vedas, but rejecting the religion from the Shruties and Smrities and the Puranas. Even from the Vedas, this sect does not accept the Brahmins. It has convinced itself that the Mantras alone are the real Veda; for the elaborate rituals in the Brahmanas would not be acceptable in modern times. The founder of this sect, Dayananda has interpreted the Vedas; and has given them a monotheistic form. The references to animal sacrifies in yajnas have been regarded as symbolic. In the eyes of Dayananda, the Vedas have a final and complete authority.

It is a futile attempt to present the old Vedic notions in a modern garb; and it has been a complete failure in its objective of reviving the outmoded Vedic concepts and giving them content useful to the modern social existence. Arya Samaj is simply a reaction to Islam. One god, one Veda, one religion cannot be the message of the twentieth century. It is not proper to talk the same language to the Hindus in the present times, because Mohamad gave a similar message to the Arabs in the twelfth century.

There are some who argue that revival of the Vedas alone can lead to the prosperity of the Hindus. The message of the pre-Buddhistic Hinduism will make the Hindus again brave and powerful. It is historically wrong, however to say that the Hindus became weak and cowardly in the post-Buddhistic period. In that period itself arose three or four important Hindu Empires. There is no historical evidence to show that similar, empires existed before the rise of Buddha. Revival of the Vedic notions on the other hand, will now further weaken the Hindu for the Vedic thought regarding life and the universe is extremely narrow and illusory. It is only a proper understanding of the laws of the universe and society that can strengthen man; harbouring illusions regarding these can only contribute to weakness. It is true that there is considerable emphasis in the Vedas on the material aspect of life but there is also a great ignorance regarding the same, underlying the belief that there are various deities in various natural objects and elements, and that they govern the behaviour of nature. There is further the futile ritual of prayers and magic. All this lumber of illusory and wrong notions can be of very little help to us today. It is entirely inconsistent with modern science and thought. The greatness of the Vedas was in the then existent peculiar social conditions and times, which need not better be compared with those of the present. Just as Bhaskaracharya is none the less important because his mathematics appears ridiculously simple when compared with that of the present, so are the Vedas. They or the Upanishads, Gita and other works have no doubt, a great historical significance, but to make them a guide in modern life is nothing short of shortsighted policy.

A number of our educated people have been attracted by the secular outlook of the Gita. Important leaders of thought and movements have written commentaries and criticism of it, trying to find in it a message of new Hinduism. But the main question in this connection would be: Is the thought in Gita to be accepted as an authority or is it to be accepted with the help of reason? Are the various ideas in that work mutually consistent? There are various complex problems tackled in that work. But its fundamental tenets of rebirth, a detached soul,

God and the doctrine of Karma (or fatalism) cannot be established with the help of reasons. Those who therefore have to accept the Gita must accept these on scriptural authority, unless they have the uncommon audacity to say that they have these as a part of their experience. But how can one, guided by reason, accept these ideas? Whether the doctrine of Gita is secular or spiritualistic, it is different matter; its basic tenets will have to be accepted with blind faith. Those who therefore donot want to accept anything on blind faith but wish to be guided by reason will see that it is impossible to logically establish these fundamentals and they have therefore to be rejected.

The real problems before us today are different. Society is stagnant and problems of its reconstruction so as to open up the way of progress have to be tackled. What can the Gita do in that respect? Idealistic expressions like spiritual or material well being have no meaning today. What is needed is a science of social dynamics, social forces and their action and reactions. The Gita talks of Karma without the desire for its results or fruits, but in fact the criterion of proper Karma (deed) itself is the effects produced by or the results obtained from it. The deeds regarded as wrong by tradition, have got to be proved to be such by reason. Social sciences and not the Gita can help in that respect. The formulations in the Gita are of the type of the Puranas. They are not rigidly logical or balanced and orderly. That order has to be discovered in them; and they are capable of variety of interpretations. All this indicates that Gita can be of very little help to us in this modern scientific age.

Some of the modern scholars donot accept the caste system and are not proud of it, they donot even accept untouchability or the rules of endogamy or the taboos of food and drinks. They have therefore argued that the caste system is not an important feature of Hinduism and have on the other hand tried to find out its higher and nobler characteristics. The attempt has been a failure. Out of these efforts based on certain semirational and pseudo-scientific concepts, a new non-existent Hinduism is arising. The present day social problems are of a profound significance and these superficial remedies cannot tackle them. Under the thin layer of rationalism in these attempts, is concealed blind faith. There is no examination of the roots of fundamentals. It will never be possible to establish a new spiritualistic religious sect, unless rationalism in the proper sense is completely rejected, and this plain truth has to be clearly grasped. If a religious sect in a new form is to be established, it can be done only on a scriptural authority. Religion disappears when proper rationalism comes in. Faith in the supernatural is the essence of religion. Both Tilak and Dayananda had recognised that there is no basis for religion excepting authority, and hence the former accepted the Gita and the latter, the Vedas.

The learned members of the Dharma Nirnaya Mandala have been trying to erect a new structure of Hinduism based on reason. But any religion must have at its root a faith in the supernatural or it is no religion at all. The rituals prescribed by this Mandals, are thus based upon an acceptance of the deity. These notions pertaining to the deities are not merely symbolic for false symbols are not needed by man. The authority of these notions is therefore the word of those who claim to have had an actual experience of God. Modern rationalism or healthy experience cannot accept these notions of God, immortality, Brahma, Maya and so on. If purely scriptural authority is not acceptable to the Mandals, it will still have to be said that their prayers and rituals do indicate blind faith. Determination and deep faith (blinds) can alone lead to the establishment of a new religion.

Various new natural and social sciences have developed in this modern age; and if they are not properly availed of, all efforts in their absence are bound to prove futile and in vain.

There are some who argue that the concepts of god, immortality of the soul or the doctrine of Karma have a value in life. Whether they are true or otherwise, whether they can be established with the help of reason or otherwise, it is not possible to act properly and couragely in life without assuming their correctness and hence that has to be assumed. The value of that assumption consists in making man feel that it is necessary and worthwhile to behave properly. The assumption is thus necessary for social order or social stability.

There are a number of flaws in this arguments in the first place, various outstanding events occur and have occurred in history without the aid of these concepts or with that of purely secular values. It is there this worldly and secular value that has the capacity of developing the various human virtues of learning, selflessness, bravery, heroism and so on. Those who carried out the French revolution were backed by secular values of liberty, equality and fraternity. In the American war of Independence people fought for the values of democracy and in the fundamental rights of man. In the Spanish civil war, men died on the battlefield for democracy, human rights, destruction of economic slavery and socialism. Where questions of life and death are involved, men have thus fought without any spiritual incentives of God or immortality. The scientist toils in his laboratory day and night, even when he has no faith in God. He works for seeking the truth or may be for love of his work or for his subsistence or for the good of humanity. When the mother works for the child, she does not do so for god or salvation; but because of her identifying herself with the child. There are very few persons who refuse to see beyond their narrow purely, personal interest. Man has been working for his family ever since ancient times and will continue to work even if he knows that god or immortality donot exist. Even the primitive tribesmen obey the tribal law in the absence of spiritual values. It is only selfishness that again prompts the religious minded person to obey the ethical laws as well as the norms of the religion. It is however a perverted selfishness for it is founded on delusions. The various ideas like well-being nationalism, socialism, glory of man are all social, not individual. Individual ends are subordinated in their pursuit; for they represent the good, stability and properity of the lives of millions of individuals. Materialism which lays emphasis on these ideals is thus definitely a better and higher type of philosophy than spiritualism which stresses the fictitious other-worldly good of individuals.

The other flaw in the argument is its ascribing a permanent value to taboos, sentiments, behaviour and thought born in peculiar historical and social conditions. Religion gives these permanent values a divine sanction; presents them as a divine message or revelation. These thought or behaviour which are important in peculiar surrounding and conditions and which have lost that importance owing to change in those conditions or surroundings become actually fetters on furher progress. It is these permanent values that open up the way for decay and fall. Religion or God created and preserved by man comes to dominate and rule man himself. It is essential therefore that we should hereafter have ideals based on reasons and capable of being revalued and changed when they have outlived their utility. The religious values must be rejected.

It may also be pointed out that these so-called spiritual values come under the influence of the dominating classes in society and thus serve as convenient tools in their hands to perpetuate the slavery of the downtrodden. The ruling classes have always used them to maintain their position, their domination and privileges. This will be borne out by the history of all religions in the world. It is religious values that have preserved the unjust laws of the caste system or untouchability. The mystic spiritual doctrine can be highly useful for attaining vulgar material ends.

It is entirely wrong to imagine that spiritualism is moral, while materialism in immoral. Mystic spiritualism generally is a cover for vulgar materialism, while scientific materialism contains within it a higher type of spiritualism. Spiritualism proper simply should mean the intellectual or mental development of man. Unless the entire society is provided with the means of physical existence, there is little or no scope for the development of art or learning; unless each one can have the path of progress opened up before him, spiritualism in the proper sense can never arise. This development of the internal and external faculties and abilities of man demands the help of all sciences and arts, which can be derived only by scientific materialism. Realisation of the higher social ideals and aims is spiritualism.

We have not examined here two philosophical camps of idealism and materialism; but simply idealism and materialism in so far as they have a bearing on life. Man is the creater of this life. Its events do not take place due to any divine dispensation. It is not possible to go into a discussion of these two philosophies in this connection.

An intellectual possessed of the spirit of inquiry when it views the enormous expanse, subtlety and gravity of the universal natural forces, is filled with a sentiment of reverence. Prof. Max Muller has styled this sentiment as the consciousness of the infinite and has called it the basis of all religion. But this is again not sound. For religious notion is not merely the notion of the infinite, of what is beyond the known, the finite world. There is in it a cobweb of delusion regarding the finite, the known. Heaven, Hell, God, Rebirth, Karma, the day of reckoning, all is not relate to the infinite, the Unknown. It is on the other hand a new imaginary world constructed out of ignorance and illusions to which they relate. These religious notions have risen out of a distortion of the reality.

The subtle, romantic, enchanting and noble sentiments regarding the universe that charm the human mind have little to do with the institutional religion which is a part and parcel of society. A traveller on board a ship looking at the unending expanse of the ocean or gazing at the starry heavens in the night in a desert may experience these sentiments and emotions. As Einsten has once observed, "it is this mysterious Universe that is the most beautiful of all other things; and is the origin of all art and science. One may be considered as a dead soul, who does not feel charmed or surprised by it. It is in this sense that I am a religious person." There is a great truth in this observation of Einsten. Kant had also expressed himself similarly when he said that human surprise knew no limits when one gazed at the starry heavens above or looked for the moral law within. This sentiments may be considered as similar to that of the poet but has little to do with heaven and hell, miracles, reincarnations, prophets and so on. Its essence is simply humality in the face of the unknown, unthought of infinite. But this humility has produced science and not religion. It encourages the search for truth and keeps on the continual march towards it. Religion, on other hand, is opposed to this humanity. It is marked by arrogance. It has always claimed domination over everything, the known and the Unknown. It has always been proud of explaining the mysteries of the Universe, rather than being humble when faced with them. Religion never had any respect for the unknown. It has always tried to impress and in doing so, seldom showed any regard for truth. Barring exceptional cases in the Upanishads and the Darshanas, it has seldom raised the questions of why and how, excepting with a view to impress. It always tried to relate the universe with the doings and misdoings of the insignificant human being, for it was endeavouring to preserve a given set of interests.

Science has demolished this influence. Astronomy, Geology, Biology, Psychology all have helped to explode this myth.

Man, moving in the light of modern science, is increasingly realising his significance. He is like a drop in the ocean. Religion has imagined man to be the centre of the Universe and made everything in it dependent upon him. It has imagined that behind all the events and happenings in the Universe, there is some scheme, some purpose. It has postulated some creator who has revised the schemes, possessed that purpose.

Man, in this age of science, is rejecting this religious thought and substituting in its place a new scientific outlook. In this view, this earth came into being sometimes due to the operations of the laws of the universe. Life and man arose on it in course of time under suitable conditions. He is being since then engaged in struggle with the world around him and has been trying to harness its forces to his own purpose; and is becoming increasingly successful in the effort. He is thus emerging from the anthropomorphic age into the scientific one. He no longer imagines the world to be what he wants it to be. He is on the contrary trying to conquer the forces around him, knowing well that what is unknown is infinitely greater than what is known. He has become more self-reliant, more confident of himself as a creator. He no longer holds god or fate responsible for the evils of poverty, inequality, starvation, ignorance, injustice and so on; but ascribes the responsibility to the social order.

Problems insoluble are pretended to be solved by religion, which simply leads to self-deception. Man with a scientific outlook will not be a party to such deception but will frankly admit his inability to solve them. The realm of knowledge is continually expanding; and it is needless therefore to rely on fantastic imaginary explanations. It is possible to him to bring heaven on earth with the help of science and reason rather than go on indulging in delusions regarding heaven and hell. The struggle for a reconstruction of the social order has already begun. The enormous amount of social energy hitherto directed in defunding religion can now usefully be canalised in this direction. The goal of human activity hereafter would therefore be the reconstruction of social order full of life, vigour, energy, vitality and happiness.

Social institutions, higher than religion are being brought into being today. And society is now endeavouring to create means and institution which would perform far more skillfully and also on much higher level, the role religion once performed in human history. A social under, unknown to all religions, is now a necessity; an order that will provide to all opportunities for full development of themselves.

These new ideals are simply a development of the old ones. Vyasa regarded human life or the social order as of primary significance and subordinated everything else to it, including the so called permanent moral values. Buddha gave again man the central position. Philosophers from the Vedic period to Shankara kept the search for Truth going. We have these, great heritage. Assimiliating it well, let us discharge our responsibility of creating a social existence which never existed before. Those who continually look to the past, while acting in the present, can have no future. It is only the new ideals and the new means of attaining them belonging to the new times that can brighten up posterity. You cannot climb up to the glory of the future unless the east is made just a step on the way.

7

The Historical Development of the Bhagavad-Gita

DAMODAR DHARMANAND KOSAMBI

The Bhagavad-Gita, "song of the Blessed One", forms part of the great Indian epic *Mahabharata,* being Mbh. 6.23-40 of the Poona critical edition.[1] Its 18 adhyaya chapters contain the report by Sanjaya of a dialogue between the Pandava hero Arjuna and his Yadu charioteer Krishna, the eight incarnation of Vishnu. The actual fighting is about to begin when Arjuna feels revulsion at the leading part which he must play in the impending slaughter of cousins and kinsmen. The exhortations of Lord Krishna answer every doubt through a complete, philosophical cycle, till Arjuna is ready to bend his whole mind, no longer divided against itself, to the great killing. This *Gita* has attracted minds of entirely different bent from each other and from that of Arjuna. Each has interpreted the supposedly divine words so differently from all the others.

The following abbreviations have been used : G–the Bhagvad-Gita; Mbh – the Mahabharata; Up – Upanishad; RV – the Rigveda, JBBRAS – Journal of the Asiatic Society, Bombay (formerly Bombay Branch of the Royal Asiatic Society); ABORI – Annals of the Bhandarkar Oriental

Research Institute, Poona; A – the Arthashastra of Kautilya; JRAS – Journal of the Royal Asiatic Society, London. For the historical background, my own introduction to the Study of Indian History has been used without detailed reference.

That the original seems far more suited to raise doubts and to split a personality than to heal an inner division. Any moral philosophy which managed to receive so many variant interpretations from minds developed in widely different types of society must be highly equivocal. No question remains of its basic validity if the meaning be so flexible. Yet the book has had its uses.

1. FOR WHAT CLASS? We know that Gita exercised a profound influence upon Mahatma Gandhi, B.G. Tilak, the thirteenth century Vaishnava Acharya Ramanuja, and the still earlier Shamkara.[2] Through contemporaries fighting in the cause of India's liberation from British rule, Tilak and the Mahatma certainly did not draw concordant guidance for action from the *Gita,* while Aurobindo Ghose renounced the struggle for India's freedom to concentrate upon study of the Gita. Lokamanya Tilak knew the Jnanesvari comment, but his Gita-rahasya is far from being based upon the earlier work. Jnanesvara himself did not paraphrase Shamkara on the Gita, nor did he follow Ramanuja; tradition ascribes to him membership of the rather fantastic Natha sect. Ramanuja's Vaishnavism laid a secure foundation for the acrid controversy with the earlier followers of Shiva who came into prominence with the great Shamkara. But then, why did Shamkara turn to the Bhagavad-Gita too?

To discover just what commons service the Gita did for these people apart from the service it renders to all readers, we have to ask what else they possessed in common. What common need did these outstanding

* ENQUIRY, VOL II (DELHI 1959), pp. 1-20. Maharashtrian reformer, Jnanesvara, the earlier.

thinkers have that was at the same time not felt by ordinary people, even of their own class? That they belonged to one class is obvious; the leisure class of what, for lack of a better term, may be called Hindus. The class bias must not be ignored, for the great comparable Poet-teachers from the common people did very well without the Gita. Kabir, the Banaras weaver, had both Muslim and Hindu followers for his plain yet profound teaching. Tukaram knew the Gita through the Jnanesvari, but worshipped Vishnu in his own way, meditating upon God and human affairs in the ancient caves (Buddhist and natural) near the junction of the Indrayani and Pauna rivers. Neither Jayadeva's Gita-govinda, so musical and supremely beautiful a literary effort charged with the love and mystery of Krisha's cult, nor the reforms of Chaitanya that swept the peasantry of Bengal off its feet are founded on the rock of the Gita. Jnanesvara ran foul of current Brahmin belief at Alandi, and had to take refuge about 1290 A.D. on the south bank of the Godavari, in the domains of Ramachandra Yadava, to write his famous gloss in the common.

We know as little of the historic action taken or instigated by Shamkara and Ramanuja as we should have known of Tilak's had only his Gita-rahasya survived. Yet, about the year 800, Shamkara was active in some manner that resulted – according to tradition – in the abolition of many Buddhist monasteries. That he did it by his penetrating logic and sheer ability in disputation is the general belief. The mass of writing left in his name, and what is given therein as the Buddhist doctrine which he refutes, make only one thing clear: that he had not the remotest idea of the Buddha's teaching. If his opponents actually held such views, Buddhism had abolished itself successfully centuries before. It had in any case degenerated into Lamaism with opulent monastic foundations which were a serious drain upon the economy of the country, and which had to be abolished. That Shamkara's activity provided a stimulus thereto, and Ramanuja's some handle against the wealthier barons whose worship of Shiva was associated in the popular mind with their oppressive land-rent, seems a reasonable conclusion on the evidence before us. Otherwise, it would be difficult to explain why the richer landholders opted for Shiva, the poorer over whelming for Vishnu, in the bitter smarta-vaishnava feuds. Neither side objected to rendering faithful service to beef-eating Muslim overlords, who knocked Brahmins off without compunction or retribution.

The main conclusion is surely the following: Practically anything can be read into the Gita by a determined person, without denying the validity of a class system. The Gita furnished the one scriptural source which could be used without violence to accepted Brahmin methodology, to draw inspiration and justification for social action in some way disagreeable to a branch of the ruling class upon whose mercy the Brahmins depended at the moment. That the action was not mere individual opportunism is obvious in each of the cases cited above. It remains to show how the document achieved this unique position.

2. A REMARKABLE INTERPOLATION. That the song divine is sung for the upper classes by the Brahmins, and only through them for others, is clear. We hear from the mouth of Krishna himself: G.9.32: "For those who take refuge in me, be they even of the sinful breeds such as women, Vaishyas, and Shudras..". That is, all women, and all men of the working and producing classes are defiled by their very birth, though they may in after-life be freed by their faith in the god who degrades them so casually in this one. Not only that, the god himself had created such differences: G.4.13. "The four-caste (-class) division has been created by Me"; this is proclaimed in the list of great achievements.

The doctrines are certainly not time-less.[3] Ethics come into being only as they serve some social need. Food-producing society (as distinct from conflicting aggregates of food-gathering tribal groups) originated in the fairly recent and definite historical past, so that the principles upon which it may work at some given stage could not have been expressed from eternity. The Gita sets out each preceding doctrine in a masterly and sympathetic way without naming or dissecting it, and with consummate skill passes smoothly on to another when Arjuna asks "why then do you ask me to do something so repulsive and clearly against this?" Thus, we have a brilliant (if plagiarist) review-synthesis of many schools of thought which were in many respects mutually incompatible. The incompatibility is never brought out; all views are simply facets of the one divine mind. The best in each system is derived, naturally, as from the high god. There is none of the polemic so characteristic of disputatious Indian philosophy; only the Vedic ritual beloved of the Mimamsakas is condemned outright. The Upanishads are well – if anonymously – represented, though only the Shvetashvatara Upanishad contains the germ of bhakti, and none the theory of perfection through a large succession of rebirths. This function of Karma is characteristically Buddhist. Without Buddhism fully developed, G.2.55-72 (recited daily as prayers at Mahatma Gandhi's ashrama) would be impossible. The brahma-nirvana of G.2.72 and 5.25 is the Buddh-ist ideal state of escape from the effect of karma. We may similarly trace other – unlabelled – schools of thought such as 'Samkhya and Mimamsa down to early Vedanta (G15. 15. supported by the reference to the Brahmasutra in G.13.4). This helps date the work as somewhere between 150-350 A.D., near the later than the earlier date. The ideas are much older, and borrowed, not original, except perhaps for the novel use of bhakti. The language is high classical Sanskrit such as could not have been written much before the Guptas, though the metre still shows the occasional irregularity (G.8.10d, 8.11b, 15, 3a, and c) in trishtubhs, characteristic of the Mbh. as a whole. The Sanskrit of the high Gupta period, shortly after the time of the Gita, would have been more careful in versification.

It is known in any case that the Mbh. and the puranas suffered a major revision[4] in the period given above. The Mbh. in particular was in the hands of Brahmins belonging to the Bhrigu clan, who inflated it to about its present bulk (though the process of inflation continued afterwards) before the Gupta age came to flower. The puranas also continued to be written or rewritten to assimilate some particular cult to Brahmanism. The last discernible reduction of the main purana group refers to the Guptas still as local princes between Fyzabad and Prayag. This context fits the Gita quite well. The earliest dated mention of anything that could possibly represent the Gita is by Hsiuen Chang,[5] early in the seventh century, who refers to a Brahmin having forged at his king's order such a text (supposedly of antiquity) which was then 'discovered', in order to foment war. The fact does remain that the Mbh. existed in two versions at the time of the Ashvalayana Grihya Sutra, which refers both to the Bharata and the Mahabharata.[6] The prologue of the present Mbh. repeats much the same information in such a way as to make it evident that the older 24,000-shloka Bharata was still current at the time the longer version was promulgated. Every attempt was made to ascribe both to the great 'expander', Vyasa, to whom almost every purana is also ascribed. A common factor is the number 18, which had some particular sanctity for the whole complex, and for the Brahmins connected therewith. There are 18 main gotra clan-groups of Brahmins,[7] tough the main rishi sages are only seven in number; many of the 18 (e.g. the kevala are difficult to fit into a rational scheme. Correspondingly, there are 18 main puranas, and 18 parvan sections of the Mbh. though the original division was into 100, as we learn from the prologue. The very action of the Bharatan war was fought over 18 days between 18 legions. The Gita has also 18 adhyayas, which is surely not without significance. That the older Bharat epic had a shorter but similar Gita is most unlikely. One could expect some sort of an exhortation to war, as is actually contained in G.2.27: "If slain, you gain heaven; if victorious, the earth; so up, son of Kunti, and concentrate on fighting". These lines fit the occasion very well. Such pre-battle urging was customary in all lands at all times (advocated even by the supremely practical Arthashastra, 10.3) through invocations and incantations, songs of bards, proclamations by heralds, and speech of captain or king. What is highly improbable – except to the Brahmin bent upon getting his niti revisions into a popular lay of war – is an obscure three-hour discourse on moral philosophy after the battle-conches had blared out in mutual defiance and two vast armies begun their inexorable movement towards collision.

The Gita, therefore, is a new composition, not expansion of some proportionately shorter religious instruction in the old version. I next propose to show that the effort did not take hold for some centuries after the composition.

3. NOT SUFFICIENT UNTO THE PURPOSE. The lower classes were necessary as an audience, and the heroic lays of ancient war drew them to the recitation. This made the epic a most convenient vehicle for any doctrine which the Brahmins wanted to insert; even better than rewriting the puranas, or faking new puranas for age-old cults. The Sanskrit language was convenient, if kept simple, because the Prakrits were breaking apart into far too many regional languages, and it was the language which the upper classes had begun to utilise more and more. Kushana and Satavahanas inscriptions are in the popular lingua franca used by monk and trader. But from 150 AD., there appears a new type of chief (oftener than not of foreign origin like Rudradaman) who brags[8] in or the 'Other Brahmans', and that local Brahmin groups are the rule, though the books and theory are in the hands of the major groups named. The Bhrigus are specially connected with the Mbh. inflation, as was shown by V.S. Sukthankar in

his magnificent Epic Studies VI (ABORI, 18.1-76; Mem. Ed. 1.278-337). It is important to note that the Bhargava inflation was independent of though not hostile to the Narayaniya inflation, which continued after the first had tapered off. So much so, that the famous benedictory stanza Narayanam namaskritya of the popular edition drops out of the critical text, but most of the properly Bhargava inflations (e.g. needless emphasis upon Parashurama) all remain. In G. 10.25, the lord reveals himself as Bhrigu among the great sages (maharsinam Bhrigur aham), though that sage occupies no position in Vedic tradition, and a trifling one even later.

Epigraphia Indica 8.36 ff. ornate Sanskrit of his achievements, including the knowledge of Sanskrit. The Buddhists had begun to ignore the Teacher's injunction to use the common people's languages; they too adopted Sanskrit. The high period of classical Sanskrit literature really begins with their religious passion-plays and poems, such as those written by Ashvaghogha.[8] A patrician class favouring Sanskrit as well as the Sanskrit-knowing priest class was in existence.

No one could object to the interpolation[9] of a story (akhyana) or episode. After all, the Mbh. purports to the recitation in the Naimisa forest to the assembled sages and ascetics by a bard Ugrashravas, who repeated what Vyasa had sung to Janamejaya as having been reported by Sanjaya to Dhritrashtra! The brahmins were dissatisfied with the profit derived from the Gita, not with its authenticity. So we have the Anugita[10] as a prominent sequel in the 14th Canto (Ashvamedha-parvan). Arjuna confesses that he was forgotten all the fine things told before the battle, and prays for another lesson. Krishna replies that it would be impossible even for him to dredge it out of his memory once again; the great effort was not to be duplicated. However, an incredibly shoddy second Gita is offered instead which simply extols the brahmin. Clearly, that was felt necessary at the time by the inflators though no one reads it now, and it cannot be compared to the first Gita even for a moment.

Secondly, the Gita as it stands could not possibly help any kshatriya in an imminent struggle, if indeed he could take his mind off the battle long enough to understand even a fraction. The ostensible moral is: "Kill your brother, if duty calls, without passion; as long as you have faith in Me, all sins are forgiven. But the history of India always shows not only brothers but even father and son fighting to the death over the throne, without the slightest hesitation or need for divine guidance. Indra took his own father by the foot and smashed him (RC 4.18.12), a feat which the brahmin Vamadeva applauds.

Ajatashatru, King of Magadha, imprisoned his father Bimbisara to usurp the throne, and then had the old man killed in prison. Yet, even the Buddhists[11] and Jains as well as Brhadaranyaka Upanishad 2.1 praise the son (who was the founder of India's first great empire) as a wise and able king. The Arthashastra (A.1.17-18) devotes a chapter to precautions against such ambitious heirs-apparent; and shows in the next how the heir-apparent could circumvent them if he were in a hurry to wear the crown. Krishna himself a Kurukshetra had simply to point to the Yadava contingent, his own people, who were fighting in the opposite ranks. The legend tells us that all the Yadavas ultimately perished fighting among themselves. Earlier Krishna had killed his maternal uncle Kamsa. The tale gains a new and peculiar force if it be remembered that under mother-right, the new chief must always be the sister's son of the old.

Thirdly, Krishna as he appears in the Mbh. is singularly ill-suited to propound any really moral doctrine. The most venerable character of the epic, Bhishma, takes up the greatest of Mbh. Parvans (Shanti) with preaching morality on three important questions: King-craft (raja dharma), conduct in distress (apad-dharma), and emancipation (moksha dharma). He seems eminently fitted for the task having administered as regent the kingdom to which he had freely surrendered his own right. He had shown irresistible prowess and incomparable knightly honour throughout a long life of unquestioned integrity. The sole reproach anyone can make is that he uses far too many words for a man shot full of arrows, dying like a hedgehog on a support of its own quills.

But Krishna? At every single crisis of the war, his advice wins the day by the crookedest of means which could never have occurred to the others. To kill Bhishma, Shikhandin was used as a living shield against whom that perfect knight would not raise a weapon, because of doubtful sex. Drona was polished off while stunned by the deliberate false report of his son's death. Karna was shot down against all rules of chivalry when dismounted and unarmed; Duryodhana battered to death after being disabled by a foul mace blow that shattered his thigh. This is by no means the complete list of iniquities. When taxed with these transgressions, Krishna replies bluntly at the end of the Shalya-parvan that the man could not have been killed in any other way that victory could never have been worn otherwise. The calculated treachery of the Arthashastra saturates the actions of this divine exponent of the Bhagavad-Gita. It is perhaps in the same spirit that leading modern exponents of the Gita and of ahimsa like Rajaji have declared openly that non-violence is all very well as a method of gaining power, but to be scrapped when power has been captured: "When in the driver's seat, one must use the whip.[12]

4. WHY KRISHNA? Just as the Mbh. could be used as basis only because people came to hear the war-story recited, Krishna could have been of importance only if his cult were rising in popularity. The cult, however, is clearly synthetic. The identification with Narayana is a syncretism, i.e., a move towards taking originally distinct cults as one. In the same direction is the assimilation of many sagas to

a single Krishna legend, whether the original heroes bore the name or epithet of Krishna or not. There would, however, be no question of creating a new cult out of wholecloth; some worship or set of similar worships must already have been in existence among the common people before any Brahmins could be attracted thereto. The best such recent example is that of Satyanarayana, 'the true Narayana', so popular all over the country, but which has no foundation whatever in scripture, and which is not even mentioned 200 years ago. Indeed, the origin seems to be in the popular legends of one Satya Pir,[13] in Bengal; the Pir himself became Satya-narayana.

The Vedas have a Vishnu, but no Narayana. The etymology seems to be 'he who sleeps upon the flowing waters (nara)' and this is taken as the steady state of Narayana.[14] It precisely described the Mesopotamian Ea or Enki, who sleeps in his chamber in the midst of the waters, as Sumerian myth, and many a Sumerian seal, tell us. The word nara (plural) for 'the water's' is not Indo-Aryan. Both the word and the god might conceivably go back to the Indus Valley. The later appearance in Sanskrit only means that the peaceful assimilation of the people who transmitted the legend was late. At any rate, the flood-and-creation myth (so natural in a Monsoon country) connected the first three avataras, Fish, Tortoise and Boar – surely related to primitive totemic worships. One performance of this Narayana is shared by Krishna in the Gita; the vishva-rupa-darshana showing that the god contains the whole universe; he individually represents the best specimen of each species in it. Though familiar to most of us as in Gita 10-11, there is a prototype version without Krishna in Mbh. 3.186.39-112, which shows that an all-pervading Narayana had been invented much earlier.

The speech-goddess vag-ambhrini, in a famous but late hymn of the Rigveda (RV. 10.125), declares that she draws Rudra's bow, and is herself Soma and the substance of all that is best. The original god whose misdeeds are never sin is surely the Upanisadic Indra who says to Pratardana Daivodasi: “Know thou Me alone; this indeed do I deem man’s supreme good – that he should know Me. I slew the three-headed Tvastra, threw the Arurmagha ascetics to the wolves, and transgressing many a treaty, I pierced through and through the Prahladiyans in the heavens, the Paulomas in the upper air, and the Kalakanjas on this earth. Yet such was I then that I never turned a hair. So, he who understands Me, his world is not injured by any deed whatever of his: not by his killing his own mother, by killing his own father, by robbery, killing an embryo, or the commission of any sin whatever does his complexion fade” (Kaush. Brah. Up.3.2). The ‘breaking many a treaty’ is again the Arthashastra King’s normal practice, though that book mentions that in olden days even a treaty concluded by simple word of mouth was sacred (A.7.17). Indra performed all these dismal feats in Vedic tradition, but that tradition nowhere makes him proclaim himself as the supreme object for bhakti; papa and bhakti are not vedic concepts. No vedic god can bestow plenary absolution as in G.18.66: “Having cast off all (other beliefs, rites and observances, yield to Me alone; I shall deliver you from all sin, never fear”. The reason Krishna could do this and not Indra was that the older god was clearly circumscribed by immutable vedic suktas and tied to the vedic yajna fire-ritual. He was the model of the ruffianly Aryan war-leader who could get drunk with his followers and lead them to victory in the fight. His lustre had been sadly tarnished by intervening Buddhism, which had flatly denied yajna and brought in a whole new conception of morality and social justice. The pastoral form of bronze age society with which Indra was indissolubly connected had gone out of productive existence.

Krishna or rather one of the many Krishnas also represented this antagonism. The legend of his enmity to Indra reflects in the Rigveda[15] the historical struggle of the dark pre-Aryans against the marauding Aryans. The black skin-colour was not an insurmountable obstacle, for we find a Krishna Angirasa as a Vedic seer. The Yadus are a Vedic tribe too, but no Krishna seems associated with them though the 'bound Yadu' prisoner of war is mentioned. There was a 'Krishna the son of Devaki' to whom Ghora Angirasa imparted some moral discipline, according to Chandogya Up. 3.17.1-7 the Mahanubhavas take Samdipani as Krishna's guru, and a few include Durvasa in the list of his teachers. Krishna the athletic Kamsa-killer could beat anyone in the arena, whether or not he was the same Krishna who wrestled down Kaliya, the many-headed Naga snake-demon that infested the Yamuna river at Mathura. Naturally the Geeks who saw his cult in India at the time of Alexander's invasion identified Krishna with their own Herakles. (The taming of the Naga has perhaps a deeper significance than Herakles decapitating the Hydra, a feat still earlier portrayed in Mesopotamian glyptic. The Naga was the patron deity, perhaps aboriginal cult-object of the place. Such cults survive to this day, as for example that of Mani-naga, which has come down through the centuries near Orissa. Nilamata-naga, for whom the brahmins wrote a special purana,[16] was the primitive patron deity of Kashmir. The Naga Shrikantha had to be faced in a duel by Pushyabhuti, king of Thanesar. Such local guardian nagas are current down to the tenth century work Navasahasankacarita). So, our hero had a considerable following among the Indian people, even in the fourth century B.C. By the later Shunga period, he was called Bhagavat, originally the Buddha's title. A Greek ambassador Heliodoros[17] proclaims himself convert to the cult, on the pillar near Bhilsa. That Krishan had risen from the pre-Aryan people is clear from Paninian reference (Pan. 4.3.98, explained away by the commentator Patanjali) to the effect that neither Krishna nor Arjuna counted as kshatriyas. But his antiquity is considerable, for he is the one god who uses the sharp wheel, the missile discus, as his peculiar weapon. This particular weapon is not known to the Vedas and went out of fashion well before the time of the Buddha. Its historicity is attested only by cave paintings in Mirzapur which show raiding horse-charioteers (clearly enemies of the aboriginal stone-age artists) one of whom is about to hurl such a wheel. The event and the painting may fairly be put at about 800 BC,[18] by which date the dark god was on the side of the angels, no longer an aborigine himself.

Finally, there was also the useful messianic aspect as in G. 4.7.[19] The many proto-historic Krishnas and current belief in transmigration made the avatara syncretism possible. It could also lead the devotee in his misery to hope for a new avatara to deliver him from oppression in this world, as he hoped for salvation in the next.

5. WHEN DOES A SYNTHESIS WORK? Like the avataras of Vishnu Narayana, the various Krishna gathered many a different worship into one without doing violence to any, without smashing or antagonising any. Krishna the mischievous and beloved shepherded lad is not incompatible with Krishna the extraordinarily virile husband of many women. His 'wives' were originally local mother-goddesses, each in her own right. The 'husband' eased the transition from mother-right to patriarchal life, and allowed the original cults to be practiced on a subordinate level. This is even better seen in the marriage of Shiva and Parvati which was supplemented by the Ardha-narishvara hermaphrodite (half Shiva, half Parvati) just to prevent any separation. Mahishasura (Mhasoba), the demon 'killed' by that once independent goddess, is still occasionally worshipped near her temple (as at the foot of Parvati hill[20] in Poona). The widespread Naga cult was absorbed by putting the cobra about Shiva's neck, using him as the canopied (hooded) bed on which Narayana floats in perpetual sleep upon the waters, and putting him also in the hand of Ganesha. The bull Nandi was worshipped by stone-age people long before Shiva had been invented to ride on his back. The list can be extended by reference to our complex iconography, and study of the

divine households. Ganesha's animal head on a human body equates him to the 'sorcerers' and diablotins[21] painted by ice-age men in European caves.

This is "in the Indian character", and we have remarked that a similar attitude is reflected in the philosophy of the Gita. No violence is done to any preceding doctrine except vedic yajna. The essential is taken from each by a remarkably keen mind capable of deep and sympathetic study; all are fitted together with consummate skill and literary ability, and cemented by bhakti without discussing their contradictions. The thing to mark is that the Indian character was not always so tolerant. There are periods when people came to blows over doctrine, ritual, and worship. Emperor Harsha Shiladitya (circa 600-640 AD) of Kanauj found no difficulty in worshipping Gauri, Maheshvara-Shiva, and the Sun, while at the same time he gave the fullest devotion to Buddhism.[22] His enemy Narendragupta-Shashanka, one of the last Gupta kings, raided Magadha from Bengal, cut down the Bodhi tree at Gaya, and wrecked Buddhist foundations wherever he could what was the difference, and why was a synthesis of the two religions, actually practiced by other (as literary references can show) besides Harsha not successful ?

Let me put it that the underlying difficulties were economic. Images locked up too much useful metal; monasteries and temples after the Gupta age withdrew far too much from circulation without replacement or compensation by adding to or stimulating production in any way. Thus, the most thoroughgoing iconoclast in Indian history was another king Harsha, (1089-1101 AD) who broke up all images[23] in Kashmir, except four that were spared. This was done systematically under a regular cabinet minister devotpatana-nayaka, without adducing the least theological excuse, though one could easily have been found. The Kashmirian king remained a man of culture, patron of literature and the arts who presumably read the Gita too. But he needed funds for his desperate fight against the Damara group of local barons. He won the particular campaign, at the cost of making feudalism stronger.

The conclusion to be drawn is that a dovetailing of the superstructure will be possible only when the underlying differences are not too great. Thus, the Gita was a logical performance for the early Gupta period, when expanding village settlement brought in new wealth to a powerful central government. Trade was again on the increase, and many sects could obtain economic support in plenty. The situation had changed entirely by the time of Harsha Shiladitya though many generous donations to monasteries were still made. The villages had to be more or less self-contained and self-supporting. Tax-collection by a highly centralised but non-trading state was no longer a paying proposition, because commodity production per head and cash trade was low; [24] this is fully attested by the miserable coinage. The valuable, concentrated luxury trade of the Kushana-Satavahana era had gone down in spite of feudal and monastic accumulation of gold, silver, jewels, and etc. Once magnificent cities like Patna, no longer necessary for production, had dwindled to villages containing ruins which people could regard only as the work of superhuman beings. There was no longer enough for all; one or the other group had to be driven to the wall. One such instance is the combined Hari-Hara cult (with an image half Shiva, half Vishnu) which had its brief day but could not remain in fashion much beyond the eleventh century. The followers of Hari and Hara found their interests too widely separated, and we have the Smarta-Vaishnava struggle instead. With Mughal prosperity at its height, Akbar could ream of a synthetic din-e-ilahi; Aurangazeb could only try to augment his falling revenue by increased religious persecution and the Jizya tax on non-believers.

So sum up, writing the Gita was possible only in a period when it was not absolutely necessary. Shamkara could not do without intense polemic. To treat all views tolerantly and to merge them into one implies that the crisis in the means of production is not too acute. Fusion and tolerance become impossible when the crisis deepens, when there is not enough of the surplus product to go around, and the synthetic method does not lead to increased production. Marrying the gods to goddesses had worked earlier because the conjoint society produced much more after differences between matriarchal and patriarchal forms of property were thus reconciled. The primitive deities adopted into Shiva's or Vishnu's household helped enlist food-gathering aboriginals into a much greater food-producing society. The alternative would have been extermination or enslavement, each of which entailed violence with excessive strain upon contemporary production. The vedic Aryans who tried naked force had ultimately recombine with the autochthonous people. The Gita could certainly not promote any fundamental change in the means of production. At best, it might reconcile certain factions of the ruling class, or stimulate some exceptional reformer to make the upper classes admit a new reality by recruiting new members.

6. THE SOCIAL FUNCTIONS OF BHAKTI. However, the Gita did contain one innovation which precisely fitted the needs of a later period: bhakti, personal devotion. To whosever composed that document, bhakti was the justification, the one way of deriving all views from a single divine source. As we have seen from the demand for the quite insipid Anu-Gita, this did not suffice in its own day. But with the end of the great centralised personal empires in sight – Harsha's being the last – the new state had to be feudal. The essence of fully developed feudalism is the chain of personal loyalty which binds retainer to chief, tenant to lord, and baron to king or emperor. This system was certainly not possible before the end of the sixth century AD. The key word[25] is samanta which till 532 at least meant 'neighbouring ruler' and by 592 AD had come to mean feudal baron. The new barons were personally

responsible to the king, and part of a tax-gathering mechanism. The Manusmriti King, for example, had no samanthas; he had to administer everything himself, directly or through agents without independent status. The further development of feudalism 'from below' meant a class of people at the village level who had special rights over the land (whether of cultivation, occupation, or hereditary ownership) and performed special armed service as well as service in tax-collection. To hold this type of society and its state together, the best religion is one which emphasises the role of bhakti, personal faith, even though the object of devotion may have clearly visible flaws.

Innumerable medieval 'hero stones'[26] commemorate the death in battle – usually a local cattle-raid – of an individual who was not on the same footing as the ordinary villager. In older days, the duty of protecting the disarmed villages would have been performed by the gulma garisoning the locality. The right of bearing arms (with the concomitant obligation to answer a call to arms) was now distributed among a selected class of persons scattered through the villages. More striking is the Ganga baron's sacrifice of their own heads in front of some idol, to confer benefit upon their king. More than one inscription declares the local warrior's intention not to survive his chief. [27] Marco Polo[28] reported of the thirteenth century Pandyas that the seigneurs actually cast themselves upon the king's funeral pyre, to be consumed with the royal corpse. This suits the bhakti temperament very well. Though barbarous, it is not the type of loyalty that a savage tribal chief could expect or get from his followers, unless his tribe were in some abnormal situation.

7. THE GITA TODAY, We shall be unable to discuss here just what underlay Jnanesvara's important decision to write on the Gita in the vernacular, rather than in Sanskrit. The main social problem was put upon a new footing by Alauddin Khilji, who defeated the Yadava king

within a couple of years of the Jnanesvari comment, and imposed payment of heavy tribute. This intensified the need for more effective tax collection, which meant powerful feudalism. Whether the tribute was actually paid or not, and even over regions not subject to tribute, the imposts and exactions grew steadily. The class that collected the surplus retained an increasing portion, so that the needs of the state could be satisfied only in the earlier period, when feudalism stimulated agrarian production. After that, the crisis deepened once again, to be resolved by another foreign conquest that introduced a totally different form of production, the bourgeois-capitalist. The modern independence movement did not challenge the productive form; it only asked that the newly developed Indian bourgeoisie be in power.

It follows that a new commentary on the Gita would accomplish nothing today. Anyone may pursue the original and appreciate it according to his leisure and his own aesthetic powers, purely as a literary exercise. To read some new social meaning into it is fatally easy, because it lumps together so many contradictory views; but it would be futile and dangerous. Futile because the inner contradictions of the bourgeois capitalist or any other class-society can no longer be solved on a world basis. The system is bound to work in India, but not very well and not for long. There is no point in justifying it or for criticising it on the basis of proto-feudal theology. The future obviously belongs to a classless society, irreconcilable to any earlier form dangerous, because any such attempt would give the Gita a spurious authority, which may then be used to divert attention from the essential problem. It would automatically lend undue weight to bhakti, which can easily be made to justify fascism, or any other cult of personality.

Individual human perfection on the spiritual plane is much easier if every individual's material needs are first satisfied on a scale agreed upon as reasonable[29] by the society of his day. That is, the main root of evil is social. The fundamental causes of social evil are no longer concealed from human sight. Their cure lies in socialism: the application of modern science, based upon logical deduction from planned experiment, to the structure of society itself. Science is at the basis of modern production; and no other tools of production are in sight for the satisfaction of man's needs. Moreover, the material needs could certainly be satisfied for all, if the relations of production did not hinder it; the most powerful country of today takes pride in growing food by the most modern technique and then destroying it to keep up prices. Any loyalty now must be to principles, not primarily to individual leaders. From sound principles, correct reasoning tested by reality will furnish guide to action. Without effective action, no philosophy has any substance.

Footnotes

1. The Poona edition of the Mbh was begun under the editorship of the late V.S. Sukthankar, and the Adi, Sabha, Aranyaka, Udyoga and Virata parvans completed under his direction. Succeeding volumes have been less satisfactory, and editorship of the late V.S. Sukthankar, and the Adi, Sabha, Aranyaka, Udyoga and Virata parvans completed under his direction. Succeeding volumes have been less satisfactory, and edition is not yet completed. For the Gita in particular, the readings generally assumed to be Shamkara's have been retained against the norm accepted for the rest of the edition. Among the many useful translations of the Gita are those of F. Edgerton (Harvard Oriental Series), K.T. Telang (Sacred Book of the East), and S. Radhakrishnan (London 1948).
2. In particular, the translation of dharma as religion, or even a Universal Law for all society was a new concept with Buddhism', not accepted even after the time of the G. For example, Manusmriti 8.41 reads 'The (king) must inquire into the laws (dharma) of each caste (jati), district (janapada), guild (shreni) and household (kula) and only then give his own legal decision (sva-dharma)'. A great deal of the confusion over the Gita derives from ignorance of reality, of the actual practices of large social groups; and from taking Brahmin documents as representative of all Indian society.

3. The standard reference work is F.E. Pargiter's The Purana Text of the Dynasties of the Kali Age (Oxford, 1913). Some of the theories have been contested. e.g. A.B. Keith's review in the JRAS, but the work has survived and gained a well-deserved reputation for its synoptic edition of the historical kernel in the major puranas.
4. The standard reference work is F.E. Pargiter's The Purana Text of the Dynasties of the Kali Age (Oxford, 1913). Some of the theories have been contested. e.g. A.B. Keith's review in the JRAS, but the work has survived and gained a well-deserved reputation for its synoptic edition of the historical kernel in the major puranas.
5. Translated in S. Beal: Buddhist Records of the Western World (London 1884, Vol. 1, pp. 184-186). The equivalent of G. 2.37 does occur on p. 185, and the association with a great battle at Dharmashetra, where bones still whitened the earth, is explicit, in an otherwise garbled account.
6. V.S. Sukthankar : The Nala episode and the Ramayana in Festschrift F.W. Thomas, pp. 294-303, especially p. 302, where he concludes that the two versions bracket the extant Ramayana. The paper is reprinted in his Memorial edition, (Poona 1944), pp. 406-415. For the mechanism of inflation, see his Epic Studies VI; and my notes on the Parvasamgraha, in the JAOS 69, 110-117; for the Bhishmaparvan and the 745 stanzas of the Gita, *ibid.* 71.21-25.
7. J. Brough: The early Brahmanical system of gotra and pravara (Cambridge, 1953), p. 27, notes that the kevala Angirasas are completely omitted by Hiranyakeshi-Satyashadha, but takes this to be a casual lacuna. So great an omission is highly improbable. My review in JAOS 73.202-208 was mistaken for a polemic, when the point being made was that theoretical works on gotra need to be checked by independent observation. For example, the shegrava (shaigrava) gotra found in Brahmi inscriptions at Mathura is not known to the books. Even more striking are the innumerable local brahmin groups whose conforming to theory has never been tested. City people in Maharashtra take brahmins to be primarily of the Sarasvat, Citpavan, Deshastha and Karhada groups. The 1941 Census caste tables for Bombay province as published show that such categories are together outnumbered by Bhargav and kevala Angirasas).
8. Ashvaghosha's Budhacarita and Saudarananda still exist, not to speak of subhashita verses scattered through anthologies in his name. The fragments of a play Shariputraprakarana

were arranged in order by H. Luders, from Central Asian (Turfan) finds. This or another play of the same name was acted by hired actors in Fa Hsien's time in the Gupta heartland, as were also similar plays on the conversion of Moggallana and Kassapa, note that all three disciples were Brahmins.

9. The Mbh. diaskeuasts proclaim their desire to include everything. In Mbh. 1.1-2, the work is successively an itihasa, a purana, an upanishad, a veda and outweighs all four vedas together. It is the storehouse for poets. Mbh. 1.56.33 boasts: yad ihasti tad anyatra, yan nehasti na tat kva-cit: 'whatever is here might be elsewhere, but what was not here could hardly ever be found!' Translated by K.T. Telang, see note 1. There is an Uttaragita, a quite modern apocryphal work.

11. This is the second sutta of the Digha-nikaya, and has served as the model, in many ways, for the later Milindpanho, questions of king Menander.

12. This was clearly stated by Mr. C. Rajagopalachari in a press interview.

13. The only published source I have been able to locate for the original cult is the Satya Pirer Katha in Bengali by Rameshvara Bhattacharya (ed. by Sri Nagendranath Gupta, Calcutta University 1930).

14. This paragraph and the next are treated in greater detail in a paper of mine on the avatara syncretism and possible sources of the Bhagavad-gita, JBBRAS: Vol. 24-25 (1948-9), pp. 121-134.

15. RV. 8.96.13-14, but sometimes interpreted mystically as part of the Soma legend. The traditional explanation is that this Krishna was an 'Asura', i.e. non-Aryan, and the fighting against Indra on the banks of the Amshumati river was real, not symbol of something else.

16. Ed. K. de Vreese, Leiden 1936. This particular naga cult had been virtually killed by the Buddhist monks (Rajatarangini 1. 77-8), while the brahmins had also been reduced to helplessness at the time of the Buddhist teacher Nagarjuna. They made a come-back by writing the purana (Raj. 1.182-6), as Kalhana informs us in passing.

17. ABORI 1.59-66, JRAS 1909. 1055-6, 1087-92; 1910, 813-5, 815-7.

18. See a forthcoming article of mine 'At the Crossroads' in the JRAS; for the cave painting (originally discovered by Carlleyle). Mrs. B. Allchin in Man, 58. 1958. article 217 + plate M (pp.153-5).

19. The assurance is unmistakable: "Whenever true belief (dharma) pales and unrighteousness flourishes, then do I throw out another offshoot of myself". The next stanza proclaims: The god comes into being from age to age, to protect the good people, destroy the wicked, and to establish dharma. It need not be further emphasised that the superfluous incarnation in Mbh. times wasted a perfectly good avatara, badly needed elsewhere.
20. The cult is coeval with the foundation of Parvati village, hence older than the Peshwa temple to the goddess who killed that demon. Cf. Bombay Gazetter, Vol. 18, pt. 3 (Poona District), p. 388.
21. Art in the Ice Age by J. Maringer and H.G. Bandi, after Hugo Obermaier (London 1953), especially figures 30, 31, 70 (with Mask and arms imitating mammoth tusks), 142, 143, and perhaps 166.
22. This shows in Hara's inscriptions (e.g. Epigraphia Indica 7.155-60); benedictory verses at the beginning of his Buddhist drama Nagananda, addressed to Gauri, Bana's description in the Harshacharita and Hsiuen Chuang's account (Beal 1.223; the stupa, vihara, fine Maheshvara temple and the Sun-temple were all close together near Kanauj, and all constantly thronged with worshippers).
23. For the iconoclasm of Harsha of Kashmir, Rajatarangini 7.1080-1098. He had predecessors of similar bent, though less systematic: Jayapida in the 8th century (Raj. 631-3; 638.9) and Shamkaravarman (5.168-70) in 883-902 A.D.
24. The Gupta gold coinage is impressive, but hardly useful for normal transactions. Their silver coinage is notoriously inferior to say, pre-Mauryan punch-marked coins and rather rare in hoards of Harsha, only one coinage is known, and even that rather doubtful, in silver. The Chinese travellers Fa Hsien and Hsiuen Chuang are emphatic in the assertion that most of the transactions were barter, and that cowry shells were also used, but very little currency. The accumulation by temples, monasteries, and barons did nothing for the circulation of wealth or of commodities.
25. This is discussed in a paper of mine to appear in the Journal of the Economic and Social History of the Orient (Leiden), on feudal trade charters. Yasodharman of Malwa uses Samanta as neighboring ruler, whereas Vishnushena (a Maitraka King) issued a chartered 592 AD where samanta can only have the feudal meaning.

26. The hero-stones carved in bas-relief are to be found in almost any village not recently settled, throughout Maharashtra and the south. A good collection is in the National Defense Academy's Museum at Khadakwasla, near Poona. The death in fending off cattle raiders seems to be symbolised in many cases by a pair of ox-head in the lowest panels. The story progresses upwards, to the funeral perhaps with a sati, and going to heaven. The top of the relief slab is generally carved in the semblance of a funerary urn, familiar since Buddhist days. For inscriptions, even a single volume (Epigraphia Carnatica X, for example): Kolar 79, feudal grant for family of baron killed in battle (about 890 A.D.):, Kolar 226 (circa 950 A.D.), grant of a field, on account of the death of a warrior fighting against cattle raiders; Kolar 232 (750 A.D.), Kolar 233 (815 A.D.), Mulbagal 92, 780 A.D.; Mul-bagal 93, 970 A.D. and C, with the hero-relief in every case.
27. Less well known than Ganga inscriptions are the minor one showing how widely the custom was spread : e.g. from the El Carnatica, Goribindnur 73 (circa 900 A.D.), the village watchman sacrifices his own head; Cintamani 31 (1050 A.D.), when the Odeya of the village of the village went to heaven, his servant had his own head cut off and a field was dedicated to his memory; oaths of not surviving the lord are taken in Kolar 129 (circa 1220 A.D.), Mulbagal 77 (1250 A.D.), Mulbagal 78 and C Occasionally, a memorial was erected to a particularly able hound, as in Mulbagal 85 (975 A.D.), and Mulbagal 162, though the dog's prowess rather than bhakti is praised.
28. Penguin Classic L 57, Travels of Marco Polo (trans. R.E. Kathim), pp. 236-8 for the cremation, and ritual suicide in front of some idol, by royal consent.
29. By 'society' is meant not only the rulers but the ruled. If the shudra should agree that he ought to starve for imaginary sins committed in some supposed previous birth, either his group will die out, or at best be unable as well as unwilling to fight against invaders. Feudal Indian history, however, is full of raids and counter-raids, not only by Muslims. It follows that the expropriated class will not show by its actions that they regard the expropriation as reasonable on religious grounds, particularly when they see the very same religion unable to defend its proponents against armed heretics. My point is simply that the fulfillment of certain material needs is as essential to health of the mind as it is to that of the body. It seems to me that the Gita philosophy, like so much else in India's 'spiritual' heritage, is based in the final analysis upon the inability to satisfy the material needs of a large number.

8

Ramayanas

Nagin Das Sanghavi

Valmiki whose Ramayan is the oldest and still the most authentic text on the legends and stories of Rama exuding robust self confidence jubilantly proclaims that "so long as mountains stand and rivers flow on this earth, this Katha of Rama will flourish amongst masses." [Part I Chapter 2 Stanzas 36-37]

But what exactly is this Katha of Rama or Ramayan as it is usually named?

If Ramayan implies a collection of legends and stories about Rama and his family, then there is nothing specifically Hindu about it nor is it confined to India alone. Over a vast span of Asia stretching from the borders of Afghanistan to the eastern shores of Japan, there is no language and no nation that does not claim to have its own collection of legends and stories related to Rama or what can be called Ramayan of their own. A collection of all such epics and poems, dramas, stories and folk literature from various countries will fill up a huge multi-lingual library. As Tulsidas mentions in his Ramcharitmanas, there are thousands of millions of Ramayanas. [Ludden. Making India Hindu]. This ocean of Ramayan literature can be classified into three groups-books written in the now unused languages like Sanskrit, Pali and Ardhamagadhi.

Ramayans written in modern Indian vernaculars in various regions of India and the literature in non-Indian languages.

Valmiki is traditionally rated as Adikavi- the first poet of classical Sanskrit literature- a claim rejected by modern scholarship, but his Ramayan [200 BC] is certainly the first narration of the life and exploits of Rama. The Vedic literature from the Samhitas to the Sutras does not mention Rama either as a hero or as a divinity though there are a few obscure references to his family of Ikshavakus and to some of the characters of Ramayan. In fact, prior to Valmiki, Rama, unlike Krishna is a totally unknown figure and we have no way of knowing from where Valmiki collected his source material. But scholars have postulated the existence of legends and stories of Rama among the folk literature.

Apart from Valmiki, the earliest mention of the story of Rama is found in Mahabharata where Ramopakhyan is narrated in answer to the anguished inquiry from Yudhishthir as to any one else has suffered as much agony as he is undergoing for upholding moral values. Sixteen out of eighteen Puranas [written between sixth to twelfth century AD] narrate the story of Ramayan- the most extensively in Padma Purana with several additions and interpolations in Valmiki Ramayan. Since Valmiki's volume was undergoing continuous revisions, some of these additions and distortions got incorporated in the original text and has now become ingrained in Hindu psyche. Ten heads and twenty arms of Ravana are first mentioned in Vayu Purana and it is Skanda Purana that makes Hanuman the son of Shiva as well as his incarnation and it is here that life long celibacy of Hanuman is mentioned for the first time. Valmiki never mentions Hanuman as a brahmachari and in fact his house is described as teeming with beautiful women. [Strijanshobhit] Bharat gifts him with 32 women and he accepts the gift. Shiva Purana makes Rama a devotee of Shiva and mentions the temple of Rameshwaram built by him. There is no such thing in Valmiki. Bhavishya Purana declared that Sita that was abducted was only her shadow and the purpose of the fire ordeal of Sita was to burn the shadow off so that Rama gets united with the real one. Mahabhagwat Purana makes Sita a daughter of Mandodari. There are endless such additions and distortions in the Puranas; but then Puranas were never very highly rated by Vedic Pandits among the Hindus.

Hindus have a flourishing tradition of deifying human heroes and thereby creating more and more gods out of nothing: the process has been going on from the days of Rama to this very day when Saibaba and Santoshi Mata are being included in the ever expanding pantheon of Hindus. Buddha and Mahavir have suffered the same fate as Rama. In Valmiki and even in Mahabharata Rama is a rare specimen of human hero who chooses to suffer for upholding moral values and traditional virtues. But he graduates from human hero to godhood and is then transformed in to the Supreme Brahma. This led to the writing of numerous sectarian Ramayanas, the best known and very highly rated one amongst them being Adhyatma Ramayan also known as Maharamayan or Arsharamayan or Gyanvashistha. The story is full of philosophical discussions but it adds a new character of a crow-Kagbhushandi who narrates Ramakatha and explains the esoteric significance of the incidents in the life of Rama. The story of earth assuming the form of a cow to complain against the atrocities of Ravan and Lakshman abstaining from food, sleep and sex for fourteen years are added to Rama story by Adhyatma Ramayan. Adbhuita Ramayan is highly influenced by Shaktaism and Sita gets more prominence here than Rama. Mandodari buried her fetus in the ground and Janaka unearthed Sita from the site. Sita warned Rama about a thousand headed Ravana and when Rama failed to fight with him, it was Sita who killed him and she kills Rama and Shiva also. Anand Ramayan declares Sita to be an incarnation of Padmalakshmi and Ravan carried her off in childhood but she was later on abandoned by him. The protecting circle around Sita drawn by Lakshman is mentioned here for the first time and Sita was suspected when she could draw an exact painting of Ravan. Sita had delivered only one child Luv but it was a Rishi who lost him, made another child out of Kush grass and called him Kush. It was a Bhushandi Ramayan borrowing the story from Padma Puran and describing in great details the story of Rama having eaten the berries tasted by Shabari.

The story of Rama, the characters and incidents of Ramayan proved to be a rich and ever attractive source for the creative writers of Sanskrit literature. So many dramas, poems and novels dealing with the theme of Rama have been produced by these masters with great literary gifts that an exhaustive list will of all of them would cover a volume. Smt. Juthika Ghosh has prepared such a list. Of nearly 10 plays about various episodes in the life of Rama, Bhavbhuti's Utterramcharita is hailed as the best by the critics and of nearly 20 short and long poems telling the story of Rama, Raghuvamsha of Kalidas is the longest and the best. There are about 15 dramas all titles Raghavas and are known as Raghava dramas. They adopted the story but added numerous incidents and episodes, not found in the original Ramayan. The story of Ahalya converted from stone to human being by Rama the meeting between Sita and Rama prior to their marriage in the garden, the presence of Ravan in Swayamvar of Sita, the peace talk of Angad with Ravan are some of such additions that have now been ingrained in the belief system of Indian masses.

Over and above such extensive literary products, the devotion to Rama has produced a flood of stotras, bhajans and padas and stuties that can hardly be compiled or even listed. Tatvasamgraha Ramayan and Ramayan Tatvadarpan of seventeenth century did acknowledge the debt of several earlier Ramayans and other books but does not name them. Tulsidas has also mentioned that he has used several sources for his Ramcharitmanas but he too avoids naming them.

The tremendous popularity of Ramayan goaded if not forced the Jains to produce their own version of Ramayan emphasising the moral values and concepts peculiar to their own creed. Jains wrote in Ardhamagashi. The oldest of Jain Ramayans is Vasudev Vahindi of Sanghdas but Vimal Suri's Paumchariyam is far better known amongst such texts. Most of Jain Ramayanas describe the escapades of Lakshman and Hanuman and portray them as womanisers. Jains have a logical explanation of ten heads of Ravan as they were his faces reflected in his necklace of nine gems. Vasudev Vahindi makes Sita the first child born to Ravan and Mandodari who was abandoned because she was declared to be inauspicious. She was put in a box and floated in a river where she was found by Janak. The sin of killing Ravan was done by Lakshman and not Rama. Vimal Suri changed the name of Rama to Padma [Pauma] and Ravan is a staunch Jain but he was overcome by his passionate yearning for Sita and there was no fighting between Vali and Sugriva as Vali handed over his kingdom to his brother. Utter Purana written by Gunabhadra also describes Sita as a daughter of Ravan. Kathavali of Bhadreshwar contains a story that was picked up by several later writers both Hindus and Jains. The sisters-in-laws of Sita made her draw an exact replica of Ravan and that created jealousy and suspicions in the mind of Rama and resulted in final expulsion of Sita.

Trishashihisalaka Purushcharitra of Hemchandra-charya mentions Dashrath as having fled Ayodhya out of fear of Ravan. There are several other Ramayans by Jain writers but they are of minor importance and are more or less copied from Paumachariya of Vimal Suri.

But it was left to Buddhist versions of Ramayan to take the Ramayan to all the countries in East Asia. These stories were written mostly in Pali which is the scriptural language for the Buddhists. In most of the Buddhist Ramayanas Sita is the daughter of Dashrath and Rama has married his own sister. Diggha Nikayya declares that Rama was exiled by Dasharath for such incestuous relationship. Shakyas are the children of this marriage and the Shakya dynasty being the family of Buddha is highly rated by Buddhists.

Dasharath was the ruler of Kashi and has married 16000 queens in Dasharath Jatak. Rama, Lakshman and Sita born of his different wives are thus siblings. Stray and indirect references to the episodes in the life of Rama are found in several Jatakas but detailed and exhaustive Ramayans in Pali are few in numbers. Buddhacharit of Ashwaghosh contains the story of Ramayan that is more or less same as Valmiki. Mahavibhash is not available in its original but as translated by Yuan Chwang contained a summary of Ramayan. Anami Jatak as translated by Kang Seng Hui tells the story in a slightly modified form. The king accepted voluntary exile to keep up his vow of Ahimsa and his wife was abducted by a demon. Monkey king helps him find his wife and the story ends in happy reunion. Dashrath Nidan as translated in Chinese also mentions Rama story in very brief outline.

It was the Buddhist version of Ramayan that was translated in various Asian languages with the spread of Buddhism but it is very surprising that Ramayan immediately became a popular story in whichever language it was translated. As Dr Brokington notes in his 'Righteous Rama' "the spread of Rama story was very much involved in this cultural diffusion to the extent of becoming a part of national tradition in several nations."

Chinese Ramayanas are mostly translations of Pali Ramayans but Japanese Ramayans are borrowed from the Chinese stories and hence one more step away from the original story. Hobutsushu's collection of Japanese folklore narrates the story of Rama who insisted on retiring to forest rather than give up his vow of Ahimsa and his wife Sita insists on going with him. She was abducted by a demon. Sambo Ikotoma mentions the killing of Shravan by Dasharath who gets revived and the story ends in a happy mood. Tun Hwang manuscripts contains many references to Rama katha where usually Sita is the daughter of Ravan who was abandoned by her parents. Rama-Lakshman are brothers and when Rama is exiled, Lakshman becomes the king. Ravan abducted Sita but Rama knew that soul of Ravan was in the head of a horse that was killed and Ravan died. When Ravan went to fight a war, Sita was left by him into a Buddhist monastery with 500 monks and she delivered Lav there. But the child was lost by a Bhikkhu who made a child out of Kush grass. Sita was exiled when accused by a washman's family but Hanuman proved the purity of Sita leading to final reconciliation. Khotan Manuscripts has a different Ram-katha. Dashrath has a son known as Sahasrabahu and his sons are named Rama and Lakshman. Sita, the abandoned daughter of Ravan, was brought up by a bhikkhu and married Rama and for her protection there was a permanent circle was drawn. Rama allied with Nanada and killed Sugriva and Nanda helped him to kill Ravan.

But it is in South East Asia that Ramayan is far more popular.

During Kohaba-Kankaria festival in Sri Lanka, the Ramayan is recited and discussed. This festival is the celebration for the birth of the third son of Sita. Rama accepted voluntary exile for seven years and Sita was abducted during this prolonged absence. Vali befriended Rama, burnt Lanka and retrieved Sita but she was deserted by her suspicious husband. She delivered Lav in the ashram of Valmiki who lost Lav and made a child out of Kush grass. But Sita doubted this story and Valmiki in order to prove, created the third son.

U Aung wrote his Ramayatry in based on the traditions prevailing in Manmyar [Burma] Dasgiri [Dashgriva] molests a female monk who commits suicide and is immediately reborn as Sita who is deserted by Dasgiri. Lakhanna and Bhadar are brothers of Rama and it is Gambhi who helps Ravan in abduction of Sita. The story of Mahiravan-Gondadipa is also narrated here. Ramayan is very popular in Thailand with its capital city named as Ayuthia [Ayodhya] and several of its kings are named as Rama. Rama I collected all the available Ramayan literature and wrote Ramkien. Dramas and dances based on Ramayan story are very popular in Thailand. Anjana wife of Khadoum [Gautam] had two sons born out of her illicit relations with Sun and Indra. One of the sons betrayed her and she made both of them monkeys named Fali [Vali] and Sukhrip [Sugriva]. Her daughter Savaha was fertilised by Indra who dropped his semen in her mouth and she gave birth to Hanuman. Fali defeated Thotukson [Dashkantha] and snatched his wife Nangmontha [Manodari] and had a son by her named Angad. Thotsaoth [Dashrath] was married to Kakeyasi and a part of his semen was taken by a crow and put in the body of Mantha who gave birth to a girl named Sida [Sita] who was abandoned and found by king Chonak. In Thailand, Ramayanas Hanuman is very sexy philanderer. It was Rama who founded Ayuthia and ruled in Thailand for forty years. Ramayan in Laos is the story of Fra Lak [Lakshman] and Fra Lam [Ramaa] Dasharatha had a beautiful daughter abducted by Ravan. Twin sons of Dasharath Lak and Lam fought with him to free their sister. Ravan escaped and founded Lanka but he stayed with Indra and seduced his queens one of whom was born to him as a daughter and stabbed Ravan. Ravan threw her away but when she got adult tried to marry her. But Janaka married him off to a shadow and gave Sita to Fra Lam. When Ravan abducted Sita, Lam searched for her but ate some fruit and became a monkey. As a monkey lam produced two Hanumanas who jointly searched for Sita and jointly constructed the bridge to Lanka. The epic of Ramkerati in Cambodia [ancient Kamboj] mentions all the characters of Ramayan in ,local dialect and a quaint humor with local flavour.

The oldest Ramayan of Indonesia is known as Kakquin by Shri Yogeshwar and is a faint copy of the poem Bhattikavya in Sanskrit language. The enmity between Shabri and Vishnu ended in the life of Rama and all the seven wives of Indrajit fought with Rama. Mandodari was the wife of Dashrath when Sita was born. Hikayat Shrirama in the Ramayan epic of Malaya and is a mixture of Islamic beliefs and folklore. Dasharath was married to Mandudaki [Mandodari] but donated her to Ravan for officiating as a priest. Sita was born out of the illicit sex between Dasharath and Mandodari on the former's visit to Lanka. Rama and Sita were transformed as monkeys and Sita got pregnant during this time. Hanuman was born of Sita. All such shocking versions of Ramayan would stun the orthodox but they signify the spread of Indian culture in what is known as Greater India to the scholars of Ancient Indian History and Ramayan being the cultural motif and the torch bearer of Indian culture. One has to add that Ramayan is still the living tradition in all these regions.

Lastly we turn to the Ramayanas that were produced in various vernacular languages of India during the medieval period. These were not the direct translations of Valmiki's epic but literary creations based on the story as depicted by Valmiki with considerable additions and distortions of the original Ramayan. The oldest such Ramayan is Kampan's Iramavatar in Tamil. For Kampan, Rama is the Supreme Deity and the creator controller of the universe. He emphasises the Ahalya story and lays great stress on the recitation of Ramanam. Hanuman could cross the ocean only because he endlessly recited the name of Rama. Pampa Ramayan in Kannada is the oldest Ramayan in that language and has been written by Nagachandra under his pseudo-name Abhnav Pampa. Sita had a twin brother who was abducted in childhood.

This Ramayan describes in great details the escapades of Lakshman during the exile in forest he inadvertently kills an ascetic. Vali is not mentioned by name but there is a Maya-Sugriva killed by Rama. The other Ramayanas in Kannada are Yogendra Ramayan and Utter Ramayan but Toran Ramayan of Kumar Valmiki is far more popular and respected. Ramcharit or Ramakathapattu, Kanvash Ramayan and Ramayan Champu are well known in Malayali but Atiyatu Ramayan of Apputtachan is much more popular. Based on Adhyatma Ramayan it narrates the story of Valmiki being a bandit for the first time and depict Ravan as a great scholar of Mahyan Buddhism. The epic does not mention the war between Rama and Ravan.

Telugu language has three Ramayanas— Ramayan of Rangnath, Bhaskar Ramayan of Hulakki Ramayan and Molla Ramayan. It tells the story of goddess of sleep granting two boons to Lakshman. He does not sleep for 14 years and his wife Urmilla sleeps for all the 14 years.

Ramayan tells the story of north Indian royalty but is far more popular in South India and vernacular Ramayanas were written first in South Indian languages. The first vernacular Ramayan in north India is Krittibas Ramayan in Bengali and it added several new incidents and episodes in Valmiki's epic. Sita was afraid of Rama marrying another wife and Ravan is made a staunch devotee of Shiva. Mahiravan, the son of Ravan abducted Rama and Lakshman and prepared to sacrifice them to Devi. Sita drew the accurate portrait of Ravan and put it in her bedroom arousing suspicion and anger of Rama and Sita was exiled again. Chandravati presents the story in slightly different way. The portrait of Ravan was drawn on a fan and while Sita was asleep the fan was put on her breasts making Rama wild with anger. There are three more Ramayanas in Bengali language. There are numerous Ramayana in Udia and Assamiya language but none is very noteworthy either as literature or for innovations.

Hindi Ramayanas come much later and the earliest of them was by Vishnudas of Gwalior but the best is undoubtedly Ramacharitmanas of Tulsidas. This has now become the standard and the most authentic text for the orthodox Hindu audience. Tulsidas is a great poetic genius and there are many other literary productions by him. Ramacharitmanas took many years in the making and Tulsidas has metamorphosed not only the contents but even the format of Ramayan. The first two parts of Ramayan—Balkanda and Ayodhyakand takes up nearly two-thirds of his volume and he has deleted Uttarkand. Tulsi begins with the discussion between Shiva and Parvati but the threads are picked up by Kakbhushandi and once again the narration is picked up by Shiva. This may be due to the long interval of years that the Manas was being composed. Kashmiri Ramayan of Divakar Bhatta is a very interesting in that it makes Mandodari bent upon destruction of Ravan. Lavkushcharit of the same language extols the exploits of Lav and Kush who killed Rama and all his three brothers.

Marathi has several Ramayanas the best known being Bhavartha Ramayan of Eknath, Mantr Ramayan of Moropant, Ramayan of Swami Ramdas, and Ramvijaya of Shridhar. Gujarati language is poor in this respect because Girdhar Ramayan is not of much value and a few stray incidents of Ramayan have been utilised by poets like Bhalan and Premanand.

SECTION - C

RELIGION AND POLITICS IN CONTEMPORARY INDIA

9

Role of Hinduism in Modern Indian Society

UDAY MEHTA

India has witnessed a massive upsurge of traditional as well as modern religio-mystical cults of God-Men, Swamis, Gurus, Shastries, Bapus and Bhagats particularly during the last three decades. Some of these cults operate at local, district or regional level, while some have established an extensive network at national as well as international levels. Along with the new cults, the hold of various traditional religious sects has acquired new dimension in recent years. Increasing politicisation of religion in last few years has posted a serious dilemma with regards to role of religion in modern Indian Society.

It is not only in India but even in Western Countries particularly even in industrially advanced nations like the USA the new along with traditional religious movements have gained an unprecedented momentum in recent years. The growing influence of religion in USSR and China has been also widely reported. The powerful influence of the church in Polish Solidarity movements and Buddhist impact on Vietnamese liberation struggle has been also widely acknowledged. The dominant role of the church in overthrow of the authoritarian regime in Philippines and the Buddhist monks' hold in recent reactionary political upheaval in Ceylon could not be overstressed. Decisive influence of Islamic fundamentalism in Iranian revolution and several other Muslim countries has been sufficiently highlighted. While the emergence and significance of the liberation theology in Latin America would call for an independent appraisal.

The persistence and extension of religious influence in advanced Western Countries, in colonial and post-colonial nations of Asia, Africa and Latin America, and even in so called socialist societies have raised some basic questions with regard to the significant of religion in human society. Large number to the sociologists and anthropologists on the basis of their survey of primitive as well as modern societies have come to the firm conclusion that it is impossible to visualise any present or even future society devoid of presence of religion in some form or the other. They feel that the need for religion would be felt in all human societies, irrespective of their cultural or technological levels, or socio-economic systems as religion fulfills some basic urges, emotional needs and provides sense of security to individuals. Several critics in this context have also pointed out the hollowness of the Marxist dictum of reducing the significance of religion as an opiate for the oppressed and exploited strata.

Marxist View

It is true that Vulgar Marxist appraisals have focused exclusively on the role of religion as opium for the poor and highlighting its reactionary significance for the toiling people. Nevertheless such dogmatic and objective approach evolved by Marx and Engels in their critique of religion.

A close perusal of the views expressed by Marx and Engels on religion as reflected in their various works, as their observations on the radical significance of the early Christianity, its peculiar origin and Jescus as messiah of the oppressed and in their writing on present war in

Germany, highlighting Munzer's effective use of the poor peasants. Their works on Hegel's philosophy of Right, the Holy Family, Jewish question and others reveal their deep concern for all relevant facts, their dynamic approach, examination and modification of their interpretations in the light of fresh appraisal and exposure to new situations, and the least dogmatic assertions, as the dominant features of their perspective on religion.

Marx and Engels in all probability were influenced by Tylor's view in tracing the origin of religion in the primitive man's sense of awe and fear, in the face of an inexplicable nature, religion emerging as fantastic reflection in man's mind of those external forces that control their daily life. It was however Engels who first pointed out that "while both magic and religion have their origin in humanity's lack of control over the forces of nature, religion however also reflects humanity's lack of control over the social forces that resulted from class domination." Marx and Engels in their concrete appraisal of the role of religion through the ages highlighted its contradictory functions, its positive as well as negative significance. While indicating that historically the primary function of religion world over had been to sanctify repressive institutions, they have also brought out the fact that rebellious movements, among the oppressed in pre-bourgeois periods and even subsequently, the aims and aspirations of social agitations have also found needs and expectations of the insurgent masses.

Such observation also throw new light on Marx's dictum that religion is the opium of the masses, which is generally presumed to mean that religion is a drug which enable the toiling strata to bear their miseries by loosing themselves in dreams that deprive them of the capacity to revolt. This is the conception of the Enlightenment philosophers and it is undoubtedly a good deal of what Marx meant, but it is not all that he meant. Immediately preceding his famous sentence is the sentence 'religious distress is at the same time the expression of real distress and the protest against real distress. Opium dream could rouse to protest and struggle, could stimulate as well as stupefy. Nevertheless, option is naves conducive could not be achieved at that time, as the struggle for it could only be an anticipation of the future, that the urge for it assumed the form of fantasy?

However, it should be pointed out that Engels thought that since the French revolution, religion has become incapable of serving any progressive class as the ideological vehicle of its aspirations. This is not come true as borne out by the heroic contribution of the liberation theology particularly in several Latin American Countries in strengthening and extending the struggles of the oppressed and exploited against the ruling oligarchy, similarly the role of catholic Church in Polish liberation struggle and recent solidarity movement of independent trade union could not be brushed aside as reactionary by any stretch of imagination. It has been also reported that Buddhist theology made significant contribution in heroic Vietnamese liberation war against American imperialism.

In this context, it should also be noted that the persistence and spread of religious influence in so-called socialist countries as well as advanced capitalist nations do not disprove the validity of the Marxist observation on religion. As indicated earlier it was Engels who first suggested that till men acquire control over social forces (which would not be possible in all class societies) religion in some or the other form would persist. In this sense, it is neither in USA, nor USSR, or for that matter even in China or in other countries, so called working class states, toiling people have acquired command over social forces nor exploitation and oppression of man by man has come to an end. This generates a climate of uncertainty and increasing insecurity leaving enough space for flourishing of religious influences.

Religion in Modern Indian Society

As indicated earlier, India is experiencing a new wave of religious revivalism especially since last three decades what is being projected as Hinduism in recent years is a novel concept based on crude amalgam of various contradictory set of beliefs, rituals and practices.

As pointed out by Romila Thaper, "The New Hinduism which is being currently propagated by the Sanghs, Parishads and Samaja is an attempt to restructure the indigenous religions as a monolithic, uniform religion rather paralleling some of the features of semitic religion.

Further, "Hindu sects unlike Buddhism or Islam are characterised by distinct and independent origin connecting them to particular founder or text. Only at a later stage attempts were made to assimilate some of these sects into dominant sects. What has survived over the centuries is not a single, monolithic religion but a diversity of religious sects which today have been put together under a uniform name."

Frequent reiteration by upper caste elites these days that Hinduism for last thousand years has passed through very severe persecution conveniently ignore the fact that in the history of last thousand years, "Hinduism has witnessed the establishment of the powerful Shankaracharya Maths, ashramas and similar institutions attempting to providing all ecclesiastical structure to strengthen conservatism, the powerful Dashnamis and Bairagi religious orders, the popular cults of Nathpanthis, the extremely significant sects of the major Bhakti teachers as Tukaram, Namdeo, Vallabhacharya, Chaitanya, Dadoo and Kabir, not to mention Nanak. The establishment of the sects, accompanied by wealthy patronage does account for the prosperity of temples and institutions. The last thousand years have been most assertive thrust of the major 'Hindu' sects.[4] As a matter of fact non-violence of Hinduism is the nineteenth century myth, largely invented as a response to requirement of nationalism stressing the spiritual superiority of Indian culture.

Romila Thaper has aptly coined the new term, 'Syndicated Hinduism' for modern Hinduism. According to her, 'Syndicate Hinduism, draws largely on Brahmanical texts, the Gita and Vedantic thought, accepts some aspects of the Dharma Sutras and attempts to present a modern reformed religion. It ends up inevitable as a garbled form of Brahmanism with a motley of 'Values' drawn from other sources, such as bringing in elements of individual salvation from the Bhakti tradition of some puranic rituals. Its contradictions are many. The call to unite under Hinduism as a political identity is anachronistic.[5]

This new Hindu phenomena has acquired strength as a result of the widening of the social base of political Hinduism in the post-independence period. The backward castes or more appropriately 'the other backward classes' who benefited from the intial phase of agrarian reforms have now entered the socio-religious spheres which were till recently preserves of the upper caste-Hindus and have developed stakes in them. This phenomenon is also described as a process of political Sanskritisation. Large scale mobilisations as the Skatmata Yagna and the Ram Janam Bhoomi Andolan, in all probability would not be possible without the actual involvement of this enlarged base. Moreover, the following observation deserves attention: "The closing of ranks between the upper castes and the backward castes in recent seeks external enemies in order to consolidate its somewhat uneasy solidarity. Hindu communalism directed against minorities and scheduled caste is one of the outcomes".[6]

Nineteenth Century Religio-Reform Movement and Modern Hinduism

The chauvinistic thrust of the new Hinduism becomes strikingly evident if one compares it with the dominant spirit of the religio-reform movement of the nineteenth century and the Bhakti Movement of the medieval period in India.

The modernisation process introduced by the British despite its distorted nature, encouraged a secular and rational outlook, scientific knowledge and technical skills, new ways if thinking and self-reliance. It was a process by which men began to breakaway from medieval customs and superstitions and the fatalism based on traditional beliefs in *karma, Maya* and transmigration of the soul and by which new occupations and new relations among men began to emerge.

As brought out by Late Damodaran "The Nineteenth Century thinker, though could not completely free himself from the concept of the supernatural but he began to interpret karma creatively instead of totalistically. The concept of karma underwent a radical change. Fatalism gave way to a new sense of strength and confidence. The new thinker asserted that caste distinctions, priest and animal sacrifices and customs like sati and child marriage were not ordained by God or karma, but were created by man's ignorance".[7]

Raja Ram Mohan Roy inaugurated the modern age in India. He opposed the caste system, idol worship, religious separatism, child marriage and the practice of sati. He advocated remarriage of widow, inter-caste marriage, supported English education and fought for freedom of speech. He founded Brahmo-Samaj. The teachings of the Brahmo-Samaj are summarised as follows:

> "The wide universe is the sacred temple of the Brahman of the supreme being. The pure heart is the place of pilgrimage. Truth is the one eternal scripture. Faith is the foundation of all religions. Love is the desire is the only form of ascetic renunciation recognised and proclaimed by the members of the Brahmo-Samaj".

Further, "This universalism appears to be a synthesis of the best elements of the upanishadic teachings and the ideas of Islam and Christianity".[8]

Ranade was also inspired by the teaching of the Brahmo-Samaj, proclaimed intense faith in individual freedom and human dignity. He instead that revival was impossible and that reform was the only alternative open to sensible people. The emphasis is of life to mundane existence. Freedom of individual was now interlinked with his social and political emancipation.

"In the middle ages' as so aptly argued by late Damodaran," self-emancipation was interpreted as an escape from the idea of sansara i.e. from social life. The ultimate aim of life was top end cycle of births and deaths, to liberate the atman from the physical body and the material environment and to modern age the concept of self-realisation assumed a new meaning. The self was no more abstracted from life. The self was the social life, the self was that could find the fullest being only in social life, self-realisation as the realisation of the identify of the individual self with the universal self, meant the identification of one self with the whole of humanity. Man could realise himself only in other man, in the totality of human existence that is Brahman." Vivekananda himself explained this truth as follows:

"The individual's happiness is the happiness of the whole; apart from the whole, the individual's existence is inconceivable. This is an eternal truth and is the bed-rock on which the universe is build".[10]

As a matter of fact, freedom, democracy and human dignity were the values of the Nineteenth Century. Old values of renunciation, denial and withdrawal began to give place to social action. Concepts like *karma* and *dharma* assumed new meaning.

Nevertheless, while the fact of freedom of the distinct contribution made by the nineteenth century religion-reform movements is true, one should not overlook the fact that the Bengal renaissance as well as its counterpart of Maharashtra were essentially sponsored by upper caste elites who were initially exposed to western liberal ideas and value and had aspiration based on democratic and scientific spirit. Although they came in sharp conflict with Sanatani orthodox Hindu religious protagonists, their impact was by and large confined to certain selected intellectual circles.

In sharp contrast to this elitist movement, it is argued that the movement led by Jotirao Phule through the Satyashodhak Samaj founded by him in 1873, should for the old social order sought by the former under the pretext of modernisation.

As pointed out by Gail Omvedt, "Their identification was in the Hindu cultural system and as modern intellectuals concerned about the Hindu developed an ideology which sought to use a revitalised Hindu tradition as the spiritual and moral centre around which the liberal modernism of the west could be created".[11] This is also bubbed as "Eastern Morals and Western Science". Upper caste elites accepted the "Aryan Theory of Race" which had implication of identifying them ethnically with their British conquerors rather than majority of their country-men, which traced civilisation in India from the Aryan conquest, and which provided a new pseudo-scientific justification for the case hierarchy. And they developed an economic theory which looked to the capitalist development of India freed from the destructive bonds of British Imperialism. Hence, they opposed foreign exploitation without considering the exploitation of workers by native capitalist or peasants by landlords and lower bureaucracy.

It is further argued that the majority of Indians were dark-skinned non-Aryans. The majority of Indians were peasants and had no hope either in the near or distant future of becoming members of the bureaucratic elite or capitalist, large or small. The liberal modernisation of Hindu culture and the capitalist development of India did not conform to their interests. Peasants, tribals, workers, low caste, untouchables were all adversely affected by the colonial regime and responded like the upper caste elites, with both renaissance and rebellion, their ideology and organisation remained in a more incident, crude, localised and in complete form. Nevertheless it may be said with Jotirao Phule the low caste, non-Aryans, peasants masses of India came to consciousness.

While taking note of the fact that Dayanand's version of Aryan culture was not racial as he stressed on acquisition of virtues of ideal vedic practices and rejected birth as determined of individual's status in society and similarly Vivekananda called for the liberalisation of women and ending of Brahmin superiority even as he bitterly attacked "westernised reformers". Gail Omvedt along with several others holds the view that those religious leaders sought to harmonise the early emphasis aof liberal and conservative Brahmins. They argued that the Hindu nation must be considered holy; but insisted as well that social evils of the present day, including caste, were not ancient religious customs. They formulated a revivalistic nationalism that was to have dangerous anti-Muslim aspects.

In dismissing totally the dominant religious traditions of India, it is further stated that, Phule accepted the assumption that something had to be put in its place; even a revolutionary culture required a moral religious centre. Hence he never rejected the idea of Dharma but rather attempted to establish a universalistic one. Sarvajanik Satya Dharma, it is suggested that expressed this concept completely: implying that the moral basis of society has to be centred on truth or rationality and it had to be one that unified all men and women as equals. The world was regarded as good and holy, in contrast to the Vedantic projection of its as an illusion.

Further the same author remarks that Phule's thinking does not show: Indian tendency to the reconciliation of opposites and is based upon the principle that an irreconcilable conflict of interest existed between the Brahmin elite and non-Brahmin masses. Secondly, Phule's theory of exploitation focuses on cultural and ethnic factors rather than economic and political ones. Although he displayed great concern for economic and political aspects of exploitation, Phule's ideology, in short was based on identification with peasant masses and on attachment to revolutionary values of equality and rationality such concern for the poor kisans also reflected in his projection of Baliraja as a peasant god, drawing on the image of the common man and his focus on the plight of woman and untouchables.

The basic question that is posed in this context is about the appropriate centre of a "national culture." If the focus is on Sanskritic Hinduism, Vedic Culture, Vedantists Philosophy, Mahabharata and Ramayan stories, this implies bias in favour of the upper caste and towards indirect support of the caste system and geographically in favour of north India. If the emphasis is towards non-Vedic culture, towards traditions of religious cultural revolt running through Buddhism and the Bhakti cults, then the bias is socially in favour of the masses and geographically in favour of the outlying linguistic regions of Indians. In scholarship and nationalist thinking the bias upto now has been towards been towards a sanskristic and therefore elite basis to Indian culture, but in fact non-sanskritic traditions have as much claims to an all-Indian spread."

Non-Brahmin movement or what was also popularised as self-respect movement in Tamil Nadu under the leadership of Periar had powerful emotional appeal for the masses. Periar preached a new secular form of marriage which would have no priest of any caste. Idol-breaking, removal of caste name plate (particularly those of Brahmins), propagating the eradication of superstitions beliefs and practices, burning the copies of Ramayana and the Puranas and demanding the expulsion of the Brahmin from Tamil Nadu, were his major programmes of anti-Brahmanism. Periar's popular methods of communication and programmes adopted by him created the popular stream in the elite N.B.M in Tamil Nadu.

Both these protest, movement against the Brahminic domination and landlord, money-lenders exploitation of poor kisans in Maharashtra, later degenerated into castists and elitists movement utilising anti-Brahmin platform for sub-serving the interest of vocal and affluent sections of backwards castes. In a sense they over a period started, articulating the aspirations and interests of the rich farmers and intermediate caste elites that had begun to emerge under the British patronage and the socio-economic changes brought about as a result of the British conquest in India. In the case of Tamil Nadu the movement was dominated by the elite right from its inception.

As a matter of fact the recent aggressive version of Syndicate Hinduism is jointly sponsored and articulated by the upper and backward castes. As observed earlier backward caste have acquired wider social and political base as a result of first hand reforms introduced after independence.

As we could see the major focus of particularly the nineteenth century religio-reform movement and even of much more radical pro-poor movement led by Phule including that of non-Brahmins movement in Tamil Nadu was on the Propagation of liberal values and rational outlook and were essentially directed against orthodox Brahminic rituals, undesirable customs as Satee, child-marriage, prohibition of widow-marriage, superstitions, monopoly of priesthood, against untouchability and for the spread of education among women, towards the improvement of women's plight and their rehabilitation against monolithic, aggressive, highly authoritarian new version of Hinduism as projected by the upper and backward caste in recent years.

The progressive liberal character of the nineteenth century religio-reform movement, though dominated by upper caste affluent section and despite is very limited impact, could be seen in its reinterpretation of traditional religious deals, Tatawam Asi, self-realisation in terms of striving for collective happiness of Indian humanity late Damodaran while tracing the genesis of the post-independence resurgence of religious revivalism remarks, "Millions of people had hoped that political independence would lead to new social order which would abolish poverty, unemployment and human degradation and guarantee opportunities and freedom for every individual to build his personality. But all these hopes believed in practice...."

The widespread poverty and unemployment, exploitation and squalor, are leading to human degradation torment sensitive hearts. Corruption, bribery and black markets have generated a "get rich-quicker" mentality and abominable "success ethics" has begun to dominate society. Moral values are sacrificed at the altar of the profits, rent and interest. The individual regards his own interest as something opposed to the interest of the people. This exaggerated pre-occupation with one's own person vitiates and distorts all human relations. It is only natural that under such conditions man is encountered with a sense of insignificance and powerlessness. He is subjected to feelings of isolation and abandonment. This situation has already produced a crisis of cultural and spiritual values leading to frustration and despair. People are left with a feeling of emptiness. The turmoil and the squalor, the anxieties and the anguish the anarchy and the violence created by the capitalist path of development make life untenable and miserable".

Vast bulk of toiling state, petty bourgeois and others gravitate towards religion out of sheer sense of helplessness and apathy. Ruling classes by effectively playing on this sense of frustration and helplessness among the masses have whipped up religious propaganda which has already become instrumental in dividing and generating animosities among the different sections of Indian population on communal lines.

As a matter of fact since Independence the ruling classes in India as pointed out by Dr. A.R. Desai have evolved a dual policy which may appear contradictory but has proved extremely effective in perpetuating their rule and consolidating and expanding the capitalist development in this country. In economic, administrative and legal spheres they have evolved logical, rational, this worldly approach that could result in maximisation of economic gains to bourgeoisie. While in social and cultural sphere they have encouraged feudal institutions and traditional, religious values which has succeeded in stupefying, confusing masses and generating pessimistic, fatalistic outlook among them. With increasing political instability and aggravation of economic crisis as reflected in growing unemployment, widespread industrial sickness, increasing population of masses, rising inflation and the total bankruptcy of the ruling party and the state in resolving them, the dominant classes are desperately seeking to regain their credibility by increasingly relying on whipping up of religious sentiments in order to retain their hold over people in recent years.

In this context, it is interesting to note that material conditions created as a result of the introduction of modernisation process by the British in the nineteenth century paved way for the emergence of religion-reform movement which in sense also articulated the aspiration of the rising bourgeois. Decadence and utter bankruptcy of the capitalist system in resolving any of the basic economic, political, social or cultural problems faced by the Indian society and the resultant crisis of the legitimacy have created conditions giving rise to new aggressive, religious fundamentalism particularly since last decade.

As pointed out earlier, the modern version of Hinduism itself is based on concoction and distortion of earlier historical traditions and unfortunate identification of nationalism with Hinduism since the nineteenth century (an outcome of peculiar historical situation). It has sufficient room for future distortion. Hinduism as popularly projected today is down right reactionary formation and rules out any possibility for the emergence of any form liberation theology within its fold.

Buddhism in its formative stage was certainly far more liberal and progressive with dialectical orientation compared to later Vedic or Upanishads traditions. Under the circumstances, Dr. Ambedkar's protest against Hinduism took the form of call to his followers to unblock conversions to neo-Buddhism.

It is also suggested that focusing on dynamic elements of earlier Buddhism, certain sects of medieval Bhakti movements, radical aspects of Satyashodhak Samaj and other non-Brahmin movement one can evolve liberation theology which may prove quite effective in mobilising the oppressed and exploited classes and ultimately might pave way for just and egalitarian social order free from all form of exploitation.

Unfortunately the entire history of social movements based on caste and sectarian loyalties drawing inspiration from some of the above traditions does not leave much room for such optimism.

In this context it is worthwhile to draw a contrast between the dominant Hindu religious traditions and early Christianity. Jesus Christ was literacy a messiah of poor and oppressed and he upheld their cause and ultimately was criticised for this 'crime'. Heroic martyrdom of Jesus for the proletarians of his time leaves enough scope for the future inspiration. Secondly, the missionary traditions in the church of working with the poor, coupled with peculiar oppressive and suffocating conditions in most of the

Latin American countries could give birth to liberation theology. In India, conditions are quite different in terms of nature of capitalist development, political set up, astute leadership of bourgeois, even in terms of history and traditions of the country. It is not surprising that one of the main architects of Indian theology of liberation had to admit that as far as India is concerned, liberation theology is likely to be in low key in the years ahead, due to specific conditions obtaining here. As he further remarks, "the parties of revolution have been tamed and absorbed into the bourgeois politics of power and expediency to a point where they scarcely differ from the parties of order. Gandhism is today a spent force, being no more than a convenient ritual. The prospects of fresh revolutionary energies springing up from the subterranean consciousness of the masses are not bright. The power of the establishment to neutralise dissent knows no bounds."

10

Undermining National Institutions to Create Regimented Minds

IRFAN ENGINEER

The students of FTII are agitated (2015) over appointment of Gajendra Chauhan as President Chair of the Governing Council of the Institute. About 150 students pursuing various courses at the FTII are on an indefinite strike against the patent political appointment because of Chauhan's affiliation with the BJP. When we google Chauhan, all the information we get is that he acted in films like *Andaaz* (2003), Baghban (2003) and *Tumko Na Bhool Payenge* (2002). Wikipedia informs us that he acted in 150 movies and 600 TV serials. However, links to only some of the movies Chauhan acted in are given and when we follow the link, often his name is not even mentioned in the star cast of the film. Chauhan claims that he has worked in 600 serials, however only one TV serial in which Chauhan acted was popular – *Mahabharat* where he played the role of eldest of Pandava brothers – Yuddhishthir. He may have acted in 600 episodes. Students felt that Chauhan lacked the vision, stature and experience and was not qualified for the post which was once occupied by Satyajit Ray, Mrinal Sen, Girish Karnad, Shyam Benegal and Adoor Gopalkrishnan. Noted film makers like Anand Patwardhan have expressed their serious concern over the appointment of Chauhan when the shortlist included Gulzar, Shyam Benegal, Saeed Mirza and Adoor Gopalkrishnan. The previous incumbents of the Chair were winner of prestigious awards, including Padmashree, Padma Vibhushan, Sahitya Akademi, Dadasaheb Phalke, Jnanpeeth and other prestigious Awards. Gajendra Chauhan has no such credentials. There is lack of transparency in the appointment.

There is no explanation forthcoming from the Ministry of Information and Broadcasting on the appointment of Chauhan. Nor has Chauhan been able to explain his eligibility for the job. All he has said is that the opposition from the students will only make him work better. He has not been able to spell out his vision for the Institute. Appointment of such a low profile person as chair of such a prestigious institute when persons like Shyam Benegal, Adoor Gopalkrishnan and Gulzar were shortlisted, can be explained only by the fact that Chauhan was special invitee to the BJP National Executive for two terms. The other explanation that is doing the rounds is that the RSS backed his appointment. The RSS involvement gains credence as four of the eight members nominated under 'Persons of Eminence' category to the society are from the Sangh Parivar. Anagha Ghaisas, has a strong RSS background and made documentary films supporting Prime Minister Narendra Modi. Her husband was a long-serving Sangh pracharak – 17 of his 21 years as pracharak were in Gujarat. Another member is Narendra Pathak who was the Maharashtra president of the ABVP for four years. Pranjal Saikia is an office-bearer of the RSS-linked Sanskar Bharati. Rahul Solapurkar was in contention for a BJP ticket in last year's State Assembly elections.

These political ladies and gentlemen, having links with the Sangh Parivaar, have been selected in the category of 'persons of eminence', on the governing council of FTII as they do not have any independent vision for the Institution. When Indian Express contacted them, they responded that they wanted the FTII students to have nationalistic (read Hindu nationalist) feeling. FTII in the past has groomed students to think freely, differently and boldly. Creative arts and aesthetics rarely come from conformist thinking, and even less from those accept hierarchies of race, caste, community, ethnicity, nationality, gender regionality or on any ground whatsoever; and accept hierarchical structures as natural and desirable. They produce conformist arts for propaganda. The objective of the FTII includes among others, "*to constantly endeavour at raising the technical standards of Indian films and television programmes so as to make them aesthetically more satisfying and acceptable; to facilitate regular inflow of* ***fresh ideas and new techniques*** *in the field of Cinema and Television and a corresponding outflow of trained personnel imbibing these ideas and techniques; to* ***create a new awareness*** *among the future workers in film and television of the potentialities of their media* ***not only as means of entertainment but also of education and artistic expression***". Does the present appointee to the Chair and the four Governing Council members seem suited to ensure these objectives of the FTII when their vision is to have students with nationalistic feeling?

Prime Minister Modi proclaimed himself to be a Hindu nationalist in his election campaign. The Hindu nationalists have always justified caste system and patriarchal traditions to be unique Indian values and superior. The Indian cinema is coming of age and moving away from the portrayal of cultural traditions of feudal upper caste elite with ethos like *pativrata Bharattiya nari*, observing *kadvachauth vrat* even if her husband was evil and indulged in all kinds of vices as the 'national culture'. There is increasing trend of films depicting live-in relations (*Cocktail; Pyar Ke Side Effects*) films with explicit and erotic scenes like (*Shuddh Deshi Romance*) bold portrayal of an assertive woman (*Dirty Picture*) questioning the motives behind wrongly accusing a Muslim as terrorist (*Khakee*) films portraying the deceits of godmen (*PK*) etc. One way of reversing this trend within the Indian Cinema is to influence and control the thinking and creativity of the students passing out of the FTII. Reduce them to be propagandist rather than creative artists questioning and critiquing what they witness around them and pushing cinematic boundaries, creating space for new creations. This can be done by ensuring, to the extent possible, that inflow of students is predominantly from elite and privileged social background as they love to be conformist; and by controlling the curricula which teaches them to be conformists and nationalists rather than creative artists. Being nationalist is to portray superior virtue of submissive wife and terrorism as the problem with terrorists belonging to one community.

NDA had earlier appointed Mukesh Khanna who had campaigned for the BJP, and was caught on camera calling Modi, "the Shaktiman (a character that he played) in Gujarat", as head of Children's Film Society. Mr. Khanna had played Bhisma in Mahabharata. Similarly, Pahlaj Nihalani, a film maker who made promotional videos on Modi was appointed as censor board chief, the I&B ministry also appointed Malayalam actor and BJP supporter Suresh Gopi as the chairperson of the NFDC, in another controversial decision. Zafar Sareshwala, a businessman confidante of PM Modi was appointed as Chancellor of Maulana Azad National Urdu University even though he has little knowledge of the language.

The larger issue

The larger concern is that not only FTII, but the Hindu Nationalist Organisation is systematically and in organised fashion percolating into the vital institutions of our democracy to undermine it, constrict the liberal secular space and promote hegemonistic Hindu nationalist ideology. The NDA Govt. is facilitating and partnering with the Hindu nationalists to achieve their objective of undermining academic autonomy and freedom to explore truth and frontiers of knowledge. The Hindu nationalists largely believe that *all* knowledge is in ancient epics, Vedic scriptures and Vedanta, and all one need to do is be immersed in these scriptures. PM Modi while inaugurating science exhibition in Mumbai University said that ancient India already knew how to make aircrafts as evident from the *pushpak viman.* Likewise Ramanand Sagar's depiction of Mahabharat on TV screen is evidence that India knew how to make nuclear missiles. Hindu nationalist would want to mythologize history and historicise mythology. Even when the BJP was not in power, the Hindu nationalists were in conflict with the academic freedom and autonomy of academic institutions. ABVP demanded that AK Ramanja's 300 Ramayans be removed, Aditya Thackeray pressurised the Mumbai University V.C. to remove Rohinton Mistry's award winning book *Such A Long Journey* from syllabus.

In order to accelerate the trend of mythologizing history and historicizing mythology, the NDA Govt. appointed Y. Sudershan Rao as chair of the ICHR, a premier body to encourage research in History. Just like the rest of the appointees, Prof. Rao is little known in history circles and was Head of Dept. of History and Tourism Management in Kakatiya University. In Prof. Rao's opinion, caste system was not such a social evil, and that rigidity and distortions had crept in after Muslim Invasion and as a result of it. This position is close to the Hindu Nationalist position.

The NDA Govt. created a situation wherein Nobel Prize winner Amartya Sen had to resign from the Chancellorship of Nalanda University only because he was critical of the policies of Modi Govt. Anil Kakodkar, former chairperson of Atomic Energy Commission of India and Chairperson of Board of Governor of IIT also wanted to resign on differences regarding selection of IIT Directors, but later withdrew his resignation. Earlier the HRD Ministry caused IIT Delhi Director Raghunath Sheogaonkar to resign on dubious grounds.

The other posts on which less eligible persons who were appointed mainly on their being camp followers of Hindu nationalist ideology are – Prof. Inder Mohan Kapahy as a member of the University Grants Commission (UGC); Vishram Ramchandra Jamdar as the head of Visvesvaraya National Institute of Technology, Nagpur; Baldev Sharma, former editor of RSS mouthpiece *Panchajanya*, as chairman of National Book Trust.

Academic freedom for students activities, an important part of academics. Under NDA Govt. even that space has been threatened. Human Resource Development Ministry made an 'inquiry' into the activities of a students' group – *Ambedkar Periyar Study Circle* in IIT Madras and caused to withdraw its recognition merely over comments being made against the Prime Minister. School Students were forced to hear PM Modi's radio talk – *Mann Ki Baat.* Hindu religion inspired culture is being forced down the throat of citizens with a circular that was issued to central schools saying that December 25 would be observed as "Good Governance Day" to mark the birthday of former Prime Minister Atal Bihari Vajpayee and the birth anniversary of Madan Mohan Malaviya. The circular asked the schools to "ensure active participation of your students". Similarly, Yoga Day is being forced even on unwilling citizens and students with Govt. involvement.

The NDA Govt. is homogenising culture and aggressively promoting Vedic and Hindu Epics based, mythologised culture of a small section of Hindu upper-caste on the entire people of India. Hindu culture is rich and diverse reflecting democratic aspirations of the people if we draw from great saints like Narsi Mehta, Tukaram, Mira, Ravidas, Gyaneshwar, Chokha Mela, Kabir, Bahinabai and many others from all regions, castes and from both genders. The great Hindu saints, particularly from the oppressed castes sang love, equality and opposed hierarchies and authorities of all kinds. Why doesn't the NDA Govt. not draw from these traditions? Are these not, according to them, Hindu traditions? Why the NDA partners like Lok Janshakti Party holding on to apron tail of the NDA Govt.? Is it only for power?

In the process of aggressively promoting Vedic-Vedanta-Hindu Epic based mythologized culture as national culture, the NDA Govt. is not only undermining autonomy of our institutions, but democracy itself. Democracy and fundamental rights of the citizens gives power in the hands of the organised citizens to check naked crony capitalism seeking to grab land, natural resources, cheap labour, and large chunk of Govt. budget spending. The NDA aggressively promotes Vedic-Vedanta-Hindu Epic based mythologized culture as it creates submissive followers accepting hierarchies and hierarchical authoritarian structures that does not question why social and economic inequalities are growing, but accepts with pride that 'nation is developing' just because a few industrialists are making super profit from exploitation of land, natural resources, cheap labour and with huge budgetary support of the Govt. Regimented, mesmerised blind followers only hero worship – they do not question. Hindu nationalists want national institutions to help create regimented minds.

11

Hindutva Politics and Democratic Norms

Ram Puniyani

The Hindutva politics took a qualitative leap from the decade of 1980s with the Ram temple movement. Its polarisation tactics around identity issues divided the society along religious lines. Its agenda of communal violence went on intensifying year by year. With this its electoral strength also went up and it came to seat of power in Centre in 1996 for the first time. The fragmentation of secular parties, the opportunism of these parties led to a state of affairs where by 2014, it could gain a simple majority in Lok Sabha. With this its affiliated organisations, increased their assertion leading to change in educational curriculum, attacks on minorities and undermining of scientific temper. With this the street violence and stifling the voices of dissent went up in the form of aggressive conversion campaign and attacks on those upholding secular, rational ideology and imposition of their agenda through the conduits of state mechanisms and through moves meant to marginalise the underprivileged and religious minorities. This essay discusses the so called Love Jehad, attacks on the rationalist-secular ideologues and also traces the transformation of Brahmanism to Hinduism and later its political hybrid the Hindutva.

(a) Hinduism: Brahmanic and Shramanic traditions

There are lot of confusions about Hinduism as a religion, its relationship with Brahmanism and Shramanism. Also the term Hindutva has come up presenting newer politics in the language of religion, adding to the confusion.

As such word Hindu came up from eighth century only. It came up as a geographical category to begin with. This term was coined by Arabs-Persians who came to this part of sub-continent. As they crossed river Sindhu, they used this river as a marker for the land on the east of this river. They pronounced it as Hindu. As such the people of this land till that time had many a religious traditions. Aryans who came here in the waves of migrations were nomads and later a pastoral society, not a 'nation state' as being asserted today. These pastorals' life and norms are reflected in the Vedas and Smritis.

The picture of social organisation of that time got articulated in Manusmriti. The hierarchical Varna and later caste system was the core of the social system. The dominance of Brahmans as *the* caste was undisputed and the social inequality was the central pillar of the society. The dominated castes, Dalits, were regarded as untouchables; they had to serve the upper caste, while other Varnas had also their privileges marked out. The upper caste had rights and the dominated castes had duties to perform. A very clear cut 'division of labour'!

It was in this context that Buddhism had come up with the message of equality and it started appealing to large sections of society, who opted for the values of social equality and embraced this religion. The advent of Buddhism; has been called as revolution by Ambedkar. This changed the social equation and caste hierarchy got a serious challenge. Apart from Brahmanism there were other religious traditions which prevailed here. Buddhism's challenge to caste system forced Brahmanism to come up with a new phase in due course of time. During this phase the cultic practices were broadened and public ceremonies and rituals were devised by Brahmanism to influence the broad masses to wean them away from Buddhism. The term Hinduism started being used for religions prevalent here. With spread of Buddhism the hold of Brahmin-landlord on low caste got weakened. Shankarachaya led the movement which opposed Buddhism at ideological level. Ambedkar calls this as *counter revolution.* This assault on Buddhism came was duly supported by the rulers, many a kings Pushyamitra Shung and Shashank being major examples.

Buddhism was wiped out from this land in the process and all the other religious traditions, from animism to atheism, came to be lumped under the umbrella of Hinduism. Hinduism as such has neither a single prophet nor a single Holy Scripture. The broad Hindu identity took shape with Brahmanism in command and other traditions on margins; subjugated to Brahmanism. From this time on the Hinduism as a religion got initial identity. The two major streams within this umbrella of Hinduism, Brahmanism and Shramanism had contradictory beliefs, values and practices.

So here we see the social process in which two diverse types of values, caste and gender hierarchy based Brahmanism; dominated and lorded over other traditions, which can be called as Shramanism. These are traditions like Nath, Tantra, Siddha, Shaiva, Siddhanta and Bhakti tradition had values which were more inclusive. These traditions were close to the poorer sections of society and had practices away from Brahmanical norms, especially caste hierarchy. As such since Buddhism and Jainism are also away from the caste hierarchy, they are also Shramanic traditions but not a part of Hinduism as they have their own prophet, and the boundaries from Hinduism are well demarcated.

Romila Thapar (Syndicated Moksha, Seminar 1987) sums up the process as "The Hindu religion as it is described today is said to have its roots in the Vedas. In any case, whatever we call the religion of these nomadic clans, it was not the religion that is today known as Hinduism. This (Hinduism in its current version) began to be formulated only in the period of Maghadha-Mauryan State..."

This process of hegemony of Brahmanism over other traditions' was further stepped up from nineteenth century onwards. As the British colonialists were not much interested in grappling multiple local traditions and as they did not understand the local diversity; they resorted to the guidance of Brahmins and recognised Brahmanism as *the* Hinduism. Their major advisors in matters of religion were Brahmins, who were employed by them. The Brahminic texts were projected to be having the key to understand the local religion and these texts formed the basis of British understanding of religion of this country. This Brahminical core got the veneer of Hinduism in a stronger way. Here the religion; Hinduism, is constructed by bringing together diverse tradition with contrary values under the single label of Hinduism. In this construct Brahminic value system dominated. This is what led Ambedkar to say that Hinduism is Brahminic theology. This formulation precisely defines Hinduism.

With the changes in the social system under British rule, with the rise of new social groups of industrialists and modern educated classes, the landlords and earlier rulers, the allies of Brahmins at social level, started feeling marginalised due to the new power equations, due to the potential of change towards democratic society, society with equality. This process also witnesses the rise of national movement, the rise of dalit-Bahujans as a nascent movement along with ideologies of liberation put forth by Jotirao Phule and later consolidated by Ambedkar. This dalit Bahujan ferment posed a serious challenge to the hegemony of Brahmanism. Buddha's preaching's and work was a threat to rulers-Brahmins, to the system prevalent at that time. Now with the dalit Bahujan ideology picking up on the social base of industrialisation-modern education; again the threat to hegemony of Brahmin-landlord became real.

At this point the landlord-Brahmin combine throws up the word Hindutva. First they shouted that education for dalit bahujan is against 'our' religion and later they formed political organisations in the name of religion to protect their socio-political interests. And with this comes in ideology of Hindu nationalism: Hindutva. This is a repacked Brahminism in political arena. So in earlier times Brahmanism undermined dalit Bahujans by adorning the label Hindu and still later the label adopted is Hindutva. In the newer definition of Hindu; as per them; has all non-Muslim, non-Christian traditions, like Buddhism, Jainism and Sikhism also incorporated in Hindu. This is political construction of Hinduism not a theological one.

Starting from Buddha to the medieval saint tradition to the movement led by Phule Ambedkar dalit-Bahujan has kept opposing caste-Varna system. Today with the ascendance to power of BJP-RSS, the Hindutva is again trying to camouflage its basic opposition to the interests of dominated castes. In the genesis of dalit Bahujan ideology one can see three major stages and also their major opponents. Buddhism opposed by Shakracharya-rulers, medieval saints opposed by ideology of Brahmin clergy (supported by rulers) and finally the Phule-Ambedkar ideology of liberation opposed by the political Brahmanism (Hinduism): the Hindutva.

While recalling non-Brahminic traditions one also needs to recall the traditions of dominated castes, dalits and Bahujans. These are traditions of rebellion and resistance in the language which keeps changing as per the context. The present phase is the one where the ideology of domination has adorned the name of Hindutva and is trying to undermine the interests of dalit-Bahujan in multiple ways.

(b) Love Jehad: Forcible Reconversion

Propaganda around conversions has been one of the major political tools during last few decades. It was Niyogi Commission report which investigated the conversions in Adivasi areas in 1950s, then the Meenaxipuram conversions of Dalits into Islam, the and then the gruesome murder of Pastor Graham Stewart Stains on the charges that he was doing the conversion; are few amongst the big spectrum related to the phenomenon of conversions.

As such the regular propaganda by communal forces that Muslim Kings converted people into Islam by sword has been made the part of 'social common sense' by now. On regular basis around Christmas time one saw the anti-Christian violence in Adivasi areas a decade ago, and in that context rather than focusing on the violence against religious minorities, the then Prime Minister Atal Bihari Vajpayee called for a National debate on Conversions.

In the recent conversions to Hinduism in Agra (10 December 2014) nearly 350 pavement dwellers-rag pickers and other destitute sections were promised that if they participate in the religious function they will be given the ration card and BPL cards. This was done by the Bajrang Dal activist and the Hindu Janjagriti Samiti both outfits affiliated to RSS. The only difference is that this process has been called as Ghar Vapasi and not conversion.On one hand this is being projected as a great valorous achievement by the RSS leaders like Yogi Adityanath, on the other it is being labeled as a master stroke by, RSS by other RSS ideologues. According to one ideologue of RSS, they had been calling for a ban on conversions, which was being opposed by the secular elements and religious minorities. This conversion nay Ghar Vapasi will bring to fore the debate to bring in the strict law against any conversion. If, as reported, the conversion of 350 odd

Muslims in Ved Nagar in Agra to Hinduism is the work of RSS, it is clear that the RSS has grown strategic, according to RSS ideologue.

As per this ideologue this move of RSS is a smart one too. It seems to have triggered a debate on conversions which it has been asking for decades but was evaded by its critics. While communal elements are crying hoarse that Meenaxipuram has been the act of conversions through petro dollars and the Christian missionaries are doing conversion through foreign money, the truth of the matter is somewhat different. Meenaxipuram conversion was triggered by humiliation of the dalit youth by the upper caste. While the propaganda that Christian missionaries are doing forcible conversions is in the peak the fact is that no evidence of the application of force has been generally reported. It is also true that while some sects of Christian do claim that they are converting; the majority sects affirm that when the conversion is sought by someone in the society and only under that voluntary request the conversion if at all takes place. Interestingly as many people have started believing that the missionaries are converting the population of Christians has been shown a marginal decline during last few decades as per census figures (1971-2.60, 1982-2.44. 1991-2.34, 2001 -2.30 and 2.30 in 2011) The Wadhwa Commission, which was appointed by the then home minister L.K. Advani in the aftermath of the burning of Pastor Stains points out that Pastor was not involved in the work of conversions and that in Keonjhar in Manoharpur of Orissa, the percentage of Christians has shown fair stability, or a statistical insignificant rise in the percentage of Christian population during the time Pastor Stains was working there.

How have conversions taken place in India? We can examine this in two stages. In medieval period as far as conversion to Islam is concerned it took place mainly due to the caste oppression, as pointed out by Swami Vivekananda "Why amongst the poor of India so many are

Mohammadens? It is nonsense to say that they were converted by the sword. It was to gain liberty from Zamindars and Priests.....” (Collected Works- Vol. 8- Page 330). Surely a small section did convert to Islam due to anticipation for reward by Muslim kings, a smaller section due to fear and a substantial chunk due to the social interaction as seen in the Muslims of Malabar coast and the Muslims of Mewat. Major conversion to Islam during medieval time was due to the influence of Sufi saints, at whose Dargah the untouchables could also visit. Since even today one-fourth of the population holds to the norms of untouchability, it is not surprising that some dominated castes do keep deciding to leave the fold of Hinduism, as was proclaimed by Dr. Ambedkar, who left Hinduism with proclamation that ‘I was born a Hindu; that was not in my hands, but I will not die a Hindu.”

The conversions to Christianity did not begin with the coming of British as propagated by some. Christianity is century’s old, entering India with the coming of St Thomas in the first century. Some doubt this version and hold that Christianity came here in fifth century. The Christian missionaries have been working here in the neglected Adivasi areas providing the health and educational services, the appeal of which prompted many an Adivasis-Dalits to embrace this religion. It is only from last six decades that communal forces have been showing their discomfort of missionaries working in the Adivasi-village areas violence has been more in those areas. Not to forget here is the point that many a Christian institutions are located in cities, where all sections of society vie to send their children. One can also concede that a few of these missions may be aiming for conversions through their prayer and healing services. The question of allurement and fraud, if at all, may be a small component of the phenomenon of conversion to Christianity. Most of the attacks and accusations which took place against Christian missionaries were at times when they were holding prayer meetings. The money they receive comes through proper FCRA channel, and many a NGOs including the organisations like RSS also receive foreign funds to be sure.

Now the assertion is that what RSS affiliates do is a Ghar vapasi! They claim so many things which are a pure political concoction. The voluntary conversions have very much been a part of caste ridden Indian society. It is another matter that even the Christian and Muslim communities could not remain free from this caste virus, but the hope of the dominated castes to get social justice has played a major role in changing one's faith. The RSS claim that the ancestors of all these converts are Hindus has no relevance in the debate. How is ancestry important in one's faith and the citizenship today? Do we have to trace our ancestry to decide today's faith? Where will this lead us? The theory of evolution apart the latest DNA studies show that human's beginning is from South Africa. The coming of Aryans to India from Arctic zone (Lokmanya Tilak) to that Aryans were original inhabitants of India is a perpetual debate, with more heat than light in it.

What was the religion of Nomads-Pagans? Some social scientists call it Indigenous culture, rather than religion for the phenomenon which was and is practiced by indigenous (Adivasi) people all over the World. Society is always changing. As caste system has been the central part of religion in India many of the dominated castes regularly kept leaving Hinduism to opt for other religions, Jainism, Buddhism, Christianity, Islam and Sikhism. People felt that they are not getting equality and so kept leaving the Hindu fold and embracing other religions. After Lord Buddha's teachings a large chunk of people became Buddhists in the sub-continent. It is another matter that later in the Brahminical reaction, Buddhism was wiped out from here. Many felt that the missions are doing service to their community so they changed their faith.

The problem, which RSS projects is due to its being hung up to the values and system of past; pastoral, agricultural-feudal societies. The changes in social system accompany the changes in systems of production and education in particular; are totally missing in its world view. India came into being through the freedom struggle led by Mahatma Gandhi, who could unite the people of all religions as he treated all religions on equal ground.

For him, there is no distinction between foreign and native religions. Three types of Nationalisms competed with each other during freedom movement. On one hand was the concept of Indian Nationalism and the accompanying concept of 'India as a nation in the making', this is what was followed by most of the people. The other was Muslim Nationalism, which located its beginning from the time of Muhammad bin Kasim's victory in Sindh in eighth century. And the third one was Hindu nationalism, 'we are a Hindu nation from times immemorial', held by the Hindu Mahasabha and RSS. Both these latter nationalisms derived their legitimacy from identity of religion had miniscule social support.

Unfortunately, Gandhi is quoted extensively by Right wing forces to oppose conversions; but his quotes which are taken support are fragments of what he said. His major quote on conversion is from collected works, Volume XLVI, pp. 27-28. In an interview dated 22nd March 1931, given to The Hindu, Gandhi apparently stated that "if in self governing India, missionaries kept 'proselytizing' by means of medical aid, education etc., I would certainly ask them to withdraw. Every nation's religion is as good as any other. Certainly India's religions are adequate for her people. We need no converting spirituality." This is the first part of the quote and the lines that follow give the totally opposite idea, the ideas, which Gandhi held. Gandhi goes on to write, "This is what the reporter has put in my mouth... All that I can say is that it is a travesty of what

I have always said and held." He goes on to explain, "I am, then, not against conversion. But I am against the modern methods of it. Conversions nowadays have become a matter of business, like any other... Every nation considers its own faith to be as good as that of any other. Certainly the great faiths held by the people of India are adequate for her people. India stands in no need of conversions from one faith to another." And then he goes on to list the faiths of India, "Apart from Christianity and Judaism, Hinduism and its offshoots, Islam and Zoroastrianism are living faiths."

As Gandhi opposed the divisive agenda of communal forces, which were using identity of religions for political purpose, Gandhi in contrast was harping on 'morality' of religions to unite the people. So while he was leading the anti-colonial struggle the communalists were spitting fire against the 'other community' and '*Shuddhi*' (Arya Samaj) and '*Tanjim*' (Tablighi Jammat) was part of their political agenda in the early part of twentieth century. The Hindu religion is not a prophet-based religion, so the concept of conversion is not there. In most prophet-based religions the call for spreading the divine word is there. So earlier Arya Samaj coined the word Shuddhi, which was for forcible conversion into Hinduism. RSS improvised on that and has coined the word Ghar Vapasi as a clever move to hide its 'forcible conversion drive'. Its claim that it is undertaking Ghar vapasi to bring the religious minorities in the mainstream is again a hoax as minorities had been equal participants in the movement for India's freedom, a struggle from which RSS remained aloof, barring one exception. To claim that adivasis are Hindus, is again does not hold water as Adivasis are animists, believing in nature worship, and in the spirit of their ancestors and spirit of Nature. All over the World indigenous people hold similar belief and have similar practice. This is unlike Hinduism where Gita, Ram and Acharya are the core part of it belief today.

The central point is that RSS does not recognise Indian nationalism and holds to Hindu nationalism so the whole maneuver for this 'forcible conversion' is being passed off as 'Ghar Vapasi' while dubbing other conversions as forcible. Rather than recognising the qualitative change in the formation of India as the nation state, it is stuck to the pastoral-feudal-preindustrial society with the values of caste and gender hierarchy. The 'Ghar vapsi' is being planned at larger scales. And an intimidating and fraudulent atmosphere is being created to execute the forcible conversions. This is a frightening message to religious minorities. This is a clever manipulation of political power to violate the norms of Indian constitution.

Then how do we distinguish between a forcible conversion and adoption of a new religion. In the present scheme of things if one leaves Hindu fold to embrace Buddhism-Jainism-Sikhism, it is OK, as they are 'Indian religions.' For communalists problem seems to be only with Islam and Christianity! The basic shrewdness is to call religions as national or foreign. As such religions are basically universal not bound by national boundaries.

Constituent Assembly had discussed this thread bare and so the right to practice and propagate one's religion is very much there. In the debate the word used is 'converting' others. Where is the place for people volunteering and adopting another religion, like Ambedkar and so many others? In a way it is a way to undermine the conscience of people that somebody is converting them. Where is the place for choice of one's religion in a democratic society believing in 'freedom of religion and conscience'?

With RSS plans for a bigger conversion nay Ghar vapasi in Aligarh this Christmas (2014) the attempt to polarize the society are being taken to a higher pitch. The heroes of RSS parivar like Yogi Adityanath are saying that those being subjected to ghar vapasi will be given the Gotra and caste from which they converted! So come what may the caste structure and rigidities remain and thrive. That's what the agenda of nationalism in the name of Hinduism is!

Do we need laws to ban conversions? We have laws to punish those who indulge in force, fraud and allurement. What we need is to distinguish between voluntary conversion and forced one's. Ghar Vapasi is a shrewd name for forcible conversions. So what we need is the political and moral will to promote freedom of religion and punish the guilty, using illegal means to achieve the change of faith. The so called 'Freedom of Religion' bills are there not to provide freedom of conscience but to curb the same by legal means.

(c) Killing a Rationalist: Silencing Reason

The killing of Professor Maleeshappa Madhivallapa Kalburgi on 30th August 2015 came as a severe jolt to all those who are for an open, liberal society, who uphold the values of reason and are against blind faith. Prof. Kalburgi was a renowned scholar with over 100 books to his credit. He had brought to fore the ideology of Basavanna; the Twelfth Century poet saint of Kannada; and had supported the idea that Lingyats, the followers of Basavanna be given the status of religious minorities as they do not belong to the Vedic tradition. His study of *Vachanas*, the teachings contained in the verses of Basavanna, was a profound contribution to the rational though.

It was his forthright reminder of Basavanna's teachings, criticism of idol worship and Brahmanical rituals, which earned him the wrath of Hindutva groups like Bajrang Dal. As there are many traditions within the broad pantheon of Hinduism, the atheist tradition has its own existence from centuries, Charvak being the one from ancient times. Even opposition of idol worship is not new to Hindu traditions as Swami Dayanand Saraswati, founder of Arya Samaj, had given the call to stop the idol worship.

Incidentally as we are receiving the news of this killing, the neighbouring Bangladesh has witnessed the murder of three young secular bloggers in recent times (2015). In Syria a Scholar Khaled al-Assad has been put to death by ISIS fanatics. Maharashtra was shaken by the murder of a rationalist of repute Dr. Narendra Dabholkar nearly two years ago. He was instrumental in getting the law against black magic and practices related to blind faith passed in Maharashtra. Another well respected activist, Comrade Govind Pansare was killed just a year ago. Pansare was working on many issues; anti-blind faith campaign being one of them. He is also the author of well known tract on Maharashtra's revered king Shivaji. Contrary to the communal presentation of Shivaji as anti-Muslim king, Pansare shows that Shivaji was the king who was very sympathetic to the farmers (*rayyat*) and that he was respecting all religions. This interpretation of Shivaji is a great eyesore to the Hindutva politics.

On the back of the murders of these two rationalists, comes the murder of Dr. M.M. Kalburgi on 30th August 2015 in his home in Dharwad. Prof Kalburgi was a very well accomplished man, ex-Vice Chancellor of Kannada University in Hapmi, and recipient of National and Karnataka Sahitya Academy Awards for his writings. The learned professor had deep study of Virshaiva, Basavanna tradition amongst others. The opposition to him was due to his criticism of idol worship, Brahmanical rituals and ritualisation of Basavanna tradition by Lingyats. Controversies followed him and so did the threats from conservative forces. The first one of which, was the publication of Marga treatise on Kannada folklore including articles on Virshaiva, Basavanna. Due to the death threats to him time and over again police protection was given. This police protection was withdrawn on his request recently. He supported U.R. Anathmurthy on the issue of stopping idol worship. When he invited VHP leaders and the pontiff of Vishveshra Tirtha Swami for a public debate;

another controversy followed. His support to Karnataka bill against practices of superstition invited anger of Bajrang Dal and associate organisations and he had to face protest; where his effigy was burnt.

There is a pattern in the murders of Dabholkar, Pansare and Kalburgi. Though there are some differences in the broad range of field of their social engagement, the similarity is very striking. They were rational, they made their voice abundantly clear and many threats were received by them. Another stark similarity is that all these three murders took place in early mornings by those who came on motor cycles, one person driving the bike and the second one pumping bullets. Strangely despite a long lapse of time the killers of Dabholkar and Pansare have not been nabbed so far.

After the murder of Kalburgi one Bajrang Dal activist Bhuvith Shetty tweeted, ***"Then it was UR Ananthamurthy and now MM Kalburgi. Mock Hinduism and die dogs (sic.) death. And dear KS Bhagwan you are next".*** This tweet was later withdrawn. Also many a person's related to Hindu right wing organisations started saying that Kalburgi had insulted Hindu gods, so anger among Hindus and so such murders. This is a subtle justification of the intolerance which our society is being gripped with. As such the attitude of communal elements in different religions is very similar. One recalls the threat to Salman Rushdie, the type of intolerance shown to Taslima Nasreen and the murder of bloggers in Bangladesh and also murder of Salman Taseer in Pakistan. Taseer had stood in defense of a Christian woman who was accused of blasphemy.

The opposition to the voices of reason has been going on in History all through. One can as well begin with Charvak, who opposed the Brahmanical understanding about the world, divine nature of Vedas in particular. Charvak said Vedas are manmade, social in nature, and was persecuted. Gradually with the power of clergy the imposition of faith on society became more institutionalised. Even teachings of Gautam Buddha, who was agnostic, and talked about the social nature of human problems, were attacked. This had led to the wiping out of Buddhism from India. The medieval Bhakti saints were also more for rational thinking, critical of the imposition of various social practices-rituals in the name of faith. Many saints like Tukaram in Maharashtra had to face persecution at the hands of those who were close to social power, the clergy.

Globally one can see the same pattern in Europe. In Europe the scientists, rational thinking had to face the opposition from organised Church, which condemned Galileo to hell for stating that the Earth is round etc. Similar was the fate of many scientists who had to face inquisitions and punishments of various types. Clergy hid behind the façade of 'divine authority': faith, and tried to stall the process of social change and halt the scientific thinking. The society over a period of time overcame the opposition to the rational thinking and so we saw the rooting of science and scientific inquiry. Clergy had maintained that they are the repository of whole knowledge; as knowledge is already there in our 'Holy books'. This is a part generalisation and it manifested in different cultures and religions in diverse ways. In Pakistan, some Maulanas asserted that the problems related to power can be solved by doing research on *djinns*, who are power houses of infinite energy; this was presented as part of the religious knowledge.

In India with freedom movement, those standing for social change and transformation did stand for rational thinking and critiqued the scriptures from that angle. The traditionalists, who wanted to retain the old social equations; resorted to 'our glorious heritage of knowledge'. Faith based understanding was counterpoised against the spirit of scientific inquiry. With independence, with Nehru being at the helm of affairs, the notion of 'scientific temper' came up in a big way paving the way for establishment of institution of higher learning and research; leading to the national growth and transformation towards democratic structures. This was the time when the nation was looking forward to all round progress and rational thinking was duly promoted. The national science resolution; based on reason and logic was passed unanimously in 1958.

Things start changing in the decades of 1980s. The politics in the name of religion came up in a very assertive manner and faith not only continued to be the emotional support system in the times of social anxiety but some political forces started asserting identity politics, faith-based politics. Identity issues and faith-based politics started getting more legitimacy. The social conservatism and undermining of rational thought went hand in hand. Incidentally it is around this time also when the groups promoting rational thought, scientific temper, groups to oppose blind faith, came up. The most prominent of these groups was Kerala Sastra Sahitya Parishad. Later in Maharashtra Narendra Dabholkar took the lead to establish Andhshraddha Nirmulan Samiti (Committee to oppose Blind faith).

This took the Maharashtra conservative elements by storm as the volunteers of this organisation started going from village to village and started demonstrating the science behind the magic tricks which were being practiced by hoards of Godmen and other of their tribe, who were taking full advantage of the social insecurity of poor villagers and exploiting them. Pansare, in addition to opposing blind faith was also disseminating the values of Shivaji, presenting him as a person respecting all religions, which Shivaji was. The right wingers could not stomach it; neither could they oppose the logical formulations presented by him. In Karnataka individual like U.R. Ananthmurthy articulated against idol worship and blind faith. Kalburgi not only supported U R Anathmurthy; he also went on the support the bill against the practices promoting blind faith. He did author papers/ books to disseminate his ideas.

Slightly back in time when the first NDA Government came to power with Dr. Murli Manohar Joshi as the MHRD minister, he introduced the courses like ritualism (*paurohitya*) and astrology (*jyotish shastra*) in the universities. This gave a big boost to the 'faith' based groups who were politically close to the politics in the name of Hindu religion.With the new government coming to power (2014) again now the mythology is being promoted as history, the *Pushpak viman*, 'plastic surgery in ancient India' etc. is being promoted; at the same time so called fringe elements, which as such are part of the Hindutva politics, are becoming more assertive. The liberal open space is shrinking and the place of debate is being taken by physical violence. The liberal values which accept the validity of differences is being eliminated by force, intimidation and even partly by state support. The murder of these '*saintly*' figures, Dabholkar, Pansare and Kalburgi, just goes to show that we are landing in a situation where those entrenched in the conservative values are becoming dominant and do not want the rational thinking to exist in our society.

The aggressive stance by the Hindutva right wing on those who are putting forward the rational thought, criticising the ills of caste system, idol worship etc. is ideological supplement to the politics of Hindu right wing. The march of this politics in recent years has been built around identity issues like Ram temple or cow slaughter. Their whole assertion is built around the Brahmanical Hinduism, which upholds the caste hierarchy. The ideology being propounded by the likes of Dabholkar, Pansare and Kalburgi stands closer to the ideology for liberation from the caste hierarchy, which is the root of Hindutva politics. This politics does target the religious minorities, while ironically Hinduism is so diverse with contradictory tendencies within same religious umbrella. Kalburgi's murder is part of the larger scheme of things where the ideologies opposed to the present *status quo* are being hounded along with persecution of those who are struggling to uphold these values.

On the other hand there has been a tremendous opposition to these brutal acts. The social groups upholding pluralism and rationalism have been agitating against these murders and the ideology of those involved in these killings. Opposition of sections of society to the murders of Dabholkar, Pansare and Kalburgi shows that there are still large numbers of people who are willing to uphold rational values and that gives a ray of hope for the times to come. In last couple of years after the murder of Dabholkar, various social groups have been coming together with a determination not only to oppose the intolerant conservative aggressive right wing politics, but also to take up the unfinished task of these slain pioneers committed to social change.

Bibliography

1. Waiting for Justice; National Peoples Tribunal on Kandhamal, Bhubaneshwar 2012.
2. Minorities in Contemporary India, Sebastian Vempeny, Kanishka Publishers Distributors, Delhi 2003.
3. Communalism and Anti-Christian Violence, Ram Puniyani, Mythri, Trivandrum 2006.
4. The Politics behind anti-Christian violence, Ram Puniyani (Editor) Media House, Delhi 2006.
5. Minorities in India Social system, Joseph Benjamin (Editor) Gyan Publishing House 2006.
6. Violenct Gods, Angana Chatterjee, Three Essays, Delhi 2009.
7. Rise of Fascism, Indian People's Tribunal, Delhi 2008.
8. Changing Gods-Rethinking Conversions in India, Rudolph Heredia, Penguin, Delhi 2007.
9. Breaking the Shackled Silence, Saumya Uma et. al, National Alliance For Women, Odisha, Bhubaneshwar, 2014.

Section - D
RELIGION AND LIBERATION THEOLOGY

12

Religion and the Left: An Introduction

Cornel West

Notwithstanding the secular sensibilities of most leftist intellectuals and activitist religion permeates and pervades the lives of the majority of people in the capitalist. And all signs indicate that the prevailing crisis in the capitalist world is not solely an economic or political one. Recent inquiries into the specificity of racism, patriarchy, homophobia, state repression, bureaucratic domination, ecological subjugation, and nuclear extremism suggest that we need to understand this crisis as that of capitalist civilisation. To exend leftist discourses about political economy and the state to discourse about capitalist civilisation is to accent a sphere rarely scrutinised by the Marxist thinkers; the sphere of culture and everyday life. And any serious scrutiny of this sphere sooner or later must come to terms with religious ways of life and religious ways of struggle.

In this introductory essay, I shall pose three crucial questions to contemporary Marxism regarding religion. First, how are we to understand the character and content of religious beliefs and practices? Second, how are we to account for the recent religious upsurges in Latin America, the Middle East, Asia, Africa, Eastern Europe and United States? And third, in which ways can these upsurges enrich and enhance-or delimit and deter – the international struggle for human freedom and democracy? In the present historical moment, these queries strike me as inescapable and important.

Religion and Marxist Theory

The classical Marxist understanding of religion is more subtle than is generally acknowledged. Crude Marxist formulations of religion as the opium of the people in which the religious masses are viewed as passive and ignorant objects upon which monolithic religious institutions impose fantasies of other worldly fulfillment and reveal more about Enlightenment prejudices and arrogant self-images of petty bourgeois intellectuals than the nature of religion. Marx and Engels understood religion as a profound human response to, and protest against, intolerable conditions. For Marx and Engels religion constituted alienated forms of human cultural practice under circumstances not of people's own choosing. On this view, religion as an opium of the people is not a mere political pacification imposed from above rather a historically circumstanced existential and experiential assertion of being (or some bodiness) by dehumanised historical agents under unexamined socio-economic conditions. Marx and Engels characterised religion as alienation not primarily because it often overlooks the socio-economic conditions which shape and mould its expression and thereby delimits human powers and efforts to transform these conditions. In short, the classical Marxist critique of religion is not an apriori philosophical rejection of religion; rather it is social analysis of and historical judgment upon religious practices. For Marx and Engels, religion often overlooks the socio-economic circumstances which condition its expression, principally because the religious preoccupation on human nature and personal morality holds at arm's length social and historical analysis. Hence religion at its worst serves as an ideological means of preserving and perpetuating prevailing social and historical realties and at its best yields moralistic condemnations of and utopian visions beyond present social and historical realities-with few insights regarding what these realities are and how to change them. The Marxist point here is not simply that religion alone is an impotent and inadequate form of protest, but also that it is without a probing and illuminating social and historical transformation. In stark contrast to crude Marxists, Marx and Engels do not claim that only a substitution of rigid Marxist science of society and history for false religion and glib moralism can liberate human kind, but rather that a Marxist social and historical analysis can more effectively guide transformative human praxis motivated, in part, by moral and/or religious norms of human freedom and democracy.

This more nuanced understanding of religion has rarely surfaced in the Marxist tradition, primarily owing to the early Eurocentric development of Marxism. In Eurpoe – where the Enlightenment ethos remained (and still remain) hegemonic among intellectuals and the literate middle classes – secular sensibilities were nearly prerequisites for progressive outlooks, and religious beliefs usually a sign of political reaction. The peculiar expression of critical consciousness in Europe focused on a corrupt and oppressive feudal order which the institutional church participated and firmly supported, and buttressed. And through the advent of Marxism itself bears traces of this Enlightenment legacy, the deep sense of historical consciousness nurtured and promoted by Marx and Engels led them to understand religious beliefs as first and foremost cultural practices generated from conflictual and contradictory socio-economic condition, rather than as a historical set of philosophical arguments of course, Kant, Fichte and especially Hegel and Feuerbach contributed to such an understanding.

The Marxism of the second International – with its diverse forms of economic determinism, Kantian moralism, and even left social Darwinism – view cultural and religious issues in a crude and reductionist manner. Karl Kaustsky's monumental work "The foundation of Christianity" (1908) is an exemplary text in this regards. The major anti-reductionist voices in this deterministic wilderness were those of the Italian Marxist Antonio Labriola and the Irish Marxist James Connolly. Lenin and Trotsky indeed undermined the crudity and reductionism of the Second Internatinal, but they confined their efforts to the realms of politics and the arts. Neither provided serious and sustained anti-reductionist formulations in regard to ethics and religion. In fact, the third International remained quite reductionist on such matters.

The centrality of morality and religion loom large in the works of Antonio Gramsci. For the first time, a major European Marxist took with utter seriousness the cultural life worlds of the oppressed. Though still tied to rationalist psychology which neglected unconscious impulses and a revolutionary teleology which uncritically privileged industrial working class agency, Gramsci highlighted the heterogeneous elements which comprise the cultural ways of life of oppressed people and the fragile, ever-changing characters of these elements in response to contradictory socio-economic circumstances.

Gramsci understood culture as a crucial component of class capacity. Like James Connolly before him and Raymond Williams in our own time, Gramsci examined the ways in which cultural resources enabled (and disenabled) political struggle among the exploited and excluded in capitalist societies. While Lukacs disclosed the reified characters of contemporary capitalist culture – the way in which processes of commodification and thingification permeate bourgeois.

From amonst thought, art, and perception – Gramsci focussed on the cultural means by which workers and peasants resisted such reification. While Karl Korsch enunciated his principle of Historical specificity – the need to acknowledge the materiality of ideology and the diversity of conflicting social forces in a particular historical moment –Gramsci applied this principle and specified the nature of these conflicting social forces with his complex notions of hegemony and historical blocs.

Ironically, the major figures of so called Western Marxism were preoccupied with culture – but none was materialist enough to take religion seriously. Whether it was Adorno and Marcuse on the subversive character of highbrow music and poetry, Sartre and Althussre on the progressive possibilities of avant-garde prose and theatre, or Benjamine and Bakhtin on the revolutionary potential of film and the novel – all rightly viewed the cultural sphere as a domain of ideological contestation. Yet none highlighted religion as a crucial component of this cultural sphere.

It is important to note that it has been primarily third world Marxists- for whom issues of praxis and strategy loom large- who have confronted the religious component of culture in a serious way. Peru's Jose Carlos Marioategui, China's Mao Tse-Tung and Guinea-Bissau's Amilcar Cabral were trail – blazers on such matters. All three shunned the reductionism of the Second International, eschewed the excessive hostility towards religion of the Third International, and transcended the Enlightenment prejudice of the Western Marxists. Mariategui, Mao and Cabral – whose cultural concerns inspire black Marxists feminists, Marxist gay and lesbian in the first world – recovered and refined the classical Marxist insights regarding the materiality and ambiguity, the relative autonomy and empowering possibilities and cultural and religious practices by grasping the existential and experiential content of such practices under capitalist conditions. In our own time such Marxist historians as Christopher Hill and E.P. Thompson in England, W.E.B.Du

Bois and Henri Lefebvre in France, Manning Clarke in Australia and Enrique Dussel in Mexico have begun to come to term with the complex relation of religious practices to political struggle. In other words the age of crude Marxist reductionist treatment of religion – along with the European secular condescending attitudes which undergrid them in passing. Concrete social and detailed historical analyses of the relations of religion to revolutionary praxis, is now a major issue on the agenda for contemporary Marxism.

Religion and Marxist Politics

The fundamental challenge of religion for Marxist politics is how we should understand religious practices as specific forms of popular opposition and / or subordination in capitalist societies. Recent religious upsurges around the world in post–industrial, industrial and pre-industrial capitalist countries – call into question the bourgeois theories of secularisation and crude Marxist theories of modernisation. The world – historical social process of rationalisation, commodification, and bureaucratisation have generated neither a widespread "disenchantment with the worlds" a "polar night of icy hardness and darkness", nor a revolutionary class consciousness among industrial workers. Instead we have witnessed intense revivalries of nationalism-ethnicity, and religion. Modern capitalist processes indeed have transformed traditional religious worldviews, intimate Gemeinschaft–like arrangements and bonds. Recent nationalist, ethnic, and religious revivals constitute new forms of these world views, arrangements and bonds, with existential intensity and ideological fervour.

There are three basic reasons for this. First, the culture of capitalist societies has for the most part, failed to give existential moorings and emotional assurance to their inhabitants. The capitalist culture of consumption – with its atomistic individualism, spectorial passivity, and outlook of therapeutic release – does not provide meaningful sustenance for large number of peoples in first world countries, religious responses is not only in nostalgic forms but also in utopian ones. Given the relative lack of long-standing ties or traditional links to a religious past, these responses are intertwined with the prevailing myths of European modernity: nationalism, racism, anti-semitism, sexism, anti-Orientalism, and homophobia. This is why religious (as well as nationalist and ethnic) revivals are usually dangerous- though there also can be occasions of progressive opportunity. Such opportunity is significant in that religious impulses are one of the few resources for a moral and political commitment beyond the self in the capitalist culture of consumption. These impulses often require commitments to neighbour, community and unknown others – though such commitments are ideologically circumscribed.

The second reason that religious revivals emerge is that they constitute popular responses to intense capitalist domination of more traditional societies. This is especially so in third world countries in which the cultural forms are either indigenous or colonial and the capital is primarily external or international. The boom-town character of industrialisation, urbanisation and proletarianisation demands that cultural ways of life, usually religious, provide strategies for new personal meaning, social adjustment, and political struggle.

The emergence of the most important third world development in religious practices – the liberation theology movement- consist of such strategies of new personal meaning social adjustment, and political struggle. This movement began in Latin America primarily in response to rapid capitalist penetration, quick yet painful industrial class formation rampant state repression, and bloated urbanisation. This response was not only rooted in Christian thought and practices, it also flowed from the major "free" space in these repressive regimes, the church, and given the overwhelming Roman Catholic character of this movement – with the monumental reforming impetus of Vatican II (1962-65) and the ground-breaking counter-hegemonic posture of the Medellin Latin American Bishops' meeting (1968) – these new strategies became more open to personal meanings, social adjustments, and political struggles informed by prophetic elements in the Scriptures and ecclesiastical tradition as well as progressive social and historical analyses.

Liberation theology in Latin America– embodied in the works of Gustavo Gutierrez, Reubem Alves, Hugo Assmann, Jose Miguez- Bonino, Victoria-Araya, Ernesto Cardenal Paulo Freire, Elsa Tamez, Jose Miranda, Pablo Richard, Juan Luis, Segundo, Enrique Dassel, Beatrice Couch, and others –is generated and sustained by popular religious opposition to the consolidation of capitalist social processes in Latin America. It is, in part, an anti-imperialist Christian mode of thought and action. Similar liberation theology outlooks – with their own contextual colourings are found in Africa (especially South Africa), Asia (especially, the Phillipines and South Korea), the Caribbean (especially Jamaica), and the United States (especially among blacks and feminists). Yet in terms of widespread concrete praxis none yet rivals that of Latin America.

The last reason such religious revivals emerge is that they constitute anti-western forms of popular resistance to capitalist domination. This is especially so in those third world countries (or pockets in the first world, as with indigenous peoples) in which a distinct cultural and religious way of life still has potency and vitality compared to western modes of religion. For example, in the Middle East and parts of Asia and Africa, Islam, Buddhism, Hinduism or traditional religions still have substances and life. Hence these religions serve as cultural sources against not simply Western imperialism but also much of

Western civilisation – especially western self-images, values and sensibility. Such resistance, like all forms of resistance, can be restorative and reactionary (as in Iran) or progressive and prophetic (as among many Palestinians)

In short, the religious revivals, along with nationalistic and ethnic ones, fundamentally result from the inability of capitalist civilisation to provide contexts and communities wherein meaning and values can be found to sustain people through the traumas of life. And since there can be no potent morality without such contexts and communities, these religious revivals represent an ethical challenge to Marxism. Instead of the promised autonomy and progress of the European Enlightenment, the modern west has bequeathed to the world – besides ingenious technological innovations, personal liberties for some, and comfortable living for the few-mere fragments and ruins of a decaying and declining civilisation. This decay and decline owes much to the captivity of its way of life to class exploitation, patriarchy, racism, homophobia, technocratic, rationality and the quest for military might. Of course, many of these remarks – and even more so in the realm of personal liberties – can be made of “actually existing socialist “civilisation”. But our focus here is the capitalist world, and as this capitalist world continues its deterioration, religious revivals will more than likely persist. The great question is: Will such revivals enable or disenable the left in its struggle for human freedom and democracy?

Religion and Marxist Strategy

Religious upsurges in the third world and second world, (as in Poland) may quite clearly contribute to the building of a left movement. As we have seen in Latin America – where over 2,00,000 base Christian communities exist as concrete praxis centres for social change, communal support, and personal sustenance –and parts of Africa and Asia, religion plays an important role in liberation struggles. The prophetic church in Nicaragua, with its tensions (both healthy and unhealthy) with the state, is the best recent examples of the crucial role.

The major contribution religious revivals can make to left strategy is to demand that Marxist thinkers and activists take seriously the culture of the oppressed. The fundamental shift in the sensibilities and attitudes of Marxists requires all kind of de-secularising and de-Europeanising of Marxists praxis, a kind of laying bare and discarding of the deep-seeded Enlightenment prejudices that shape and mold the perspectives and perceptions of most Marxist. This shift does not yield an anti-technology view-point but rather an anti-technologist. Nor does it reduce a rejection of reason but rather a specifying of liberating forms of rationality.

Such a shift is necessary because after over a century of heralding the cause of the liberation of oppressed peoples, Marxists have little understanding and appreciation of the culture of these people. This means that though Marxists have sometimes viewed oppressed people as political or economic agents, they have rarely viewed themes cultural agents. Yet without such a view, there can be no adequate conceptions of the capacity of oppressed people to change the world and sustain the change in an emancipatory manner. And without a conception, it is impossible to envision. Let alone create, a socialist society of freedom and democracy. It is, in part, the European Enlightenment legacy- the inability to believe in the capacities of oppressed people to create cultural products of value and oppositional group's of values-which stands between contemporary Marxism and oppressed people. And it is the arrogance of this legacy, the snobbery of this tradition, which precludes Marxists from taking seriously religion, a crucial element of the culture of the oppressed.

Needless to say, shedding the worst of the Enlightenment legacy does not entail neglecting the best of this European tradition. Relentless criticism and historical consciousness remains the crucial ingredient of any acceptable emancipatory vision – just as protracted class struggle and an allegiance to socialist democracy remain indispensible features of any recognisable Marxism. So the call for an overcoming of European bourgeois attitudes of paternalism towards religion does not mean adopting religious viewpoint. Religious affiliations are neither the mark of ignorance not intelligence. Yet, it is the mark of wisdom to understand the conditions under which people do or do not have religious affiliations. In this sense, science neither solves nor dissolves the issue of religious beliefs. Instead history provides us with traditions against which we must struggle yet in which we must critically abide. The grand query for truth is a thoroughly historical one which takes the form of practical judgments inseparable from value judgment upon, and social analytical understanding of prevailing socioeconomic realities. There indeed are standards of adjudication, but such historically constituted standards include multiple viewpoints worthy of adoption. Hence, the quest for truth continues with only human practice providing provisional closure.

If Marxists are to go beyond European bourgeois attitudes towards the culture of the oppressed without idealising or romanticising these cultures, it is necessary to transcend a hermeneutics of suspicious and engage in hermeneutical combat.*

In other words, Marxists must not simply enact negative forms of subversive demystification (and, God forbid, more bourgeois forms of deconstructions), but also positive forms of popular revolutionary construction of new personal meanings, social adjustments and political struggles for human freedom and democracy. These new forms can emerge only after traversing, transforming and building upon the crucial sphere in society – religion, family, labor process, state apparatuses – in order to consolidate an unite multiple organisational grouping for fundamental social change.

So to take seriously the culture of the oppressed is not to privilege religion, but no enhance and enrich the faltering and neglected utopian dimension of left theory and praxis. It is to believe not simply in the potential of oppressed peoples but also to believe that oppressed people have already expressed some of the this potential in their actual products, their actual practices. To be a person of the left is not only to envision and fight for the radically free and democratic society: it is also to see this society in the making as manifest in the abilities and capacities of flesh and blood people in their struggles under conflictual and contradictory socio-economic conditions not of their own choosing. This is the fundamental message regarding the relation of religious practises which is an evolutionary praxis beyond capitalist civilisation.

Courtesy *Monthly Review*

13

Religion, Ideology and Liberation Theology: An Islamic Point of View

Asghar Ali Engineer

I

The people of Asia and Africa are struggling today to transform their societies. Struggle for socio-economic transformation is by itself a stupendous task. However, before we get on with the subject it is important to answer three relevant questions. The right perspective to the subject can be obtained only if we answer these questions.

First important question is transformation for whom; second question is transformation for what and thirdly how to bring about this transformation. As far as the first question is concerned I have no hesitation to say that transformation through modernisation and change or otherwise, if it is to be meaningful, must be primarily for the weakest sections of the society. In other words, mere elite-oriented transformation would not only be hardly beneficial to the weaker sections of the society but – and it is important dimension of the problem to be taken into account – it would also lead to development of highly authoritarian structures in the society. The elite-oriented development can be sustained only if protest from below can be stifled and only an authoritarian regime- whatever its democratic pretensions – can 'successfully' crush such a protest.

Many Asian and African countries started, after their liberation from the clutches of western imperialism, with a democratic model but were soon transformed into authoritarian regimes as their socio-economic development was designed to fulfill the aspirations of upper class elites. In such a model of development all the surplus extracted from the toil of the weaker sections is invested in high-tech projects designed to benefit the elites. High tech and westernisation thus become not only the main idiom of development process but also become the touchstone of progress and change.

Here I would like to draw the attention to yet another phenomenon consequential to this model of development. Westernisation and elite oriented modernised development is not rooted in the native society and culture and thus sets the process of religio-cultural alienation in motion. It also gives momentum to the process of migration from rural to chaotic urban areas where the rural population lands itself in slums further deepening the process of alienation. The social change, which is neither meaningful to them nor beneficial and also becomes incomprehensible creates a sense of frustration and fatalism and develops deep conservative tendencies and are ready to fundamentalists to exploit them for their own political ends. Like the Khomeini of Iran they might even use radical religious rhetoric to entire them.

The Shah of Iran, it must be noted, followed the policy of westernisation and modernisation immensely benefiting the social elite of Iran in turn breeding corruption – both moral as well as material. This process of modernisation not only left the rural and urban poor high and dry but created among them a strong sense of resentment towards his regime. The rural poor, victims of the Shah's 'land reforms' policy which only facilitated deeper penetration of American agro-business corporations, were compelled to migrate to the urban areas and swell the ranks of urban poor. In urban areas they experienced nothing but poverty, unemployment, giddying heights of inflation and rank corruption. Thus, their alienation was complete. They developed deep antipathy towards westernisation and western ways of living and thinking.

The religious tradition was the only prop they could resort to and draw psychological strength from. Ayatollah Khomeini, both through his suffering at the hands of the Shah and radical religious rhetoric, provided an alternative model which greatly inspired the people of Iran, specially the rural and urban poor and the traditional mercantile classes of Tehran and other town and cities. In the given circumstances in Iran at the time, this model had tremendous appeal and provided the greatest thrust for change. It would be wrong to reject Iranian revolution as a sudden outburst of religious frenzy or sheer fanaticism inspired by the charismatic personality of Ayatollah Khomeini. The whole development, on the other hand, must be seen in its proper socio-political and development context. There is much to learn from what happened in Iran and to devise proper developmental strategies for the struggling people of Asia and Africa.

II

It is also necessary to analyse and understand why in the given situation like the one prevailing in Iran, religious rhetoric succeeded and Marxism failed to make any impact. Here we would also like to take up the second question raised in the beginning- development for what and also the third question how to bring about this transformation i.e. what strategy to be followed. As for the second question, it must be borne in mind that the process of development should not be seen by the masses as being amoral, let alone being immoral. Again, going back to Iranian situation, the whole process of socio-economic transformation was perceived by the people as immoral and hence incited deep revulsion. In the rapidly developing situation, even the westernised middle classes joined the ranks of those so perceiving the situation. Again, as pointed out earlier, it would not do to seek explanation in religious bigotry, obscuranticism and liberalism. This is precisely the idiom employed by western liberals who are the main beneficiaries of the process of development and who are looked upon by the masses with a sense of hostility, if not with a sense of downright hatred.

The process of development should be so designed as not to be perceived as violative of conventional morality, if it is to inspire and enthuse the masses. The sense of hostility increases manifold if the process of development is seen not only as breeding corruption but if it also leaves them out completely. This is what is happening today in most of the Asian and African countries. This is precisely the reason why religious fundamentalism is striking deeper and deeper roots in all these countries leaving most of us wondering as to why greater degree of economic development and spread of modern education results in strengthening, rather than weakening religious conservatism. More educational and economic development, howsoever rational and with scientific outlook, remains elite oriented and also amoral, even if not immoral.

This brings us to the third basic question posed earlier i.e. what developmental strategy to be followed. The foregoing discussion makes it clear that the strategy is to be devised that firstly, it provides greatest benefit to the weakest sections of the society, does not uproot them from their socio-cultural environs and secondly, does not deeply hurt their religio-cultural sensibilities. This, however, does not mean leaving superstitions or certain spiritually hollow, petrified conventional practices untouched, let alone encouraging them, far from it. They must be attacked and eliminated. But such attacks would produce result only if the process of development is really beneficial to the masses and also if the campaign is so devised as to combine attack on such practices with emphasis on certain positive aspects given cultural complex which are rich and creative.

III

MARXISM AND RELIGIO-CULTURAL TRADITIONS

Marxism thinkers and ideologues in India in particular and in other countries of the third world in general have not shown much appreciation for native cultural sensibilities, let alone religious feelings. They too adopt western cultural idiom and elitist approach. Marxism is by and large defined in terms of economic goals rather than aiming at enriching spiritual and cultural life of the people, in an idiom which appeals to them. Thus, there has not developed a genuine Marxist idiom, rooted in native cultural ethos. Marxism remains, more or less, a middle class elitist ideology and workers and peasants are drawn to it for limited economic goal and are left cold as far as their spiritual and cultural ethos are concerned. No wonder then, if they remain under the spell of fundamentalist, conservative and reactionary forces as far as the latter needs are concerned and, make no mistake, these needs are, in their case, as compelling and powerful as their economic needs. As such they remain religiously under the influence of highly conservative elements and are unable to change their outlook in this respect. Also, such conservative religiously-oriented parties like the Jamat-e-Islami float own trade unions to keep workers under their total influence.

It is therefore highly necessary for the Marxists to evolve an integrated approach in religio-cultural and economic spheres rooted in the native ethos. It requires great deal of original and creative thinking and ingenious theorising. Western-oriented Marxists with all its paraphernalia would not cut much ice. It would also not do to ignore religion, let alone opposing it. It is highly necessary to do some hard thinking on this subject. It is very short-sighted approach indeed to depict religion as 'opium' for the people and discard it. Religion, it must be remembered, is a powerful instrument and could be used either way – as opium or as a revolutionary ideology. It becomes opium, as Marx puts it, only when it becomes 'sign of the oppressed', the 'heart of the heartless world' and 'spirit of spiritless situation'.

Religion, however, is not always the sigh of the oppressed; it also becomes sword in their hands. It does not always act as opium to benumb the fighting vigour of the exploited; it also provides a powerful motivation to overthrow the status quo. There are many such instances. Buddhism, Christianity as well as Islam, all were powerful revolts against status quo. All three helped establish new revolutionary orders. Even Judaism earlier was a revolt led by Moses against Pharoah. Even in our own time what happened in Iran and in the Philippines proves this point. Islam in Iran and Christianity in the Philippines stood against Shah and Marcos respectively.

It is true that these religions, in times to come, once again became powerful establishments and allies of status quo. But the same can be said of political revolutions as well and hence many revolutionaries often talked of 'Permanent revolution'. Any revolution can degenerate if there is no constant watch and if men of unquestionable integrity are not in charges of its affairs and if revolution is allowed to turn into an establishment.

In fact, it is no use discussing religion *per se* shorn of its socio-political context. Religion *per se* can be discussed only in philosophical sense. Thus, Marx rightly points out in *Capital:* "Every history of religion even, that fails to take account of material basis, is uncritical. It is, in reality, much easier to discover by analysis the earthy core of the misty creations of religion, than, conversely, it is, to develop from the actual relations of life corresponding celestialised forms of those relations. The later method is the only materialistic and therefore the only scientific one".[1] However; no Marxist has ever tried to develop such a corresponding celestialised form from actual relations of life. In other words, religion has to be seen in the concrete sociological conditions and its critique to be attempted only in the sociological context.

Religion, in my opinion, must be seen both in its sociological as well as its philosophical context. Religion can become opium or a revolutionary force depending firstly, on concrete socio-political conditions and secondly, who it is made to ally with: revolution or status quo. Religion in a philosophical sense is a different proposition altogether. It is then primarily a question of how one wants to relate oneself with the cosmos and how one wants to draw spiritual sustenance through this relationship and also how one gives meaning to one's life. Reason and science can help in exploring and understanding the universe but not in relating oneself with it. Theism and atheism both after all are philosophical positions. One chooses one or the other depending on his/her philosophical disposition and intellectual inheritance. Neither theism always implies rejection of material objectivity and scientific approach to empirical exploration; nor atheism means doing away with spiritual aspects of life. Still an atheist or a theist may radically differ from each other in relating himself to the universe.

Religion, therefore, must be studied as a serious intellectual's spiritual and historical enterprise, rather than being brushed aside as a spiritual fraud, as often done by many rationalists. Engel's rightly observes about Christianity: "A religion that brought the Roman world empire into subjection and dominated by far the larger part of civilised humanity for 1,800 years cannot be disposed of merely by declaring it to be nonsense gleaned together by frauds. One cannot dispose of it before one succeeds in explaining its origin and its development from the historical conditions under which it arose and reached its dominating position. This applies to Christianity."[2]

He further observes very significantly, "The question to be solved, then, is how it came about the popular masses in the Roman Empire so far preferred this nonsense – Which was preached, into the bargain by slaves and oppressed – to all other religions that the ambitious Constantine finally saw in the adoption of this religion of nonsense the best means of exalting himself to the position of autocrat of the Roman world."[3]

IV

LIBERATION THEOLOGY

If religion is to be taken pretty seriously and an ally of revolution, progress and change, it must be divested of those theological aspects – which at best are later accretions – and were made part of it to serve not the oppressed but the oppressors. In other words, liberation of theology is needed to develop theology of liberation. Theology today by and large is monopolised by those who swear by status quo. It, therefore, trends to be highly ritualised, dogmatised and incomprehensibly metaphysical. It is only in this form that it can develop mystique of its own and keep the masses hypnotised. The theology of liberation must radically purge many of these elements. It is undoubtedly a challenging task, though of course, highly necessary. Religion cannot cease to be celestial but it cannot cut itself adrift from earthly matters too, from mainstream of life, if it has to retain its relevance.

The historicity and contempraneity of religion on one hand, and, its mundane and celestial elements, on the other, must be fused into a living, dynamic reality. Theology today is mere bundle of soulless rituals as far as toiling and oppressed masses are concerned. It is an abstract intellectual and metaphysical or mystical exercise for the middle class elite. In both these forms it serves the cause of status quo. It must be jettisoned of these soulless rituals as also of sheer metaphysical abstractions. It must become a soulful motivation for the oppressed to change their condition and a spiritual force to relate oneself meaningfully with and comprehend higher, spiritual aspects or reality.

V

ISLAM AND LIBERATION THEOLOGY

Islam was both a religion in technical sense and also a social revolution which posed powerful challenge to the oppressive structures of its time in and outside Arabia. Its basic thrust was towards universal brotherhood, equality and social justice. Firstly, it emphasised unity of mankind through the Quranic verse "O mankind, surely we have created you from a male and a female, and made you tribes and families that you may know each other. Surely, the noblest of you Allah is the most pious of you."[4] The verse clearly demolishes all notions and concepts of racial, tribal, national or familial superiority with one stroke and puts emphasis on piety. Piety, as far as the Quran is concerned is no mere ritual piety. The Quran defines piety in terms of justice – "Do justice; it is closest to piety."[5]

Secondly, as it can be seen from the above verse, Islam lays great emphasis on social justice in all its aspects. There can be no justice without the liberation of, and giving leadership to, the weaker and marginalised sections of the society. The Quran does not hesitate to entrust leadership of the whole earth to the *mustad'ifin* i.e. the weak. According to the Quran, they are the leaders and the inheritors of the earth.[6] It also enjoins on the faithfuls to fight for the liberation of the weak and oppressed. "And what reason", says the Quran, "have you not to fight in the way of Allah, and for the weak among the men and the women and the children, who say: Our Lord, take us out of this town, whose people are oppressors, and grant us from There a friends and grant us from Thee a helper."[7]

Thus, it would be seen from the above verse that the Quran puts forward a theory of what can be termed as 'liberative violence'. The oppressors and the exploiters persecute the weak and readily use force to defend their interest. It is not possible to liberate the persecuted without fighting. In another verse the Quran enjoins upon the Muslims to fight until there is no more persecution.[8] The Quran categorically denounces *zulm* (oppression) and wrong doing. Allah, the Quran says, does not approve of harsh crying except by one who has been oppressed.[9]

In the context of Pharoah also the Quran, denouncing him as *zalim* (oppressor) and *mustakbir* (powerful, arrogant) again repeats that the weak shall inherit the earth: "And we made the people who were deemed weak to inherit the eastern and the western ones which we had blessed. And the good word of the Lord was fulfilled in the Children of Israel – because of their patience. And we destroyed what Pharaoh and his people and wrought and what they had built."[10] It thus can be seen that Allah does not tolerate the structures of oppression and destroys them and this destruction is brought about through the oppressed themselves, Moses is projected as the leader so the oppressed by the Quran and he launches struggle to liberate the oppressed children of Israel.

If Mose was liberator of the enslaved Israelites, Muhammad was liberator of the whole of mankind through liberation of the weak among them. He launched powerful struggle right at the outset against the rich and the mighty of Mecca. Even before he was commissioned as the prophet, he took active part in hilf al-fudul (association of the meritorious) which was formed to get justice for the weak and he ever remained proud of having joined this association.

Through the inspired words of Allah he threw challenge to the rich by strongly denouncing accumulation of wealth as it is this lust for accumulation which leads to exploitation and oppression. It describes accumulation of wealth as burning fire which rises over the hearts and closes in on the accumulators.[11] This accumulation will thus put the whole society on fire and break it into pieces. Muhammad warned Meccans, and through rich Meccans the whole humanity. However denunciation of accumulation of riches should not be misunderstood. Islam did not preach, like some other religions, renunciation in its place. It, on the other hand, encourages reasonable consumption provided it is legitimate and not earned through exploitation, injustice or fraud. In this connection the verses 10:93, 16:73, 17:70, 20:81, 23:51, 40:94, 45:16 are indicative of the Quranic outlook.

In all these verses, the key term used for consumption is *taiyyib* which literally means good, agreeable, healthy and pleasant. However, the context of these verses clearly shows that the Quran uses this term for social health and social good. The Quran thus permits consumption provided it is agreeable physically and such as not to disturb social health. The concept of social health is very fundamental to an Islamic society and it can be achieved only through distributive justice. Thus, the Quran says: "Eat of the good things *(taiyyibat)* wherewith we have provided you, and transgress not in respect thereof lest my wrath come upon you...."[12]

It would be seen here that Allah clearly warns that consume good things but do not transgress as transgression invites his wrath, i.e. if few rich in the society consume in excess whereas others are deprived of it would lead to great turmoil in the society which is described as 'Allah's wrath' in a theological idiom. This is not my own construction. It is more clearly stated in another verse: "And when we would destroy a township we send commandments to its people who lead easy lives and they commit abomination there in and so the word (of doom) becomes effective and we annihilate it with complete annihilation."[13]

Here it is less of theological and more of a secular idiom and it is made clear that a town gets destroyed when its rich (those who lead easy lives) transgress all limits in consumption and hence it is distributive justice which can prevent such disaster. In yet another verse the Quran make it clear that all that is more than one's basic needs should be given away for the needy and the poor.[14]

Here another important question arises. How the objective of social justice to be achieved, through charity or through compulsory extraction of surplus? Islam rules out neither. It must be remembered that fundamental values remain unchanged whereas instrumental values change with the changing material circumstance. Equality is fundamental value whereas the institution through which equality is achieved represents instrumental value. In medieval ages the institution of charity was used to bring about semblance of socio-economic justice. In modern times the same can be achieved through either state welfarism or socialistic planning or by restricting, or even abolishing, right to property in certain spheres.

The Quran does talk of charity in the socio-economic context in which it was revealed but does not glorify it as an ultimate or permanent institution. It is aware of the fact that it can injure human dignity and cautions accordingly. It says, "Those who spend their wealth for the cause of Allah and afterward make no reproach and injury to follow that which they have spent; their reward is with their Lord..."[15] It also says, "A kind word with forgiveness is better than alms giving followed by injury."[16]

Charity was indispensable in the context of time and has remained indispensable until our own time especially in the capitalist society. In socialist society, too, it has not disappeared completely through of course causes are quite different. In Russia, for example, donations are made for the peace movement as well as for privately run religious institutions like churches and mosques. Such causes would continue to motivate human charitable instinct in future too. Thus, charity may not be done away with altogether. Thus, the Quran also encourages it but does not approve of causing any injury to human dignity.

To cause least injury to human dignity, the Quran levied *zakat*, a form of wealth and income tax combined. It was made a compulsory levy for all faithfuls. The Prophet established state treasury – *bait al-mal* - to collect and distribute the levy to the needy, the poor, orphans; widows, to pay off the debits of the indebted and to free the slaves. It was made obligatory for the state to look after the needs of the weaker sections of the society. However, for the reasons not to be discussed here these liberative aspects of the Quran and the Prophet's *sunna* (practice) were soon pushed aside and main emphasis laid on rituals and personal laws as formulated by the latter theologians. These aspects unfortunately came to be accepted as the main thrust of Islam. It was not so during the Prophet's lifetime and for a brief period thereafter. The liberative aspects of Islamic theology came to be discarded with the emergence of dynastic rule first of the Umayyads and then of the Abbasids. The liberative aspects never came to be emphasised again as far as the mainstream Islam was concerned. However, it did see its emergence in the heterodox movements like those of Khawarji, Quramita and others.

Right to property is not absolute as far as the Quran is concerned. Notionally the land as well as all other properties belong to Allah and through Allah to the society as a whole. Private property as means of production was not permitted by the prophet. Land was the main form of means of production then. The Prophet not only prohibited share cropping, he also prohibited retention of land by those who do not cultivate it. Shafi I, an eminent jurist and founder of one of the four schools of jurisprudence maintains in his *Kitab al-Umm* that if a person gives a bare land to a tiller with the stipulation that the latter will get a share of the crop-it is muhagala, mukhabara, and muzara'a (i.e. Terms for share cropping) which were prohibited by the Prophet. (See *Kitab al-Umm*, Vol. VIII, p. 102). Ibn Hazm, another eminent jurist of literalist persuasion (Zahiri School) argues on the basis of the Quranic doctrine *al-hurumat qisas*[17] that inviolable rights must be paid for in equivalent wages. Thus, a tiller's rights is as inviolable as that of a landlord.[18]

It would also be of great interest to mention here the views of prominent companion of the Prophet, Abu Dharr. He had caught the real revolutionary spirit of Islam. To him Islamic brotherhood was meaningless without its emphasis on socio-economic equality. It was its very core. He was highly critical of the Umayyad's policy of appropriating large estates. He strongly protested against Mu'awiyah's[19] attempt to change the nomenclature *mal at-muslimin* (wealth of Muslims) to *mal al-Allah* (wealth belonging to Allah) for obvious implication that is then could be easily appropriated without accountability to the Muslims.

Justice, in economic, social and political matters is very central to the teachings of Islam. Ibn Taymiyya, a distinguished jurist of medieval period considers justice so central that he says, "The affairs of men in this world can be kept in order with justice and certain connivance in sin, is better than pious tyranny. This is why it has been said that God upholds the just state even if it is unbelieving, but does not uphold the unjust state even if it Muslim. It is also said that the world can endure with justice and unbelief, but not with injustice and Islam."[20] These are but some of the aspects of liberation theology in Islam. There are several other matters which cannot be dealt with here in view of limitation of space. Suffice it to say that one cannot conceive of Islamic teachings and their real thrust, if divorced from the concept of socio-economic justice, equality of sex as well as race, freedom and dignity of man.

References

1. See Karl Marx and Friedrich Engels, *On Religion* (New York, 1964), p. 137.
2. Frederick Engels, *Brune Bauer and Early Christianity, On Religion,* op.cit., p. 195.
3. *Ibid.*
4. *The Quran,* 49:13.
5. *Ibid.,* 5:8.
6. *Ibid.,* 28:5.
7. *Ibid.,* 4:75.
8. *Ibid.,* 8:39.
9. *Ibid.,* 4:148.
10. *Ibid.,* 7:137.
11. *Ibid.,* 104:6-8.
12. *Ibid.,* 20:81.
13. *Ibid.,* 17:16.
14. *Ibid.,* 2:219.
15. *Ibid.,* 2:262.
16. *Ibid.,* 2:263.
17. *Ibid.,* 2:194.
18. Zia-ul-Haque, *Landlord and Peasant in Early Islam* (Delhi, 1985). p. 80.
19. Mu'awiyah was the first Umayyad Caliph.
20. Ibn Taymiya, *Public Duties in Islam,* English tr. Muhtar Holland. (U.K., 1983), p.95.

14

Sufism – Its Origin and Impact on Indian Islam

Asghar Ali Engineer

Sufism has recently gained in popularity outside Muslim circles, particularly Sufi music. Sufi music is attracting attention internationally. Sufi music congregations are taking place in several western countries, particularly in USA. Maulana Rumi, a great Sufi saint has become tremendously popular in USA in post-9/11 situation when Islam is being targeted as religion of jihad.

What is Sufism and when did it originate? What are its doctrines? What is its relation with orthodox Islam? Does it reconcile with it or not? These are some important questions we will take up in this article.

Sufism, some scholars maintain during the Prophet's (PBUH) life-time itself. It is not something different from Islam or different from Islamic teachings. It is more a question of attitude than teachings. Then the question arises is it in any way different from Islam and if so, in what respect?

Due to historical circumstances of Islam's origin, it got associated with state power and some even began to theorise that political power cannot be separated from Islam. The two must go together. Thus, struggles for political power unfortunately became part of Islamic state and this created a sense of alienation among many Muslims who did not see approvingly of these kept themselves aloof from power struggles and were instead drawn to spiritual side of Islam.

The Prophet (PBUH) of Islam himself was a unique combination of statecraft and spiritualism. For him statecraft was not meant for domination or exploitation but for providing just rule. However, this could not be expected of other Muslim rulers. Lust for power became their goal. Thus, in a way Sufism originated with the Prophet himself as spiritual aspect dominated his life.

In fact, some scholars have suggested that the word Sufism has its origin in *suffa* – a piece of rock – on which some of his followers used to sit outside his mosque and discuss religious matters. Some consider them as the first Sufis who were deeply concerned about spiritual aspects of life and were known in Islamic history as ahl-i-suffa.

Some Sufis were also concerned with just governance and setting up just social order in keeping with the Qur'anic teachings and hence participated in political struggles for this purpose but not in struggle for political power. However, most of the Sufi saints maintained their distance from political Islam and concentrated on spiritual side.

As Sufis had maintained distance from political Islam, there were also differences with orthodox Ulama who concentrated on Shari'ah Islam i.e. legal Islam. The orthodox Ulama were so rigid that anyone who deviated from Shari'ah (i.e. from a particular legal school) was considered as kafir. Thus, to these Ulama legal Islam was central, not spiritual Islam. Though many Sufis followed Shari'ah their emphasis was spiritual, not legal. Thus, Sufis chose spiritual rather than political or legal Islam.

Since Sufis were concerned with spiritual more than legal, they were much more open to other spiritual traditions. Religion ultimately results in forming a community of believers and hence it leads to formation of an identity whereas spiritualism is not confined to any narrow boundary and does not result in identity formation. Sufis never hesitated in accepting other spiritual traditions.

In India too Sufis who mainly came from Central Asian regions whole-heartedly accepted Indian spiritual tradition and cultural practices. Many of them like Baba Farid preferred to write in local languages instead of Arabic or Persian. They even adopted local rituals and tradition. This made them quite popular among people and that is why they attracted Hindu masses.

Since these Sufi saints preferred to be in the company of poor and weaker sections of society instead of courtiers and upper class nobles, and they did not observe religious boundaries they could acquire much popularity and they came to be deeply venerated by the masses both Muslim as well as Hindu. It is due to them that many low caste Hindus converted to Islam as they found more dignity and acceptability at their hands.

The Sufis became bridge between Hindus and Muslims and brought about the birth of composite culture at lower rungs of society. The Sufis of Chishti *silsila* (chain) believed in the doctrines of *wahdat al-wujud* (unity of Being) and *sulh-i-kul* (total peace, peace with all) and both these doctrines are quite helpful in building bridges between the communities. In fact the doctrine of wahdat al-wujud demolished all barriers between communities as real Being is One and all human beings are manifestation of this Real Being.

Sulh-i-kul (total peace and peace with all) was another doctrine that brought about cordial relations with all communities. No doubt that Sufis commanded respect from all communities and their dargahs (hospices) and their mausoleums became centres of attraction for people of all communities, especially the poor and downtrodden.

The Sufi mausoleums even today attract large number of Hindus along with Muslims, be it dargah of Ajmer Sharif or dargah of Baba Gesu Daraz or that of Nizamuddin Awliya in Delhi.

Sufi Music

The orthodox Ulama considered music as *haram* (forbidden) but music was an integral part of Sufi Islam. The Sufis developed a special genre of music known as qawwali. Khusrau, the celebrated disciple of Nizamuddin Awliya composed qawwalis and Nizamuddin would listen to these qawwalis and fall into a trance. Khusrau was a great poet as well as musician. Qawwali became the powerful instrument of inducing spiritual trance. It is so soothing to the human soul. It transports one into inner world.

More the Sufis acquired popularity, more they came to be opposed by the orthodox Ulama. In fact, orthodox Ulama considered them to be heretics. Moreover the Ulama jockeyed for positions in king's court and maintained their distance from the poorer masses denouncing them as 'impure' and bad Muslims. They held these Sufi saints responsible for keeping them 'impure' and polluted with un-Islamic way of life. They also denounced the doctrine of *wahdat al-wujud* (Unity of Being) as un-Islamic as it demolished religious boundaries between Muslims and non-Muslims.

Also, the Wahabi Islam, founded by Abdul Wahab in eighteenth century in what is now known as Saudi Arabia (Najd), opposed Sufi Islam and denounced it as *kufr* (unbelief) and all those Muslims who visit Sufi mausoleums as kafirs. Abdul Wahab played same role in Arabia as in nineteenth century India, played by founder of Arya Samaj Dayananda Saraswati. Dayanand denounced idol worship and gave slogan for back to Vedas. Abdul Wahab, denounced visit to dargahs and mausoleums and gave slogan for back to the Qur'an.

Thus, there is direct clash between Wahabis and Sufis. Wahabi doctrines are rigid, narrow and lay stress on 'purity' and denounce any deviation for rigid dogmas as kufr. It is interesting to note that poor masses never accepted narrowly interpreted Wahabi Islam but readily accepted Sufi Islam with all its openness and liberality.

Thus, Sufi dargahs, as pointed out above, till today remain shared sacred spaces.

Since Sufi Islam lays stress on spiritualism, rather than on rigid dogmas it is becoming more acceptable in western countries despite their hatred of political Islam. The Sufi music because of its strong appeal to heart and soul is becoming so popular. As bhakti always attracted lower caste Hindus throughout ages in history, Sufism appealed to the poorer masses.

The fast and tense pace of life in modern societies makes sufism a soothing balm for the soul. Consumerism of modern capitalist society brings more tension rather than happiness in life. Instant pleasure of modern consumerism cannot provide inner and lasting happiness. Thus, Sufism becomes popular both for idle classes in modern society as well as to poor suffering masses.

To both these classes Sufism acts as a soothing balm and much more so the Sufi music. Sufi singers like Abida Parveen and Nusrat Fatehally have made Sufi singing tremendously popular and their cassettes and CDs sell by thousands in the market. There are also groups like *Junun* from Pakistan, which combine Sufi music with today's pop appeal.

In USA, Maulana Rum's *Mathnavi* (long epic poem) is selling briskly. Rumi is a Sufi poet and his poetry is full of spirituality and wisdom. Maulana Rum was a great scholar and an Alim but one spiritual encounter with Shams Tabriz, a wandering Sufi from Persia, transformed Rumi completely. Rumi gave up his high status as an alim and began to roam around madly in love with Shams Tabriz and it was in this state of total involvement with Shams Tabriz he composed his Mathnavi.

Thus, Sufi Islam which is opposite of political and legal Islam, is much more appealing to the people than rigid, doctrinaire orthodox Islam. And it is this spiritual appeal of Sufi music, which stirs our soul.

15

Syncretism – Indian Context: A Sociological Appraisal

Uday Mehta

Syncretism essentially implies the permeability and fluidity of religious situations. The Dictionary of Sociology as suggested by Fairchild defined Syncretism as "The process of amalgamation of conflicting, or at least different, parties or principles of cultures – more specifically assimilation of foreign groups. The foreign elements disappear as psychological and cultural entities into the majority and the majority adopts both the individual and a selection and adoption of their cultural traits".

Generally speaking, syncretism has been associated with Folk religion with reference to practices of primitive societies. It has been also equated with popular religion, more evident in relatively non-modern societies.

Syncretism: Variety of Interpretations

Both the views presented above reflect as per Rama Shyam a deep prejudice regarding the sociology of religion. Fairchild's explanation of the disappearance of the foreign elements, somewhere suggests only the immigrants or the minorities getting synchronised. One has seen in the case of India how syncretism or adoption of religious traditions has been an all embracing phenomenon. Even second view of syncretism mostly evident in non-modern societies also appears to be rather high-browed and tilted in favour of the world religions. (Roy Burman, 1993, 70[1]).

As rightly suggested by Peter der Veer (1994, p. 208[2]) as a broad process every religion is syncretistic, since it constantly draws upon heterogeneous elements to the extent that it is often impossible for historian to unravel what comes from where. Eliade (1987[3]) also opines that social presupposition for the rise of syncretism can be the co-existence of various groups.

Roy Burman further classifies Syncretism in terms of power dimension. According to him syncretism could be classified into five categories: (a) Defensive Syncretism (b) Aggressive Syncretism, (c) Recessive Syncretism, (d) Adaptive Syncretism and (e) Pragmatic Syncretism. These categories are based on the nature of relationship and pattern of interaction among various groups exposed to this process:[4]

> While referring to syncretism Peter Vander points out that in India syncretism is a trope in discourse of multiculturalism and that scholarly discussion of syncretic phenomena such as Hindu worship of Sufi saints usually omits consideration of conflict or of the processes of expansion and contraction.[5]

Concepts Contesting Syncretism

While referring to syncretism, Mayaram argues, that it tends to ignore multiplicity of meaning which human agency seeks to comprehend in the cosmos around. It restricts itself to a binary opposition of 'Syncretism' and 'anti-syncretism'. Hence, Mayaram prefers to use the term liminality – a term that takes into account a third space that seeks to transcend the binary mode of thought and understanding. In a sense, it also does away with the sacred – profane categorisation through a peculiar combination of reverence and irreverence to the gods. This is evident in traditions where gods as she suggests, are made fun of through poetic burlesque (In Mayaram's account, Bhim is associated with much of the comic relief in the Mewati Mahabharata. (Mayaram Shail : 'Rethinking Meo Identity : Cultural Faultline, Syncretism, Hybridity or Liminality in comparative studies of South Asia, Africa and the Middle East, Vol. XVII, No. 2, 1997)[6].

Liminality as a concept has been developed by Victor Turner in rethinking approaches to anthropology. Drawing from William Dilthey's theories, Turner expounded the thesis that the fundamental basis of human knowledge was the lived experience of human beings. Turner suggests that though we may attempt to understand society in terms of its structures and their functions, yet what forms meanings is the way people interact and experience within this structure. Hence, an understanding of the relationship between thoughts, symbols, actions and interactions is the key to making of people and their experiences. Within this framework, Turner talks of the things that happen between the structures - instances of heightened emotions and their impact. He defines these as the liminal and interstitial spaces where people come out of the routine. He departs significantly from traditional anthropology in that in his analysis it is not so much what happens within the confines of social structures but what happens between and outside them that is important.

Linking the concept of liminality to rituals and festivals, Turner puts forward the idea of communities – people spontaneously emerging as social groups with love for each other and sense of solidarity.

According to Turner, communities come into play during "collective religious or political phenomena. He explains that people who are normally divided and antagonistic can come together and transcend their differences in their common experience or humanity which in this case is defined within the liminal spaces.

For Turner, these spaces may be a threat to social structures and cohesion, but he celebrates them to represent positive potential that reaffirms solidarity and social bonds between people.[7]

Another concept which comes closer to this controversy is that of 'hybridity' evolved by Homi Bhabha (cited in Mayaram 1997) that expresses the intercultural encounter. Hybridity implies how two entities combine to produce a third, with specific reference to cross-cultural kinship / marriage. However, even this concept as argued, by Mayaram, falls into the trap of the pure verses the 'hybrid' thus implies a racial understanding of the universe.[8]

Sila Khan proposes a more interesting classification of Syncretic traditions accordingly to their significance with regards to various quotidian practices among religious communities.

(1) Divine power or charisma (Sakti in the Hindu tradition, barakat in the Islamic one) may attract devotees regardless of their origin, around a particular religious figure, for example, the worship of a Sufi saint like Moinuddin Chisthi by Hindus and the cult of a goddess performed by Muslims, with the hope of securing a boon.

(2) There is in some situations a tendency to cling to one's former beliefs. For instance, some Muslims continue to worship a Hindu deity as they did before their conversion.

(3) All over the sub-continent a number of Muslim Saints are still regarded as the guardians and protectors of a Hindu or Jain Shrine – Angar Shah for instance, at the entrance of the Jain sacred complex of Shatrunjaya near Palitana in Gujarat, Vavar is the guardian deity of the god Ayyappa at the Shrine of Sabarimalai in Kerala.

(4) Apart from this, there are syncretic cults, where Hindu and Muslim elements seem to co-exist within

> one single tradition and where the saints have a duel identity. Sila Khan illustrates this phenomenon through practices recorded by scholars in different places for example, the Legend of Satya Pir in Bengal recorded by Roy and the celebrated cult of the Panch Pir or Ramdev Pir.[9]

Syncretic cults are very prominent in the villages of Sunderban in West Bengal where the vagaries of nature take a heavy toll. Similarly cults related to healing practices are also abundant.

Since time immemorial syncretic practices are common around agricultural cycles as food abundance is the basis of human existence.

Important shrines similarly continue to remain decisive meeting points of religious communities in the Indian landscape. These shrines determine the importance of sacred places vis-à-vis religious syncretism and continue to be centre of power, interaction and legitimacy in the realm of the lived religious experience of people.

Cultural syncretism is also quite evident in art forms and festivals, Kabirpanthis for instance, celebrate in Kabir's hymns the single God. Similarly the Sikh reintegrate the teachings of Kabirpanthis into Hinduism in their Adi Granth and also hymns of Sufi Saints.

Mount Mary festival a celebrated in the month of September, in Mumbai also attracts huge crowd for day's together coming from all religious communities in India.

The syncretic discourse - Its relevance

Appraisal of the discourse on syncretism is quite important against the backdrop of extensive violence and communal disturbances in last two decades in Indian society. Much of the violence as Rama Shyam suggests in her unpublished Ph.D. dissertation stems from religious intolerance; such bigotry fails to take into account the day-to-day interactions in the human society that translates into an ethos of mutual aid akin to the innate nature of human beings. Upholding this principle, terms as syncretism or liminality pose a challenge to the Eurocentric way of looking at faith. A. Nandy argues (1990: 71) the Eurocentric perception gradually came to be associated with the dominant culture of the colonial states in the region, it subsumes under it a set of clear polarities; centre vs. periphery, true faith vs. its distortions, civil vs. primordial and great traditions vs. local or little traditions.

Rooted in the secularisation debate, Nandy's (1990) argument revolves around two aspects of South Asian religion: Faith and ideology. By faith he implies religion as a way of life, a tradition that is 'definitionally' non-monolithic and operationally plural. He prefers to use the term definitionally because unless a religion is geographically and culturally confined to a small area, it has a way of life, in effect, to turn into a confederation of number of ways of life which are linked by a common faith that has some theological space for the heterogeneity which everyday life introduce (Nandy, 70). It is in this light that he establishes the difference between Iranian and Indonesian Islams, two cultures which can be divided by the same faith, two forms of Islam that are interlocking, not isomorphic, in relation to each other. By religion as ideology, Nandy means religion as a sub-national, national or cross-national identifier of populations contesting for or protecting non-religious, usually political or socio-economic interest. Such religions as ideologies then get identified with one or more texts, rather than ways of life of the believers and come to denote the relatively purer forms of the religion.

It is this religion as ideology approach that the secularisation debate aspires to counter. However, in attempting to do so, it discounts the multiplicity of meanings that emerges out of daily social interactions and human situations. What becomes evident is the discomfort of the notion of secularism with the fluid definitions of self, characteristic to many South Asian cultures.

Nandy suggests that such a self, which can be conceptually viewed as a configuration of selves, invokes and reflects the configurative principles of religions as faith and is incompatible with the idea of secularism that chalks out an area in public life where religion is not admitted. Qualifications of this aspect of religion lies in slogans like "we are Indians First, Hindus Second". Religion is constantly relegated to the private background by the public arena which has no space for faith.[10]

Similarly as Rama Shyam argues Sociology of Religion has come long way from rigid categorisation in terms of Great-Tradition of Urban elite and Little tradition of folk, despite ample instances of that refute claims of "either / or" configuration, we find this tendency wields sway over much scholarly writings.

Syncretism çomes across as a process that is ongoing and very much a part of all religious traditions. It is as Veer (1994) indicates an aspect of religious interactions over time. Every religious tradition goes through certain adaptations and accommodations; it originates, takes root and develops through exchange of belief systems over a period of history, while moving from one locale to the other. It needs to be driven home that despite efforts at homogenising religious beliefs, what has sustained is the syncretic appeal of religious experiences that bring people of different faiths together in a celebration of their mass consciousness that surpasses normative dogmas usually laid down in scriptural texts or orthodox directives one feels closer to the spirituality of the divine and seeks comfort in what Rabindranath Tagore calls the religions of man.[11]

When it comes to every day religious experience, scriptural directives are modified as Rama Shyam suggests suiting the more practical needs of human beings. This leads to complete dissolution of the boundaries between the so called 'Great' and 'Little' traditions. Theocracy gives way to spiritualism and the quest for happiness and solace translates into quest for the divine and this amalgamation finally results in a form of religion that emerges from the daily lives of human beings and it is virtually impossible for institutionalised or codified doctrines – that are supposed to remain constant to deal with such spontaneity of social upheavals. (This appraisal of syncretism is entirely based on unpublished thesis of Rama Shyam submitted for Ph.D. in Tata Institute of Social Sciences. Chapter-II of the dissertation)

Ashish Nandy in his critique of religion as ideology also holds the view that secularism in India not only irrelevant but has proved harmful to Indian society. He blames secularism and modernity for the new religious violence witnessed by this country in recent years. He characterises secularism as a child of modernity and colonialism product of Western science and rationality. It functions as the ideology of the modern state, which Nandy thinks as a source of most contemporary problems. He argues that it is the secular state and its elite, with its instrumental rationality and a moral and manipulative technocractic managerial ethos, that has been responsible for the greatest atrocities of this century from the Third Reich to the Gulag to Hiroshima to the anti-Sikh riots in Delhi. Thus, Nandy's rejection of secularism, as Joseph Tharamangalam sums up, is rooted in a two-fold critique, a critique of modern culture and society that approvingly and respectively draws on the Gandhi of Hind Swaraj and critique of the secular state. Nandy advocates that the Indian Secular state has much to learn about morality from Hinduism, Islam and Sikhism, while Hinduism, Islam and Sikhism have nothing to learn from the secular state in this respect. As an alternative to secularism, Nandy stands for the recovery of India's traditional religious tolerance. The greatest representative of such tolerance was Gandhi, but it is still widely practiced by the masses of non-modern, peripheral believers, in contrast to the modern, secular rationalists and the semi-modern zealots.

Nandy further argues that for secularists, which has its own principles of tolerance and intolerance. He also thinks that the imported idea of secularism has become increasingly incompatible with the fluid definitions of the self, shared by several South Asian cultures, such more fluid definition of the self, he feels, is more compatible with religion as faith and depends more upon a distinctive set of the non-self and anti-selves. Nandy argues that the anti-selves are counter-points without which the self just cannot be defined in the major cultures of South Asia.

Akeel Bilgrami, while focusing on Nandy's work aptly brings out that such contemporary critique of Nehru begins by drawing a fundamental distinction between religions as faiths and ways of life on the one hand and as constructed ideologies on the other. This is intended as a contrast between a more accommodating, non-monolithic and pluralist religious folk traditions of Hinduism and Islam and the Brahmanical BJP and the fundamentalist Muslim League versions of Islam, which amount constructed religious ideologies, that is intolerant of heterodoxy within themselves as well as of each other. Nandy's target obviously is modernity itself, with its modern conception of nationhood and its statecraft, which is the source of such ideological constructions that distort those more innocent aspects of religion "as ways of life".

Likewise, Hindu nationalism, Nandy argues is nothing but an offshoot of Nehruvian state imposed secularism which leaves people no choice. Thus, secular tyranny breeds Hindu nationalist resistance, with its own form of tyranny.

As Bilgrami suggests, nationalism is for more omnibus and vague formulation to analyse, than Nandy or the Hindu Nationalists allow. There are a variety of ingredients that go into a particular nationalism at different stages and sometimes even at the same state one can't lump together Palestinian nationalism with Zianist or for that matter German nationalism. It can have instinctive tie to social democracy, liberal democracy, autocracy or fascism. In this country nationalism, during its anti-Imperialist struggle phase to post-Independence stage, with its major thrust on capitalist consolidation exhibit different characteristics.[12]

Similarly, monolithic, majoritarian, Brahminic version of Hinduism as popularised by the Sangh Parivar is just not offshoot of, or reaction to state imposed secularism or modernity, as its construction 'process goes long way into the recesses of Indian history and has helped to perpetuate the most remarkably resilient inegalitarian social formation in the world. As Bilgrami suggests, it is the product of sustained efforts over centuries on the part of the upper castes to sustain their hold over the Hindu Psche.[13]

Likewise, Nandy and several other scholars pleading for syncretism or liminal movement, idealise indigenous religious tradition, its tolerance and its extensive acceptance among masses. Indian society, historically, right from early period, has not only witnessed multiple religious and social traditions, but also clash of traditions at different levels at various historical junctures right from the Vedic period till the advent of the British rule in this country Nandy's justification and blanket support to Hinduism, betrays his bias and indifference to subaltern traditions in this country. Hinduism, as it is now widely understood, is a predominantly upper caste, Brahminic version, popularised in medieval period, especially after the advent of the Muslim rule in this country. This was projected as an ideological construction in the context of the vulnerability of the orthodox Brahminic traditions, in the face of growing popularity of the Bhakti movement and egalitarian values of Islam, as projected by Sufi saints.

Our slightly elaborate appraisal of Nandy's critique of secularism and its irrelevance for this country is imperative as those who exclusively uphold the importance of syncretic and liminal practices also knowingly or unknowingly extend concurrence to such presumption about the irrelevance of secularism in Indian context and disapprove of its application in this country also under the pretext that the concept is Eurocentric. Unfortunately those who advocate such argument are not aware or quite conveniently ignore the fact that there is no monolithic model of secularism that could be applied to Europe. Within Europe also England, France and Germany social, political and religious traditions are so different that it is impossible to locate any uniform process or model of secularism for these nations. Even within one nation, historically the process of secularisation has proceeded in such uneven manner that one cannot mechanically apply uniform abstract model for even one single country. There are upward and downward curves in secularisation process that it is impossible to mechanically fit them in uniform pattern. We have no intention of belittling the great significance of syncretic practices in this country. As a matter of fact it is because of extensive prevalence and appeal of syncretic religious practises in this country that communal forces have not been able to strike deeper roots in this country, despite open indulgence and blatant promotion of communal divide by practically all mainstream political parties in this country in recent years.

People who throng such shrines, or dargah in large number visit them largely for the fulfillment of their this worldly material aspirations, ranging from desire for progeny, to employment, success in examination, to proper life partner, physical or mental ailment to material prosperity. Aspirations for spiritually, divinity or mental peace certainly could be an important element of their visit to such sacred spots. But it would be extremely difficult to sort out clear cut distinctions between the two expectations.

In our concluding observation, we like to point out two glaring instances where communal passions were razed to a point which vitiated the communal amity at a national level, first is the recent case of Amarnath Yatra in Jammu and Kashmir. Where the debate over the control of Amarnath Trust and ownership of land around the shrine took such bitter turn that the whole state was divided on communal lines and deep unrest around this issue led to aggravating the communal tension and antagonism over the whole country.

Second, is the case of demolition of Babri Masjid and national campaign for the construction of Ram temple at that site. For almost over a decade communal tension, bitterness were created and the BJP successfully exploited this opportunity for registering massive victory in parliament and several other states in late nineties. Even now attempts are made to utilise this issue for electoral purpose.

It is widely recognised that at the local level of networks, Hindus and Muslims interacted and enthusiastically participated in Amarnath Yatra and Amarnath was a classic illustration of communal harmony where both communities a depended on each other for Yatra. Similarly, it is noted by many scholars that many temples in Ayodhya are looked after by Muslims and Ayodhya never had any problem of communal antagonism. In both cases communal forces and mainstream political parties including Indian National Congress were instrumental in aggravating communal tension with their populist policy.

Our contention in citing this two glaring instances of communal tension and divide is that despite long history and syncretic traditions and communal amity in these two places, political forces were quite successful in wiping out such syncretic traditions and disturbing communal harmony at a national level leaving permanent scars and nation facing consequences of such opportunistic indulgence. Hence unless we keep in mind the socio-economic and political forces operating at macro-level, our exclusive focus on syncretic traditions at micro-level would not help us to properly comprehend and find solution to problem of communal peace and harmony. Syncretic traditions are very important and as we noted earlier, but for deeper roots they have acquired in this country since medieval Bhakti and Sufi movement, communal forces would have succeeded in shaking the prevailing democratic set up and replacing it probably with creation of "the Hindu Rashtra".

References

1. Roy, Burmann J.J. 1993 : "Syncretism and some reference to the Disputed Shrine of Ayodhya", Journal of the Indian Anthropological Society 28 (1) : 69-82.
2. Veer Ven der Peter – 1994 : "Syncretism, Multiculturalism and the discourse of Tolerance, pp. 196-211 in Steward and Shaw (ed) Syncretism / Antisyncretism : The politics of Religious Synthesis. London and New York : Routledge.
3. Eliade Mircea (ed) 1987: "Syncretism" in The Encyclopedia of Religion, Volume 14, pp. 218/227, New York. Macmillan Publishing company.
4. Roy Burman *Ibid.*
5. Veer, *Ibid.*
6. Mayaram Shail : "Rethinking Meo Identity : Cultural Faultime, Syncretism, Hybridity or Liminality in comparative studies of South Asia, Africa and the Middle East" Vol. XVII, No. 2, 1997.

Turner Victor – 1973 : "The Centre out there : Pilgrim's Goal" in History of Religions 12 (3) – 191-230.

8. Mayaram, *Ibid.*
9. Khan, Dominique – Sila 2004: "Liminality and legality" A contemporary Debate among the Imam Shahis of Gujarat, pp. 209-232 in Ahmad Imtiaz and Reifeld Helmut (ed). Lived Islam in South Asia: Adaptation, Accommodation and Conflict. Delhi, Social Science Press.
10. Nandy, Ashis 1990: "The politics of secularism and the Recovery of Religious Toleration" in Das Veena (ed). Mirrors of Violence: Communities, Riots and Survivors in South Asia. New Delhi, Oxford University Press.
11. Veer, *Ibid.*
12. Nandy Ashis, *Ibid.*
13. Bilgrami Akeel : Two concepts of Secularism, published in Economic and Political Weekly, July 9, 1994, pp. 1937-53.

Bibliography

Basham, A.L. : The wonder that was India, Pan Macmillan. London 2004, Third Edition.

Engineer Asghar Ali Mehta Uday (Ed): State Secularism and Religion. Ajanta Publication. New Delhi : 110007, 1998

John Lewis : Max Weber Value Free Sociology. Lawrence and Wishar't. London Reprinted, 1980.

Karen Armstrong : Islam 2002. Modern Library, Paperback Edition, U.S.A.

Lele Jayant : Hindutva, The Emergence of the Right. Earthworm Books Madras 1995.

Poddar Arabinda : Renaissance in Bengal. Indian Institute of Advanced Study : Simla 1977.

Mehta, Uday : Modern Godmen in India, Popular Prakashan, Bombay 1993.

Malik, S.C. (ed) : Indian Movements : Some Aspects of Dissent, Protest and Reform- Indian Institute of Advanced Study – Simla 1978.

Madan, T.N. (Ed) : Religion in India, Oxford University Press. New Delhi 110001, 1992.

Majumdar, A.K. : Bhakti Renaissance, Bhartiya Vidya Bhavan, Bombay – 400 007, 1979.

Syed, A.J. (Ed) : D.D. Kosambi on History and Society. University of Bombay, 1985.

Sergie Tokarev : History of Religion. Progress Publishers, Moscow, 1989.

Sharma, R.S. : Sudras in Ancient India, Motilal Banarsidas publishers, Delhi, Reprint - 2002.

Thapar, Romila : Ancient Indian Social History, Orient Longman Ltd., New Delhi - 110002, 1978.

Thapar, Romila : Recent Perspectives of Early Indian History. Popular Prakashan, Bombay, 1995.

Engineer Asghar : Islamic Perspective Ali (Ed) A Special Issue on Religion and Liberation. Institute of Islamic Studies, Bombay - 400 055. July-Dec. 1988.

Bahm, Archie, J. : The World's Living Religions. Arnold - Heinemann, New Delhi, First Indian Edition, 1977.

Banerjee, N.V. : Buddhism and Marxism. Orient Longman, 1978.

Benchfod, James A. : New Religious Movements and Rapid Social Change. Sage, 1986.

Brent, Peter : Godmen of India. Penguin Books, 1973.

Castro, Fidel : Fidel and Religion. People's Publishing House, 1987.

Caudwell, Christopher : Studies and Further Studies in a Dying Culture, Modern Reader, New York, London, 1971.

Chattopadhaya Deviprasad : What is Living and What is Dead in Indian Philosophy. People's Publishing House, 1976.

Chattopadhaya, Deviprasad : Lokayat. People's Publishing House, Fifth Edition, 1981.

Chattopadhaya, Sudhakar : Reflection on Tantra. Motilal Banarsidass, 1978.

Chinmayananda, Swami : Vedanta, The Science of Life. Vol. I, 1982, Vol. II, III, 1983, 1986, Central Chinmaya Mission Trust, Reprint.

Damodaran, K. : Man and Society in Indian Philosophy. People's Publishing House, 1970.

Devaraja, N.K. : The mind and Spirit of India. Motilal Banarasidass, 1967.

Dobb, Lawrence A. : Redemptive Encounters. Oxford University Press, 1986.

Fitzgerald, Frances : Cities on a Hill. PICADOR Pan Books, USA, 1986.

Gordon, James : Golden Guru. The Stephen Greene Press, Massachusetts, 1987.

Gross, Bertram : Friendly Fascism.

Howard : American Now.

Joshi, Laxmanshastri : A Critique of Hinduism. Modern Age Publications, Bombay, 1942.

Kakar, Sudhir : Shamans, Mystic, Doctors – A Psychological Inquiry into India and its Healing Traditions. Oxford University Press, Delhi, 1982.

Kavoor, Abraham : Gods, Demons and Spirits. Jaico Publishing House, Second Edition, 1984.

Kavoor, Abraham : Begone Godmen. Jaico Publishing House, Fourth Edition, 1984.

Kirtananda Swami Bhaktipada : On his Order. Bhakti Books 1987, Palace Publishing, New Vrindaban Community.

Kolakowski, L. : Religion. Fontana Paperback, 1982.

Kosambi, D.D. : Introduction to the Study in Indian History. Popular Prakashan, 1975.

Krishnamurti, J. : The First and Last Freedom. Victor Gollancz Ltd., London, 1958.

Lexine, Faye : Strange World of the Hare Krishna. Fawett Publications, Greenwich, 1974.

Ling, T. : Karl Marx and Religion. The Macmillan Press Ltd., 1980.

Mangalwadi : World of Gurus. Vikas Publication, 1974.

Marx and Engels : On Religion. Progress Publishers, Moscow, 1975.

Mehta, Gita : Karma Cola.

Milne, Hugh : Bhagwan Rajneesh – The God that Failed. Sphere Books, London, 1987.

Muktananda, Baba: Siddha Meditation. Gurudev Siddhapeeth, Ganeshpuri, 1977.

Prabhu Pada Swami Bhaktivedanta : Krishna – ISKCON, 1970.

Prasad, Ramchandra : The Mystic of Feeling. Motilal Banarsidass, Second Revised Edition, 1978.

Rajneesh : Tantra, Rajneesh Foundation, Poona, 1975.

Rajneesh : A New Vision of Women's Liberation Neo-Sannyas International, 1987, The Rebel Publishing House, Cologne 1, West Germany.

Rajneesh : The Mystic Experience. Motilal Banarsidass, 1977.

Rao, Raghavendra K. : Religion, Society and State. ICSSR, New Delhi. 1985.

Rochfod, Jr. : Hare Krishna in America. Rutgers University Press, New Jersey, USA, 1985.

Ruhela, S.P. and Robinson, D. : Sai Baba and His Message. Vikas Publishing House, 1976.

Seigel, Paul : Meek and Militant, Oxford University Press, 1988.

Shireen, Jamail : The Mind of Bhagavan Rajneesh. Jaico Publishing House, 1983.

Smart, Ninian : The Science of Religion and The Sociology of Knowledge, Princeton University Press, 1973.

Vivekananda : What is Religion. Advaita Ashram, Calcutta – 14, 1972.

Vora, Batuk : Between You and Me. California Publishing Co., San Fancisco, 1989.

Yatishwarananda, Swami : Meditation and Spiritual Life. Sri Ramakrishna Ashram, Bangalore, 1979.

Index

B

I

J

K

L

M

O

P

W

Y

Z